W9-AAZ-486

The Eagle on the Cactus
El Águila encima del Nopal

World Folklore Advisory Board

The Eagle on the Cactus
Traditional Stories from Mexico

El Águila Encima del Nopal
Cuentos Tradicionales de Mexico

Retold by Angel Vigil

Translated by Francisco Miraval

2000
Libraries Unlimited, Inc.
Englewood, Colorado

See p. 215 for a list of permissions and credits.

Text illustrations: Carol Kimball
Icon design: Alfredo Cárdenas
Spanish proofreader: Enrique Mejía Hernández

Libraries Unlimited, Inc.
P.O. Box 6633
Englewood, CO 80155-6633
1-800-237-6124
www.lu.com

Library of Congress Cataloging-in-Publication Data

Vigil, Angel.
  [Aguila encima del nopal. English]
  The eagle on the cactus : traditional tales from Mexico / retold by Angel Vigil ;
translated by Francisco Miraval.
    p. cm. -- (World folklore series)
  Includes bibliographical references and index.
  ISBN 1-56308-703-0 (cloth)
  1. Indians of Mexico--Folklore. 2. Indians of Mexico--Social life and customs. 3.
Tales--Mexico. 4. Legends--Mexico. I. Title. II. Series.

F1219.3.F6 V54 2000
398.2'089'97072--dc21
                                                                          00-027130

THIS BOOK IS DEDICATED TO MY SISTERS,
THERESE AND SUSAN,
AND MY BROTHER, TOM.

World Folklore Series

Folk Stories of the Hmong: Peoples of Laos, Thailand, and Vietnam. By Norma J. Livo and Dia Cha.

Images of a People: Tlingit Myths and Legends. By Mary Helen Pelton and Jacqueline DiGennaro.

Hyena and the Moon: Stories to Tell from Kenya. By Heather McNeil.

The Corn Woman: Stories and Legends of the Hispanic Southwest. Retold by Angel Vigil.

Thai Tales: Folktales of Thailand. Retold by Supaporn Vathanaprida. Edited by Margaret Read MacDonald.

In Days Gone By: Folklore and Traditions of the Pennsylvania Dutch. By Audrey Burie Kirchner and Margaret R. Tassia.

From the Mango Tree and Other Folktales from Nepal. By Kavita Ram Shrestha and Sarah Lamstein.

Why Ostriches Don't Fly and Other Tales from the African Bush. By I. Murphy Lewis.

The Magic Egg and Other Tales from Ukraine. Retold by Barbara J. Suwyn. Edited by Natalie O. Kononenko.

When Night Falls, Kric! Krac! Haitian Folktales. By Liliane Nérette Louis. Edited by Fred J. Hay.

Jasmine and Coconuts: South Indian Tales. By Cathy Spagnoli and Paramasivam Samanna.

The Enchanted Wood and Other Tales from Finland. By Norma J. Livo and George O. Livo.

A Tiger by the Tail and Other Stories from the Heart of Korea. Retold by Lindy Soon Curry. Edited by Chan-eung Park.

The Eagle on the Cactus: Traditional Stories from Mexico. Retold by Angel Vigil.

Selections Available on Audiotape:

Hyena and the Moon: Stories to Tell from Kenya. By Heather McNeil.

The Corn Woman: Stories and Legends of the Hispanic Southwest. Retold by Angel Vigil.

Thai Tales: Folktales of Thailand. Retold by Supaporn Vathanaprida. Edited by Margaret Read MacDonald.

Folk Stories of the Hmong: Peoples of Laos, Thailand, and Vietnam. By Norma J. Livo and Dia Cha.

Contents

*Stories marked with an * are translated into Spanish.*

Preface xiii
Acknowledgments xvii
Introduction..xix
    History of Mexico...xix
    Mexican Folk Arts...xxxiv
    The Stories in This Book...xlii
    A Guide to the Pronunciation of Aztec and Mayan Names xlvii
    Color Plates appear after page xlviii

Essential Legends..1

Background About The Eagle on the Cactus....................................3
    The Eagle on the Cactus 4
Background About *Nuestra Señora de Guadalupe*
    (Our Lady of Guadalupe) 5
    Nuestra Señora de Guadalupe (Our Lady of Guadalupe).....................7
    Nuestra Señora de Guadalupe...12
Background About *La Llorona* (The Weeping Woman)..........................17
    La Llorona (The Weeping Woman) 19
Background About *La Flor de la Noche Buena*
    (The Legend of the Poinsettia) 21
    La Flor de la Noche Buena (The Legend of the Poinsettia).................23
Background About *La China Poblana* 27
    La China Poblana...29
    La China Poblana...31
Background About The Legend of the Two Volcanoes 33
    The Legend of the Two Volcanoes 34
    La leyenda de los dos volcanes...36

Creation Stories from Indigenous Mexico 39

Background About The Five Suns..41
    The Creation of the World: An Aztec Myth....................................43
    Los cinco soles (La creación del mundo): Un mito azteca..................45
    The Flowing Waters (The Creation of the Earth): An Aztec Myth.......48
    Into the Fire (The Creation of the Sun and the Moon): An Aztec Myth 49

Creation Stories from Indigenous Mexico (*cont.*)

The Trail of Stars (How the Milky Way Came To Be): An Aztec Myth......51

The Broken Bones (The Creation of People): An Aztec Myth 52

*Food from the Gods (How Maize Came to the People): An Aztec Myth......54

Alimento de los Dioses (Cómo el maíz llegó a la gente): Un mito azteca 56

*Music from the Gods (How Music Came to the World): An Aztec
Myth 58

Música de los Dioses (Cómo la música llegó al mundo): Un mito
azteca...61

El Nopal (How the Cactus Came to the World): An Aztec Myth........64

*The Murmur of the River (How Music Came to the World): A
Mayan Myth 66

El murmullo del río (Cómo la música llegó al mundo): Un mito maya.....68

The Possum's Tail (How Fire Came to the World): A Mazatec Myth 70

The Gift of the Toad (Why People Use Sticks to Make Fire): A
Yaqui Myth..72

Badger Names the Sun (Why the Badger Lives Underground): A
Yaqui Myth..74

*The Bridge of Many Colors (The First Rainbow): A Zapotec Myth.....75

El puente multicolor (El primer arco iris): Un mito zapoteca 78

Song to Three Stars (Why Coyote Howls to the Sky): A
Tarahumara Myth...81

The Comet and the Tiger (Why the Tiger Has Black Spots): A
Mexica Myth 83

The Rain of Five Years (The Story of the Creation of the World):
A Huichol Myth..85

Stories from Spanish Colonial Mexico
Stories from Spanish Colonial Mexico 87

Trickster Tales 89

*Pedro and the Money Tree 89

Pedro y el Arbol de Dinero..92

Pedro and the Pig Tails...95

*Pedro and the Magic Pot..97

Pedro y la olla mágica...100

Pedro and the Mule Drivers 103

Pedro and the Giant 105

Pedro and the Hanging Tree 108

Pedro Goes to Heaven...110

Tales of Transformation, Magic, and Adventure................................112

*The Wonderful Chirrionera..112

La maravillosa chirrionera 118

The Waterfall of Wisdom..124

The Miracle of Mirajel 127

The Green Bird..133

The Enchanted Forest..138

The Jewels of Shining Light...146
Background About Juan Oso..153
Juan Oso...153
Dos Compadres Stories...164
*Ashes for Sale 164
Se venden cenizas 169
The Magic Cap 174
The Art of Lying 178
Animal Fables 181
*The Fox and the Coyote...181
El zorro y el coyote 186
*The Lion and the Cricket 191
El león y el grillo 194
The Mouse and the Ant 197
*The Owl and the Painted Bird 199
La lechuza y el pájaro pintado 201
The Ant Who Learned to Play the Flute 203
The Burro and the Fox...206

Glossary of Spanish Words...209
Suggested Readings 211
Permissions and Credits...215
Index 217
Author's Biography 223

PREFACE

For many Latinos living in the southwestern United States, a constant cultural connection is made with Mexico. For 250 years, from 1598 to 1848, the territory that currently comprises the American southwestern states belonged to Mexico, either as part of New Spain (the Spanish colonial era of Mexico), from 1598 to 1821, or as part of independent Mexico, from 1821 to 1848. After 1848, when Mexico lost a disastrous war with the United States and ceded half of its northern land to the United States, the northern frontier of Mexico eventually became the states of California, Arizona, Nevada, Utah, New Mexico, Texas, and Colorado. To this day, these southwestern states continue to be home to descendants of the Spanish colonial and Mexican families that have been living there for generations. In addition, immigrants from Mexico continue to infuse the area with Mexican culture.

One legend that has helped Mexican Americans to define their cultural ancestry with Mexico involves the origin of the Aztec Indians. This legend tells of the Aztec Indians as having originated from a mythical homeland called Aztlan, an area in the northern part of Mexico. The popular belief among Mexican Americans is that Aztlan is located somewhere in the southwestern United States. However, debate continues as to the actual site of Aztlan, with Mexicans placing it inside present-day northern Mexico.

I begin this preface with these facts in order to illustrate that Mexico is an important and undeniable part of the history of the southwestern United States. This close, influential connection between Mexico and the southwestern United States became even more evident to me as I was doing research for my books on southwestern Hispanic culture. Latinos living in the American southwest share a religion, a language, a spiritual sentiment, a history, a cuisine, and a variety of cultural and artistic traditions, including oral traditions, with Mexico. Like many Latinos living in the American Southwest, I also consider Mexico to be a constant cultural reference point and a continuing source of cultural and artistic inspiration.

The oral traditions of the Hispanic Southwest are especially tied to those of Mexico—a fact I became aware of when I was writing my first book, a collection of southwestern Hispanic stories and legends. Almost every story in the book had a Mexican version or source, effectively doubling my total amount of stories. In fact, when I had finished the book, I had so many stories left over that I could have easily written a second volume. Instead, I decided to expand my knowledge and storytelling performance bases with further research on Mexican oral traditions.

This book is the result of that work. The stories in this book are traditional tales from the eras of pre-Conquest indigenous Mexico and Spanish colonial Mexico. Many of these stories exist in both a Mexican version and a southwestern United States version. The tales in this book are especially associated with Mexican oral traditions.

Another impetus for this book was my work as a professional storyteller. My storytelling performances, for both school-age and adult audiences, include a mixture of stories from the Hispanic Southwest and Mexico. At many of my performances, especially in schools, it is common to find Mexican nationals in the audience. Because of this, I have deliberately expanded my performance repertoire to include stories from Mexico.

Often, after one of my storytelling performances, audience members will approach me to share their versions of one of my stories. While these moments would not meet the standards of academic field research and story collection, they have provided me with many personal variations of traditional stories. Members of my audiences who are Mexican nationals living in the southwestern United States have been particularly helpful in this manner. I have often felt that they were just happy to hear one of their own stories while being so far from home.

It is always a great pleasure for me to have an audience member come forward and tell me a snippet of another tale or recommend a story for me to add to my repertoire. In this way, I have learned new versions of *historias*, *mitos*, and *leyendas* from my Mexican friends. These experiences proved influential while I was formulating the list of stories to include in this book.

I have often added to or adjusted my own versions of these stories based upon an especially interesting element from one of these shared versions. This sharing of stories is also another way in which the oral traditions remain a living part of a culture and escape the rigidity that occurs when traditional culture exists only in museum or archival collections.

As an active storyteller, I construct my stories into modern retellings of traditional tales. I work firmly within the belief that each generation of *cuentistas*, or storytellers, retells the traditional stories to meet the artistic sensibilities of its own audiences. Oral traditions thrive and prosper as individual storytellers pass stories along from generation to generation, with each storyteller adding his or her own embellishments to the stories.

While I am faithful to and respectful of the form and content of the traditional story, these versions are my own adaptations. In the storytelling community, there exists the concept of respecting a story's core of authenticity. The concept refers to the practice of modern *cuentistas* retelling traditional stories and ensuring that the core of the tale remains untouched and true. I have strived to respect these traditional stories so that any listener or reader would recognize the Mexican story at the center of my retelling. The stories in this book are the written versions of the stories I tell in my performances. They reflect the evolution of the traditional tale as it lives as part of an active oral tradition.

One of the unfortunate consequences of modern life is that people seldom have the opportunity to experience storytelling as a live art form. Listening to traditional stories was once a part of a person's regular experience—part of their cultural heritage. Generations of adults have passed on their wisdom and values to younger generations through these stories. My hope is that a parent, teacher, or student will find one of these stories, fall in love with it, and tell the story to someone else.

I tell my audiences that I am giving these stories to them. I want them to hear them and read them over and over until they know them by heart. Then I ask them to be part of the great storytelling tradition—the tradition that can still be an important part of their culture and their family's life. As storytellers and authors from all cultures collect and write down their own beloved traditional tales, their modern retellings will help keep alive the great legacy of the oral tradition, which is at the heart of every culture.

My greatest pleasure as a *cuentista* is to hear a child laugh at a funny turn of a story or to see an adult nod their head in recognition of an especially moving part of a story. My greatest satisfaction as an author is to know that these stories will continue to be available to people in written form, especially because so little opportunity is available in modern life to hear the story in its oral form. My most sincere desire is that the readers of this book will better appreciate and understand the people of Mexico and their magnificent culture. My greatest hope is that perhaps, one day, a story I have preserved in written form will be rediscovered and will resurface, transformed anew by a storyteller back into the living oral tradition.

ACKNOWLEDGMENTS

I wish to thank my publisher, Libraries Unlimited, for its support of my books on Hispanic culture and its continuing commitment to publishing culturally diverse books about the Hispanic culture. This is my third book published by Libraries Unlimited, and I am proud to be one of their authors.

I also wish to thank my editors, Susan Zernial, Barbara Ittner, Mary Cullen, and copy editor Louise Tonneson Rodriguez. As any author will confess, working with great editors is essential in the book-making process. I was fortunate to work with not one, but four great editors. I appreciated their creative ideas, their professional advice, and their dedication in guiding this book to completion.

I also wish to thank my longtime collaborators, artists Al Cárdenas and Carol Kimball. Their great talents and willingness to participate in these literary projects continue to bring beauty and artistry to my books. They have contributed to every one of my books, and I am very thankful for the opportunity to work with them on a continuing basis.

In addition, I wish to thank Lorenzo Ramírez and Indalesia Gonzales, the models for the Mexican *folklórico* costumes; Judy Miranda, the photographer of the Mexican *folklórico* costumes; Rod and Kim Warner and Ted Thomas, owners of Mexican import art galleries; and Spanish translators, Francisco Miraval, Stefanie Bakken, Peggy Salisbury, and Enrique Mejía Hernández for the contributions they made to this book. Their support and help greatly enhanced its quality.

INTRODUCTION

HISTORY OF MEXICO

The history of Mexico can be divided into three distinct eras. The first is the pre-Conquest indigenous era, covering thousands of years in ancient history until the arrival of the Spanish *conquistadores* in 1519. The second period, the Spanish colonial era of New Spain, three centuries of Spanish rule and influence, lasted until 1821. The final period, the era of the independent nation of Mexico, began in 1821 when Mexico gained its independence from Spain.

Pre-Conquest Indigenous Era

Archaeologists believe that humans first entered the Americas sometime between 40,000 and 20,000 B.C. These nomadic Stone Age people came from Asia and crossed over the Bering Strait, the land bridge that connected Siberia to Alaska at the end of the last ice age. These first people of the Americas then began their long journey into North America, Central America, and South America. By 10,000 B.C., these nomadic hunters had reached the central plateau of Mexico. By 3000 B.C., the inhabitants of the region of central and southern Mexico, which is known as Mesoamerica, or middle America, had learned to cultivate *maize* and had established farming villages. Centuries later, these early village settlements would become the great cultural centers of Mesoamerica.

The northern part of Mexico had been too barren and dry to support the foundation of large civilizations. However, the land to the south, in the central plateau region of modern Mexico and Central America, was a fertile region capable of sustaining large settlements. By 1000 B.C., the people of Mesoamerica had established the foundations of civilization: large ceremonial centers, intensive farming, and a stratified social system with elite rulers.

Specifically, the term Mesoamericans refers to the pre-Conquest indigenous people living in the regions of present-day Mexico, Belize, Guatemala, Honduras, and San Salvador. Mesoamerica was the site of the rise and fall of several significant civilizations, the final of which was the Aztec civilization that the Spanish eventually conquered.

When the Spanish first set foot in the New World, the population of Mesoamerica was at its height, at around 17 million people. In addition, Mesoamerica was one of two areas—the other being the central Andes—that had highly developed civilizations when the Spanish arrived.

The history of Mesoamerica is the history of advanced cultures with highly developed artistic and architectural accomplishments. It is also the history of cultural groups that shared a geographic area and influenced the evolution of each other's cultures over thousands of years.

For the purpose of this short overview of pre-Conquest indigenous history, this section will concentrate on the major civilizations that developed in Mesoamerica. These are the Olmecs, the Maya, the Zapotecs, the Toltecs, and the Mexicas/Aztecs. These civilizations, which flourished in Mesoamerica, share similar characteristics. These characteristics include the cultivation of *maize*, beans, and chiles; the use of complex calendars consisting of a sacred 260-day calendar combined with a 365-day calendar; a ritual ball game; hieroglyphic writing; large markets; ancestor worship; human sacrifice; an institutionalized priesthood, and monumental temple pyramids. The peoples of these cultures shared a complex religious belief system that included many of the same gods and also developed an extensive trade network over vast areas. Mesoamerican people never developed the wheel or metal tools for practical use and did not use draft animals.

The people of Mesoamerica built their cities in a wide variety of geographic areas of present-day Mexico: The Olmecs built cities in the eastern coastal lowlands; the people of the mysterious city of Teotihuacan, the Toltecs, created their cities in the highlands (as did the Aztecs); and the Maya planned their cities in both the lowlands and the highlands of southeastern Mexico.

The Mesoamerican age can be divided into three periods. The pre-classic period, which lasted from approximately 2000 B.C. to A.D. 250, was dominated by the Olmec civilization, the mother culture for the following Mesoamerican civilizations. The classic period, which lasted from A.D. 250 to A.D. 900, saw the development of the great Teotihuacan and Mayan cultures. Also taking place during this period was the establishment of large state-level civic and political organizations, hierarchical class systems with an elite ruling class, large market systems, tributary economies, and full-time craft and agricultural specialization. The end of the classic period brought with it a sudden decline in population and the abandonment of major city centers. The cause is uncertain, but scholars theorize that ecological deterioration, drought, famine, overpopulation, warfare, and disease are likely culprits. Finally, the post-classic period, which lasted from A.D. 900 to the arrival of the Spanish, saw the rise of the militaristic and warring civilizations of the Toltecs and the Aztecs.

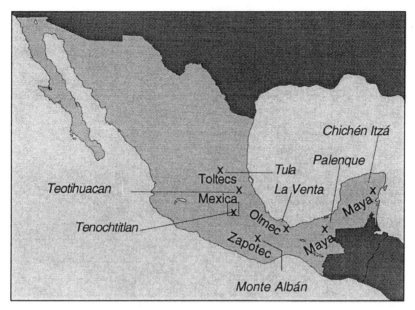

Figure 1 Mesoamerican cultural areas and cities.

The Olmecs

The Olmecs, Nahuatl for "rubber people," represented the first major civilization in Mesoamerica. Their civilization, beginning around 1500 B.C., was centered in the tropical, forested lowland along the gulf coast of Mexico near present-day Veracruz. Over a thousand years they built a culture that served as the mother culture for future civilizations. The Olmecs constructed the earliest temple pyramids; developed number systems and picture writing, which consisted of glyphs; and developed the Mesoamerican calendar. Other Mesoamerican cultural features that first appeared in Olmec culture include: complex settlement and ceremonial systems; large ceremonial and religious centers; the ball game, a ceremonial team game played with a rubber ball; extensive use of carved jade; highly organized social systems; and well-established trade systems.

The Olmecs' art forms were distinctive and included realistic athletic figures, stylized reliefs, and fine jade jewelry. They are also known for their extraordinary basalt stone head sculptures, which measure from five feet to over nine feet tall and weigh over 20 tons. The heads resided in the Olmec sites of La Venta, San Lorenzo, and Tres Zapotes. These sculptures share similar facial characteristics, and all of them wear helmetlike headdresses. The apparent African features on the faces of these stone sculptures gave rise to the theory of early contact between peoples of the African continent and the Olmecs—a theory now contested.

Teotihuacan

The mysterious city of Teotihuacan, which is located 30 miles to the north of Mexico City, flourished between about A.D. 250 and about A.D. 750. In Nahuatl, Teotihuacan means "Abode of the gods." Part of the mystery of Teotihuacan is that scholars do not know who founded this great city. Teotihuacan had become the first urban civilization with permanent accommodations for a large population, a powerful centralized government, and a large ceremonial center. It was the largest Mesoamerican city, with a population of about 200,000. It was also the most influential Mesoamerican city, which made an impression on both the Toltecs and the Aztecs.

Figure 2 Olmec stone head.

Teotihuacan was noted for its great mural paintings that covered all public buildings. Two immense pyramids, the Pyramid of the Sun, which was almost 200 feet tall, and the Pyramid of the Moon, formed the ceremonial center of this highly developed city. Like other Mesoamerican cities, Teotihuacan experienced a mysterious decline. For unknown reasons, Teotihuacan was totally abandoned by A.D. 650. Possible causes for this decline include an earthquake, an epidemic, and crop failure.

The Toltecs

The Toltec culture emerged after the fall of Teotihuacan. Its capital city, near modern-day Tula, was Tollan, "Place of the Reed." The Toltecs ruled central Mexico, which is located north and west of Mexico City, from about A.D. 900 to about A.D. 1200. They were a mighty race of warriors, builders, and artists, who worshipped the god Quetzalcoatl, God of the Morning Star and creator of people. The civilization experienced a sudden collapse in the twelfth century, similar to that of Teotihuacan.

One myth of the Aztecs that may explain the downfall of the Toltec empire is that the Toltec ruler Quetzalcoatl was drugged by the dark god Tezcatlipoca. As a result, Quetzalcoatl was disgraced and forced to flee the city of Tula. Tezcatlipoca then ruled the people, and eventually, the Toltec empire disintegrated.

The departure of Quetzalcoatl was an important aspect of the story for the Aztecs. According to the story, when he fled Tula, Quetzalcoatl went to the East with a promise to return one day. Hundreds of years later, when the Aztec emperor Moctezuma heard of the arrival of strange men from the East (explorers from the New World), he believed that this event was the prophesied return of the god Quetzalcoatl. Because Moctezuma believed that Quetzalcoatl had returned to rule again, he initially did not oppose these men.

The Toltec capital city, Tula, was resplendent with stone carvings and statues of warriors. Their most famous warrior statues are located atop the remains of the Temple of Quetzalcoatl and demonstrate the warrior aspect of Toltec life and the Toltec devotion to the worship of the god Quetzalcoatl. The statues, known as *Telemones,* are 15 feet high. These imposing statues once served to hold up the temple roof. The warrior statue depicted in Figure 3 holds an *atlatl,* or spear-thrower, and wears a feather headdress and a butterfly breastplate.

The Zapotecs

The Zapotecs lived in the Oaxaca Valley in southern Mexico. Their civilization developed from 300 B.C. and lasted until about A.D. 950. They were contemporaries of the Maya to the east. The word Zapotec is derived from the Nahuatl "Tzapotecatl," meaning "people of the *zapote* tree," a tree that grows in abundance in the Oaxaca area. The Aztecs first used the word in the fifteenth century in referring to the native inhabitants of Oaxaca.

Figure 3
Toltec warrior statue.

The Zapotec capital city was Monte Albán, a ceremonial and religious center dedicated to the gods. This city, founded on a mountaintop near the center of the Valley of Oaxaca in about 500 B.C., was famous for its plazas and large stone carvings. The most recognized of these stone carvings are the *danzantes.* The *danzantes*—more than 150 huge stone reliefs—depict people in a dance-like pose. They show an Olmec influence in the deep slant of the mouth, the thick nose, and the helmetlike headdress. Various people from the Zapotec society are depicted on the *danzantes.* Because the figures appear to be in motion, the Spanish gave the stone carvings the name *danzantes.* However, more recent analysis has suggested that the figures could be corpses (as their eyes are closed), priests in rituals, or even prisoners of war.

Monte Albán also contained an observatory, a ball court, and temples decorated with frescoes. The Zapotecs also excelled in feather work and gold jewelry and developed one of the first hieroglyphic writing systems.

The most famous Zapotec is Benito Juárez, who was the president of Mexico from 1861 to 1863 and from 1867 to 1872.

The Maya

The Maya lived in southern Mexico, in the southeastern Yucatán Peninsula, and in present-day Central America, specifically, Guatemala and Honduras. They were an extremely accomplished and brilliant people known for their soaring temple pyramids. The Maya excelled in architecture, astronomy, and mathematics. In addition to their accurate 365-day calendar, which they used for astronomical observation and lunar cycle notation and which was more accurate than any calendar until modern times, they also developed a counting system

Figure 4
Zapotec *danzante* figure.

that included zero a thousand years before the Hindus. Their sophisticated and highly detailed stone carvings were unrivaled in Mesoamerica. The Maya also built domed observatories and shared a system of hieroglyphic writing similar to that of the Aztecs.

Religion dominated Mayan life in a manner similar to the Aztecs, with whom they shared many gods. And their mythic cosmology equaled in its complexity the Aztec cosmology. The Mayan sacred texts contained in the *Popol Vuh*, or "The Collection of Written Leaves," include this culture's myths and creation epics. *Popol Vuh* is the only indigenous work that originates from the pre-Conquest era of Mexican history. It was written in the Quiche language, the language of the Maya at the time of the Conquest.

The Maya flourished between A.D. 250 and A.D. 900, during the classic Mesoamerican period. Two of their grandest cities were Chichén Itzá and Palenque, but they were mysteriously abandoned around A.D. 900. Scholars believe that the Mayan culture declined due to overuse of a fragile environment and military pressures from surrounding warrior groups.

The most recognized of the Mayan stone sculptures is of Chac Mool. These reclining figures reflect the influence of the Toltec culture and are thought to be sacrificial altars. These sculptures are thought to represent the Mayan rain god

Chac. Another explanation of their purpose is that they represent various divinities. The first Chac Mool was discovered in the Mayan city of Chichén Itzá. These sculptures may also indicate a cross-influence of Toltec and Mayan cultures, for Chac Mools have also been discovered in the Toltec city of Tula.

Figure 5 Mayan Chac Mool.

The Mexicas/Aztecs

The Mexicas, later called the Aztecs, arrived in the central plateau of Mexico in about A.D. 1325. They were a nomadic people, and their legends told of their origin in a mythical land to the north, Aztlan. The Aztecs believed that Aztlan, meaning "Land of White Herons," was an island in a lake in northwest Mexico. In the early twelfth century, they left Aztlan and wandered for almost 200 years, led by their god Huitzilopochtli, searching for a promised land. According to the legend of Aztlan, the Aztec god Quetzalcoatl had told his people to look in their wanderings for a lake with an island in the middle of it. On the island would be a *nopal* cactus, and on top of the cactus would be an eagle with a snake in its mouth. By this sign they would know that they had found the place to establish their empire. Legend, of course, has the Aztecs finding this island with the cactus, eagle, and snake. Centuries later, the nation of Mexico would adopt this miraculous Aztec symbol of the eagle on a cactus with a serpent in its mouth for the central image of its flag.

After their visionary prophecy was fulfilled, the Aztecs settled on a marshy lake, Lake Texcoco, and there they founded their capital city, Tenochtitlan, which eventually became Mexico City. The city was named after their chieftain who had led them there, Tenoch, and for the word cactus, *nochtli*.

The Spanish marveled at Tenochtitlan, for they had never seen a city of its size and complexity before. To them, it rivaled any in Europe in size and grandeur. The Spanish were amazed by this elegant city's towering pyramids, floating gardens, flowing canals, and busy marketplaces. Tenochtitlan was designed with a water system and parkways and was surrounded by ingenious canals and fields for growing an abundance of food.

The Aztecs had constructed a sophisticated system of time measurement and kept accurate records of commerce and history. They also had an education system and an established literary tradition. Their cosmology was based upon myths of a pantheon of gods, most associated with their existence as an agricultural and warrior society.

By the mid-1400s the Aztecs had become the dominant civilization in the region. During their 200 years of wandering, they had conquered other nations in the Valley of Mexico, eventually forming a civilization that incorporated many of the conquered nations' religious and mythological customs. For their demanding and complex religion, the Mexicas/Aztecs maintained a severe practice of human sacrifice. At the height of their power, their territory ranged from central to southern Mexico. Moctezuma was the Aztec ruler at the time of the Spanish arrival in 1519.

Like the Toltecs, the Aztecs were a warrior society that elevated the status of its successful warriors. Success meant capturing prisoners in answer to religious demands for ritual sacrifice. One of the most prestigious military orders was the order of the eagle. The eagle symbolized the Sun, to which all sacrifices were made. The eagle warrior statue depicted in Figure 6 was one of two found guarding the doorway to the Great Temple in the Aztec capital of Tenochtitlan. The statue portrays a warrior wearing a helmet on his head that is shaped like an eagle's beak, wings on his arms to imitate eagle wings, and imitation eagle talons wrapped around his knees.

Coined by Alexander von Humboldt in 1813, the word Aztec represents a combination of the word *Aztlan*, in reference to the mythical homeland of the Mexica people, and the word *teca*, literally meaning "people of." Today, the name Aztec refers to the Nahuatl-speaking people of the Valley of Mexico and neighboring valleys. It also refers to the Aztec empire that dominated central and southern Mexico when the Spanish arrived in the New World. A more exact use of the word Aztec refers to the people of pre-Conquest Mexico, while Nahua or Nahuas refers to the Nahuatl-speaking Aztec descendents of post-Conquest times. The name Mexica was the source of Mexico's name.

Spanish Colonial Era of New Spain

The history of the Spanish colonial era of New Spain is the story of the blending, over three centuries, of the European Spanish culture the *conquistadores* brought with them to the New World with the indigenous cultures that existed when they arrived. Columbus' voyage of exploration represented the birth of European expansion in the New World. His discovery of the New World led to the conquest of indigenous cultures by European powers and forever changed the world. It was a brief 29 years between Columbus' discovery of America and the defeat of the Aztec empire in Mexico.

Figure 6 Aztec eagle warrior.

The first *conquistadores* who came to the New World in their *caravelas* (Spanish galleons) were explorers looking for gold and personal glory. Following them were the colonists, and later, religious missionaries. These military adventurers, colonists, and missionaries would create a New Spain, based upon the cultural heritage of their country in the Old World.

The history of New Spain begins with the epic story of the defeat of the Aztecs by Spanish explorer Hernán Cortés. With only 400 men, Cortés entered the Aztec capital of Tenochtitlan. Unbelievably, in spite of their highly sophisticated culture, the dominance of their empire, and their great power as a warrior culture, the Aztecs would not prevail against the Spanish. With his relatively small band of soldiers and aided by his consort and interpreter, the woman the Mexicans would later refer to as the traitorous *La Malinche*, he succeeded in defeating the glorious Aztec empire.

Several important factors contributed to the rapid conquest of the Aztec people by Cortés. One was the help of *La Malinche*, an indigenous woman from the Tabasco tribe, who as his translator, facilitated his first contacts with native populations. Another was the *conquistadores*' use of the horse, which had never been seen by the Aztecs. A third was the Spanish use of firearms and metallic armor, also never seen by the Aztecs. Also, because of their sacred legend foretelling the return of their god Quetzalcoatl from the east, the Aztecs originally believed that the Spanish were gods, and that Cortés was their returning god, Quetzalcoatl. A final factor in the eventual Spanish conquest of the Aztecs was their vulnerability to the diseases the Spanish brought with them to the New World. By the end of 1521, many thousands of Aztecs had died from smallpox, a disease unknown in the New World and for which the Aztecs had no immunity.

With the conquest of the Aztecs, the Spanish became the dominant European power in the New World and began systematic colonization of New Spain. Their territories extended from the Yucatán Peninsula to as far north as present-day Oregon and Missouri. The viceroyalty of New Spain was the world's largest political system in its time.

The Spanish set up governmental and economic systems in order to control the new lands and the people they found on those new lands. These feudal systems created huge landholdings, which were operated with the use of Indian labor.

The New Spain economic system was based upon the *encomienda*, a system of land distribution that allotted land and native workers to Spanish settlers who had given governmental or military service to the crown. The land estates were *haciendas*, the landowners were *patrones*, and the native laborers were *peones*. The laws of the *encomienda* system were supposed to protect the native workers, but common abuses occurred, resulting in a condition close to slavery for the native workers. Although it lasted for centuries, this system and its harsh injustices were eventually replaced after Mexican Independence from Spain in 1821.

The colony of New Spain was a society of strict social hierarchy. A descriptive system of bloodline nomenclatures created classes within Spanish society. *Peninsulares* were people of pure Spanish heritage born in Spain, and *criollos* were people of pure Spanish heritage born in the New World. Over time, intermarriage took place between native people and the Spanish, which gave rise to additional societal classes. *Mestizos* were people of mixed Indian and Spanish heritage, *mulatos* were people of mixed Black and Spanish heritage, and *zambos* were people of mixed Black and Indian heritage. During the colonial period, the greatest discrimination, after *Indios* and Blacks, fell on the people called *mestizo* and *zambo*.

The missionaries from Spain came to the New World determined to convert native people to Catholic Christianity. They established missions dedicated to educating the native people and teaching them the Spanish religion, language, and culture.

For 300 years, the Spanish ruled Mexico as a colony of Spain. Mexico became the most prized colony of Spain, and Spain dedicated itself to making Mexico a replica of itself in the New World. The Spanish even designed their cities based upon the traditional Spanish city: a *plaza* was located at the center of the city, around which were public buildings and the church.

Mexico's vast natural resources and riches were solely for the enrichment of Spain. Agriculture and the mining of gold and silver made New Spain a rich colony for Spain. Spanish-born officials lived a lavish, European-style existence, patterned after the opulence of Paris. The era of Spanish colonial New Spain created the circumstances for the inevitable Mexican revolution for independence from Spain. The extravagant and privileged lives of the *peninsulares* had created an explosive political and social situation.

The Independent Nation of Mexico

The history of the independent nation of Mexico is marked by several significant events. These include the War for Independence from 1810 to 1821, the Mexican War with the United States from 1846 to 1848, the Battle of Puebla, which was won by Mexico in 1862, and the Mexican Revolution of 1910.

By 1810, the Spanish had ruled Mexico for almost 300 years. During that time, they had instituted a tribute system that put *peninsulares* in the elite ruling class. Under them were the *criollos*, who, although they were of pure Spanish descent, but born in Mexico, were considered second-class citizens. And for the Mexican Indians, a system of near-slavery existed.

During the nineteenth century, *criollo* priests led the movement for Mexico's independence from Spain. They were educated members of colonial society; thus they were aware of Enlightenment ideas of individual worth and freedom from autocratic governments. France's occupation of Spain in 1808 filled the *criollos* with the French ideals of *liberté, égalité,* and *fraternité* (freedom, equality, and brotherhood). They resented *peninsulares* who kept them from rising in the Church hierarchy. Although they were *criollos*, they viewed themselves as equals to the *peninsulares*. They held grievances against the Church, which favored the *peninsulares* and were sympathetic to the plight of the Mexican Indians.

The city of Querétaro was one of the centers of the Mexican independence movement. Its conditions as a mining area and the harsh treatment of the Indian laborers in the mines contributed to Querétaro's aggressive stance toward independence. Leaders of the independence movement formed the Querétaro Society.

Father Miguel Hidalgo y Costilla, a *criollo* Catholic priest, was born in 1753 near Guanajuato. As a priest, he worked in Dolores and eventually became involved with teaching the Indians. He had mastered the Otomí Indian language of his parishioners and worked hard to improve their lives. He was also a member of the Querétaro Society and shared the belief that Mexico had a right to independence.

Father Hidalgo was an active participant in a plot to gain Mexico's independence from Spain. The plotters had planned on forming an army, seizing towns, and expelling the *peninsulares*. The members of the Querétaro society chose Father Hidalgo to lead the independence movement.

The group's plan was discovered on September 15, 1810. Father Hidalgo, along with three other independence leaders, decided to immediately begin the fight for independence. On September 16, Father Hidalgo rang the church bells at Delores to gather his parishioners. He called for the expulsion of the *peninsulares*, the independence of Mexico, and the end of the Indian tribute system. His followers went on to capture Guanajuato and other small towns, eventually marching on Mexico City. He is remembered for the *El Grito de Delores*, the Cry of Dolores, which called for all patriots to begin the struggle for Mexican independence.

Father Hidalgo did not live to see Mexico's independence, for he was eventually captured and executed. Mexican independence fighters struggled in their attempts to defeat native Spanish forces and to establish an independent government. It would take 11 years before Spain recognized Mexico's independence. Finally, in 1821, Mexico gained her freedom from Spain and became a sovereign nation.

Figure 7 Father Miguel Hidalgo y Costilla at Delores, Mexico, ringing the church bell and standing before a flag of the Virgin of Guadalupe to begin the Mexican fight for independence.

To this day, on the night of September 15, all of Mexico remembers Father Hidalgo's *Grito de Delores* and calls out "*!Viva Mexico! Viva La Independencia!*" (Long Live Mexico! Long Live Independence!) Father Hidalgo is known as the father of Mexico, and *El Diez y Seis de Septiembre* is celebrated as Mexican Independence Day.

But Mexico's great victory of independence would be short lived. Mexico was soon to lose half of its lands to the United States, which was operating in the Americas under manifest destiny, a militant policy driven by a vision of a country with borders spanning from sea to sea. This policy empowered the United States to claim Mexican land.

In 1844, U.S. President James K. Polk was elected on a policy of western expansion. In 1846, U.S. troops confronted the Mexican army at the Texas-Mexican border, and thus began the Mexican-American War. The war ended in 1847 after American armies captured Mexico City in the Battle of Chapultepec Castle.

In 1848, the Treaty of Guadalupe Hidalgo ended the Mexican-American War. This treaty ceded the northern portion of Mexico to the United States. As a result, the area containing all or parts of the present-day states of California, Arizona, Nevada, Colorado, New Mexico, and Texas became part of the United States.

Despite Mexico's independence from Spain, the concentration of wealth had remained in the hands of the elite class of government and church rulers. The life of the Mexican Indian remained as poor as it always had been under the *encomienda* system of the preindependence era.

Benito Juárez, a Zapotec Indian who would later become president of Mexico, realized the injustice of the political and social system and fought for equality for all Mexicans. Because of his efforts to win equal justice for Mexican Indians, he has been referred to as the "Abraham Lincoln of Mexico." Juárez had helped to institute the constitution of 1857, which ended special privileges and political power for the church and the ruling elite. This constitution also called for the freedom of religion, education, assembly, and the press. But Mexican conservatives opposed the new constitution, and Mexico found itself in another war with its own people and government. Juárez was elected president under a republican form of government, which had been established in the constitution.

By the time Juárez assumed leadership of Mexico in 1861, it was an economically bankrupt country torn apart by years of internal hostilities. Mexico had experienced great civil strife and economic struggle under a series of governments and leaders. It had also lost a disastrous war with the United States to which it ceded half of its land. Even the great silver mines had been allowed to stop production by former governments. In order to have time and resources to rebuild the Mexican economy, one of Juárez's first acts as president was to suspend the interest payments on the country's foreign debts.

Mexico's refusal to pay the interest on its debts angered the European powers of England, Spain, and France. Juárez felt that he could assure the three countries that Mexico would eventually honor its debts but needed time to establish a new government and rebuild its economy. Mexico owed the largest debt to England—69 million *pesos*. Ten million *pesos* were owed to Spain and two million *pesos*—the smallest amount—were owed to France. The Mexican Congress voted to support the debt moratorium, and both England and Spain eventually agreed to Mexico's request to delay debt payment. Only France denied the request for a debt moratorium and demanded payment of its debt.

Mexican conservatives who were not in agreement with the idea that a republican form of government, like that of Juárez, was best for Mexico, created political unrest in the country. They tried to change the government of Mexico back to a conservative form of government, with power in the hands of a ruling elite and the Church. The conservatives also sought supporters in France to aid them in the overthrow of the elected Juárez government.

At the same time, France was seeking to establish an extension of its empire in the Americas. France knew that the United States was engulfed in its own civil war at the time. And although one tenet of the Monroe Doctrine of the United States was that no European power would establish a governmental presence in the Americas, France seized the opportunity and sent an invading force to Mexico.

Mexican conservatives, led by General Juan Almonte, the Mexican Ambassador to France, had convinced Emperor Napoleon III to invade Mexico and establish a conservative government to rule in France's name. Napoleon agreed to send a French army of 6,000 troops to invade Mexico, under the leadership of the famous French General Charles Latrille.

Although the French forces were vastly superior, the Mexican forces were in a desperate battle for their country. This realization and their courage prepared the Mexicans for an astounding victory. Roberto Cabello-Argandoña (1993), in his book *Cinco de Mayo: A Symbol of Mexican Resistance*, reports the stirring words Mexican General Ignacio Zaragoza used to encouraged the Mexican fighters:

> "Today you fight for something sacred. You shall fight for your Fatherland, and I promise you that this day's journey will bring glory. Your foes are the first soldiers of the world. But you are the first sons of Mexico. They have come to take your country away from you. Soldiers, I read victory and faith on your foreheads. Long Live Independence! Long Live the Fatherland!" (61)

The French army was the greatest military force in the world at that time. Its soldiers were professional, well trained, well equipped, and experienced in battle. The Mexican army, in contrast, was a peasant army, ill equipped and assembled solely to fight the invading French army.

On May 5, 1862, the French army attacked the Mexican town of Puebla, expecting to easily defeat the Mexican defenders and continue its march to Mexico City. The French attacked the forts surrounding Puebla three times; and three times, the Mexican army, under the leadership of General Zaragoza, repelled the French army. Fighting valiantly, the Mexican army finally succeeded in defeating the vastly larger French army and forced its retreat. The French army was stunned by its defeat. The Mexican army had won one of the most astounding victories in military history.

But Napoleon III was determined to conquer Mexico. In response to the defeat of his forces at Puebla, he sent an army of 30,000 troops to restore France's efforts to conquer Mexico. Eventually, just by the sheer size of the French forces, France was able to triumph. A year later, Napoleon III placed Count Maximilian in Mexico City and established a French monarchy in Mexico. Juárez fled Mexico City with the vow to never give up the fight for his country.

In 1867, Juárez and his Mexican loyalist followers finally succeeded in reconquering the country and once again established Mexico as an independent nation. Maximilian was executed, the French left Mexico, and Juárez resumed leadership of his country.

The victory at Puebla came to symbolize the strength, determination, and national pride of the Mexican people. It was an important historical moment for the new country. Juárez's own words best represent the spirit of *Cinco de Mayo:* "Between two individuals as between nations, respect for another's rights is peace!"

After the French withdrew from Mexico, the independence of the country was assured. Juárez would serve in the office of president until his death in 1872. General Porfirio Díaz, one of Juárez's generals, assumed the presidency in 1876 and ruled Mexico for the next 35 years. While Juárez had anchored his leadership of Mexico around the principles of democracy and economic development, Díaz believed that the stability of a dictatorship would benefit the economy of Mexico best. In many ways, the rule of Díaz did greatly benefit Mexico. He increased foreign investment and balanced the national budget. His control of the army and police also acted as a stabilizing force against the social strife of revolutions and coups that had been part of the early history of independent Mexico.

Although Díaz recognized the need for the modernization of Mexico, he created social systems of great inequality that eventually led to his downfall and another Mexican revolution. His policies of preference for the wealthy landowners, industrialists, and foreign investors and his regranting of former privileges to the Church, army, and traditional aristocracy eventually caused the Indian peasants to be as abused by the economic and political systems as they had been in the days of Spanish colonialism. In 1910, Mexico erupted in a revolution to overthrow Díaz.

The Mexican revolution was led by Pancho Villa in the north and Emiliano Zapata in the southern state of Morelos to win justice and equality for Mexicans. Their revolutionary struggle led to the resignation and exile of Díaz and to the eventual creation of the Constitution of 1917, which granted Mexicans new rights as citizens of their nation. This constitution is based upon principles of land redistribution, the nationalization of Mexico's natural resources, the recognition of increased rights of citizenship, education for all Mexicans, and the right of poor people to own land.

In 1929, the National Revolutionary Party was created. It later became known as the PRI, the *Partido Revolucionario Institucional.* Essentially, Mexico became a one-party democracy with the PRI winning every election since its inception.

Today Mexico is a thriving modern nation. The formal name for the country is *Estados Unidos Mexicanos*, the United Mexican States. It has 31 states and one Federal District similar to the District of Columbia in the United States. Mexico's capital, Mexico City, is projected to reach a population of 25 million by the year 2000, making it the largest city in the world.

Figure 8 The states of modern Mexico.

1a Baja California Sur
1b Baja California Norte
2 Sonora
3 Chihuahua
4 Sinaloa
5 Duranog
6 Coahuila
7 Nuevo León
8 Zacatecas
9 San Luis Potosi
10 Tamaulipas
11 Nayarit
12 Aguascalientes
13 Jalisco
14 Guanajuato
15 Querétaro
16 Hidalgo
17 Colima
18 Michoacán
19 México
20 Morelos
21 Tlaxcala
22 Puebla
23 Veracruz
24 Guerrero
25 Oaxaca
26 Chiapas
27 Tabasco
28 Campeche
29 Yucatán
30 Quintana Roo
31 Distrito Federal (Federal District)

Modern Mexico continues to be a mixture of Spanish and indigenous influences. The language, religion, and culture of Spain remain dominant characteristics of Mexican life, while indigenous peoples contribute active and significant aspects of their culture to Mexico's society.

Mexico is a country that has survived conquest, colonialism, and revolution. It has successfully created a culture combining powerful aspects of two cultures— the indigenous and the European. The history of Mexico cannot adequately be told in a series of encapsulated stories about historical events and people. But the preceding stories still reveal the great character of its people, the strength of their vision, and the truth of their history.

MEXICAN FOLK ARTS

In the introduction to his book *Folktales of Mexico*, Américo Paredes (1970) writes:

> "Mexico is deeply and passionately a land of folklore. One author has said that over half of her people live folkloric lives." (xi)

The author he refers to is the renowned folklorist and unchallenged authority on Mexican folkways, Frances Toor. Toor (1947) further describes the vast variety of Mexican folk arts in her classic text *A Treasury of Mexican Folkways:*

> "The Mexican folk arts are among the most varied and beautiful in the world. Every region has its own kinds, styles, and designs. Humble objects are touched with beauty." (39)

In their books, both Paredes and Toor speak to the incredible richness and diversity of Mexican artistic and folk culture. Their writings also document the importance of Mexican folklore in the lives of the Mexican people.

The subject of this book is the representation of oral traditions of Mexican folklore culture through the traditional tale. In order to present further aspects of Mexican folklore culture and to give a small indication of the great range of Mexican folk arts, I have selected four important and easily accessible types of folk arts for illustration in this book's color plates. Of course, these are by no means meant to represent the full spectrum of Mexican folk arts. I have selected these four types because they can be easily researched if a reader wishes to pursue this area more fully, either through study or travel, and they are typical of the folk arts available to students and aficionados of Mexican folk culture in the United States.

The color plates presented in this book are not meant to cover the immense variety of Mexican folk arts and dance costumes. They are simply illustrative of the beauty and spirit of Mexican folk arts.

The bibliography lists many excellent texts for the reader interested in further study and more comprehensive discussions of Mexican folk arts. Especially recommended are *Oaxacan Woodcarving: The Magic in the Trees* by Shepard Barbash, *Mexican Masks* by Donald B. Cordry, *Mexican Indian Costumes* by Donald B. and Dorothy M. Cordry, *Arts and Crafts of Mexico* and *Mexican Costume* by Chloë Sayer, and *A Treasury of Mexican Folkways* by Frances Toor.

The Wood Carvings of Oaxaca

Oaxaca, home of the Zapotec Indians, is one of the most prolific states in Mexico for folk arts. From a vast variety of folk arts created in Oaxaca, the wood carvings of Oaxaca are one of the most common Mexican crafts found in the United States. In his book *Oaxacan Woodcarving: The Magic in the Trees*, Shepard Barbash (1993) comments on the popularity of Oaxacan wood carving and folk arts:

"Stretching out from the capital, the Oaxacan village nurtures an astonishing diversity of crafts. There is black pottery, red pottery, green-glaze pottery, fireworks, ornamental tin, and jewelry. There are serapes, belts, blouses, baskets, combs, candles, and puppets. Indeed, it is a testament to the region's inexhaustible reserve of creativity that wood carving—one of the best-selling Mexican crafts in the United States—is just one more star in the valley's dense, swirling galaxy of artistic traditions." (14)

The Oaxacan carvers use wood from the *copalillo*, or copal, tree for their creations. The benefit of using *copalillo* wood is that it carves easily, sands to a smooth finish, and absorbs little paint, which is common acrylic house paint. The carvers use this type of paint because it holds its bright color and does not easily fade. For tools, the carvers use simple machetes and kitchen or pocketknives.

Mexican carvings have a fanciful name: *alebriges*. The name itself was an invention of Pedro Linares, a papier-mâché artist in Mexico City. Barbash relates the legend that the name *alebrige* came to Linares in a fever-induced nightmare of an antenna-covered monster carving. Over time, the name *alebrige* transferred to other export craft, including Oaxacan wood carving.

Oaxacan wood carving is an ancient pastime similar to the recreational wood carving folk arts of rural cultures worldwide. In earlier times, the Oaxacan wood carvers created utilitarian household objects and toys for their families. They also carved objects they needed for their religious ceremonies. In time, the influence of the tourist market, with its desire for objects with cultural authenticity, began to dominate the work of the wood carvers. The poverty of the rural lifestyle also persuaded the wood carver to create his folk arts for the tourist and collector markets.

Unlike the Huichol bead art and yarn weaving, Oaxacan wood carving does not carry symbolic or religious meaning. In truth, it is a colorful folk art satisfying tourist and American markets. The great success of the Oaxacan carvers is due to their expert craftsmanship and to their ability to imagine a host of fanciful subjects for carving. Color Plates 1 and 2 show examples of Oaxacan wood carving.

The Yarn Paintings and Bead Art of the Huichol Indians

The Huichol Indians of the west central Mexican states Nayarit and Jalisco are one of Mexico's indigenous groups who have most successfully held on to their traditional ways, in particular, their religious practices. They live a rural life in inaccessible mountain areas.

One important aspect of Huichol religion is the use of peyote for shamanistic communication with their gods. The Huichol Indians believe that their peyote dreams are sacred visions allowing them to experience the truths of the physical and spiritual world. For the Huichol, the "*mara'akame*," the shaman, is the guide for their spiritual pilgrimages.

Traditional Huichol art is a form of prayer expressing the peyote visions of the Huichol shaman. Contemporary Huichol art remains an expression of these religious foundations, but it has expanded to address the needs of the contemporary Huichol. As with Oaxacan wood carving, these contemporary needs include the tourist and collector markets.

Huichol art is also a symbolic art. The vivid colors and figures expressed in the art are symbols of the wisdom gained from the Huichol Indians' peyote dreams. These motifs are the Huichol artists' expressions of their religious worship and cultural wisdom. Common artistic and religious symbols used in Huichol art include birds, deer, snakes, wolves, flowers, the Sun, fire, shaman spirit guides, and prayer arrows.

Huichol yarn paintings were originally simple yarn decorations placed around small stone tablets called *nierika*. The Huichol placed these *nierika* in sacred caves or used them in their religious pilgrimages and ceremonies as sacred offerings to their gods. The *nierika* evolved into elaborate yarn paintings filled with symbolic imagery reflecting the Huichol sacred knowledge.

The Huichol make contemporary yarn paintings by first drawing their designs on a wooden board. Next, they cover the board with a thin layer of beeswax. Starting with the borders, they push yarn into the wax. They then form the main figures and images of the painting, finishing with the background colors.

An inscription on the back of Color Plate 3, the large yarn painting, reads:

> "This picture tells us of the five colors of corn that represent to us a child of five days, who is baptized in the holy water of the gods. We see well two leaves of natural water and two eagles, which represent all the beauties of the Huichol art." (Translated from Spanish.)

The Huichol artist wrote this inscription as an explanation of the painting's symbolism. Color Plates 4 through 6 are close-up views of the primary images in the painting: the Sun, the eagle, and the corn.

Huichol bead art (see Color Plates 7–10) evolved in a manner similar to the yarn paintings. The Huichol beadwork has its origins long before the Spanish conquest. The Huichol used shells, seeds, and stones colored with insect or vegetable dyes to decorate gourd prayer bowls used as offerings to their gods. These prayer gourds evolved into the symbolic sculptures covered with glass beads that the Huichol make today.

In making their bead art, the Huichol begin by carving the base figure out of wood. They then cover the figure with a mixture of beeswax and pine pitch and press glass beads into it. The Huichol artist applies each bead individually with the end of a beading needle. Some artists begin by drawing the designs on the figure, and others work in a freehand style.

The Huichol believe that their beaded masks are mirrors that allow them to see into the sacred world of religious visions. They do not wear the masks, but rather they see the masks as another form of religious art that expresses the holy wisdom of their visions.

The Huichol use their art to express a vision of their everyday life and, at the same time, to keep their traditional beliefs and practices alive. Part of the Huichol effort, like the Oaxacan wood carver, is to meld traditional folk art practices with the realities of economics and the desires of the tourist and collector. The struggle these modern-day traditional artists face is with using their traditional arts to answer the necessity of providing a livelihood for their family and community.

The Masks of Mexico

Donald Cordry (1980), in his magnificent and scholarly book *Mexican Masks*, writes about the profound artistic expression shown in the design of Mexican masks:

> "The masks of Mexico are an expression of the fertile artistic imagination and skill of the Mexican people. Although these highly individualistic works are not rigidly bound by traditional styles, they reveal the past, the religious beliefs, the archetypes, and the culture of their makers. As such, these masks clearly show two basic aspects of the Mexican people: the Christian face of European tradition, and the older face of the Indian world, whose miraculous survival provides a window to the past." (253)

Mexico's mask culture equals that of the great mask cultures of the world, which include the African, the Balinese, and the Native American. The mask traditions of Mexico date far back into the pre-Conquest history of Mexico. Striking historical mask artifacts made of stone, wood, and mosaic give testimony to the powerful use of masks for ceremonial, ritual, and magical purposes in indigenous Mexico. The masks of the post-Conquest era are equally powerful in their great visual diversity. For the reader interested in further study on the subject of Mexican masks, Cordry's *Mexican Masks* is especially recommended.

The color plates described below provide illustration of the wide range of Mexican mask styles. The first three masks, Color Plates 11 through 13, were all produced by the same carver from the village of Tocuaro, in the state of Michoacán. The masks in Color Plates 14 through 17 are from the state of Guerrero. Guerrero has long been recognized as one of the most active and renowned states for mask carving in Mexico. The masks in Color Plates 11 through 17, like most modern Mexican masks, are carved from wood. The masks in Color Plates 18 through 20 are painted coconut shells.

The Costumes of *Folklórico* Dance

The folk dances of Mexico are as varied as the country itself. Every region and state has its own traditional dances, as well as accompanying music and costumes. Each Mexican *folklórico* dance reflects the character and climate of its own region.

In this section, the various types of traditional *folklórico* costumes will be described as presented in the color plates. The costumes, selected from several states, represent a wide geographic sampling of Mexican regions, from the Pacific coast to the gulf coast, and from the central states to the southern states. While these costumes represent the most well known dances from the selected states, keep in mind that each region or state has other dances and costume styles.

Michoacán Costume

The men's costume (see Color Plate 21) is peasantlike. It has embroidery on the shirt and the pants and is white to reflect the sun. The men wear big, round, brimmed hats that have a little tassel on the back of them. The cross-ribbon work on the hat is representative of the region.

The women wear flowers on their hats (see Color Plate 21). The women's costume also includes an apron, which is decorated with embroidery. Slips, which are decorated with ribbon work, are worn underneath the women's dresses. The black *rebozo*, tucked into the dress, is typically part of the women's costume. The *rebozo* is a common rural folk garment, and it appears in many folk costumes. It can serve as a shawl, a head covering, a blanket, or when wrapped over the shoulders and crossed in front, for adornment. The red sash is also typical of these rural peasant costumes.

The *Michoacán folklórico* dance is usually performed barefooted, but it can be done wearing sandals.

Michoacán Viejito Costume

The Michoacán dance of *los Viejitos* is one of Mexico's most recognized dances. In the dance, young men, costumed and masked as old men, dance a comic, energetic dance. The costume is similar to the traditional men's Michoacán costume described above. The characteristic items for this dance are a comically smiling old man mask, a cane, a *poncho*, and a wide-brimmed hat decorated with hanging, colorful ribbons (see Color Plate 22).

Sinaloa Costume

Sinaloa is a state on the Pacific coast of Mexico, and the costumes of this area reflect the state's tropical climate (see Color Plate 23). The women's dress, which is decorated with bright floral patterns, is very colorful. The women wear head wrappings of a color matching the dominant color of their dresses. Over the head wrappings, they wear small, cowboy-like hats, which have flowers on the side of them. Their blouses have ruffles on the front and are short-sleeved or have no sleeves at all. Showing one shoulder is typical of how the women wear their costumes.

The men's costume consists of white pants and a shirt of the same color as the women's dominant dress color. The shirt's sleeves are worn rolled up. The men also wear Panama style hats typical of tropical regions. The men's costume is completed with a brightly woven belt.

Jalisco Costume

These costumes are more accurately called Jalisco *ranchera* costumes because they represent the costumes of rural Jalisco (see Color Plate 24). The men's costume is a *charro* suit similar to those worn by musicians in *mariachi* bands. The *charro* look is characteristic of a Mexican cowboy, rural horseman, or rodeo performer. The primary difference between this dance costume and the musicians' costume is in the decorations on the *charro* pants and jacket. A *mariachi* musician's *charro* pants are typically decorated with silver buttons on each side of the legs, while the dance costume from this region is typically decorated with decorative suede patterns. The men also wear suede boots to match the suede patterns on the pants. The straw hat also indicates the rural nature of this costume. The glittery *mariachi* hat is more urban and contemporary.

The women's costume includes a dress with puffy sleeves. Each dancer wears a dress of one basic color. The *ranchera*-style dress is fitted high up the neck and is all one piece. The ruffle work is sewn into the dress. The costume is designed with contrasting colored ribbons and decorative lace. The dress is full-length and worn with lace-up boots. Braids made of yarn to match the dancer's hair are usually doubled to form a headpiece. The sides of the headpiece are decorated with ribbon. The hairpiece and hairstyle indicate the correct Jalisco *ranchera* style.

Nayarit Costume

The women's dance costumes from Nayarit resemble those of the Jalisco *ranchera*, except that the Nayarit women's dress is fuller, with a more rounded shape, and the ruffles and sleeves are more exaggerated. The Nayarit costume dress is also fuller than the Jalisco dress. The dress fabric is also typically a flower print instead of a solid color. The bright colors on the dress reflect the influence of the Nayarit Huichol Indian brightly colored art.

The men's shirt is a peasant shirt of a color to match the dominant color of the women's dress. (A silk shirt, tied at the front, is often used for festive dances.) Peasant pants are also part of the men's costume. Other men's costume items include a red sash and black boots. The men do not wear hats for this costume, but they do wear headbands that match the dominant color of the women's dresses. The machete and palm fan are characteristic of the rural nature of the *Jarabe Nayarita* dances (see Color Plate 25). *Jarabe* means a syrupy sweet drink in Spanish, but it also is the name of a style of dance introduced to Mexico by the Spaniards.

Veracruz Costume

Veracruz, which means the "true cross" in Spanish, is on the Mexican gulf coast. The Veracruz region was the first place the Spanish landed in Mexico, and the dance costumes reflect this Spanish colonial influence (see Color Plate 26). It is especially evident in the style of the women's dress (see Color Plate 27), with its train, rich lace, embroidery, and ribbon decoration. The dress is very full and is usually white, but it can also be pastel colored. The black apron reflects the indigenous Indian influence in the region. Headpieces worn by the women are brightly colored. The costume also includes white shoes, a fan, and gold and silver jewelry—again, a Spanish colonial influence.

The men wear white pants, white shoes, and white shirts, which are called *guyaberas*. A *guyabera* is a very traditional men's shirt from this region. A red silk scarf and a hat, which is typical of the Veracruz style, complete the costume.

Guerrero Costume

The Guerrero women's costume (see Color Plate 28) is a full, pastel-colored dress that has lighter and darker ribbons sewn into it. The dress also has a flower print on the top neckline and around the full bottom of the dress. Lace also decorates the bottom and the top of the dress.

The men wear peasantlike shirts (see Color Plate 28) that have decoration on the tops and sleeves. Decoration is also found on the bottoms of the men's pants. The men's costume also includes black boots, a straw hat, and a handkerchief, which is used in the dance.

Yucatán Costume

The costumes of the Yucatán display a Mayan influence (see Color Plate 29). The women's costume includes the Mayan *huipil*, a sleeveless tunic dating to the pre-Conquest era of indigenous Mexico. The *huipil* used in Yucatán dances is a square-cut blouse, with embroidery on the top and bottom (see Color Plate 30). (For fancy wear—not for dance—the *huipil* can be made of embroidered silk.) Square skirts are worn underneath the *huipiles*. The women's hair is fixed with simple headpieces and combs tucked in the back. The costume includes a red *rebozo*.

The men wear simple, buttoned-up, white shirts called *filipinas*. They also wear white shoes or white sandals, straw Yucatán hats, and scarves tucked into the sides of their pants. The dancers pull out the scarves and use them in the dance.

THE STORIES IN THIS BOOK

Scholars of oral traditions and storytellers define stories according to several general categories. While the casual storyteller or audience member does not care about the technicalities of story classification, and indeed, knowing the proper story classification does not guarantee that the story or the storyteller will be any good, it is important to understand the differences between one story type and another. The more educated a storyteller, educator, or audience member is about story types, the better they can appreciate the vast variety of oral traditions and the more they can enjoy and understand the differences between stories. As one's knowledge about oral traditions increases, so does one's understanding of the cultural sensibilities contained in stories.

Folklorists and story collectors have documented that similar stories exist in cultures throughout the world. Stith Thompson (1946), the foremost authority on the folktale, writes in his book *The Folktale*:

> "Even more tangible evidence of the ubiquity and antiquity of the folktale is the great similarity in the content of stories of the most varied peoples. The same tale types and narrative motifs are found scattered over the world in the most puzzling fashion. A recognition of these resemblances and an attempt to account for them brings the scholar closer to an understanding of the nature of human culture." (6)

Folklorists present two general theories about the similarities of stories among cultures. One theory holds that stories originated with a single protoculture and then spread by diffusion throughout the world. Another theory contends that similar stories develop in separated lands because stories spring from a common deep well of human spirituality and unconsciousness. This theory explains that while every culture has its own defining and characteristic stories, the material of traditional stories is universal because people throughout the world share the same wishes, desires, dreams, and fears and create similar stories to express these feelings. Those who hold these two differing theories do agree, however, that story categories worldwide are very similar, and that it is possible to sort the stories of any culture into several general categories.

In this book I have retold stories representing several dominant story types. I have placed stories in categories according to their primary themes. I do acknowledge that other storytellers and writers might place particular stories in other categories.

For example, some legends and creation stories can also be considered myths. Myths are the grandest of stories. They are stories from the beginning of creation—a time of prehistory when the Earth was still new. Another characteristic of myths is that they are sacred to the people who originated them. Often, they are about supernatural heroes and gods. In this way, myths can be religious tales or sacred narratives that reflect a people's spiritual beliefs about their gods and the creation of their world.

Legends are much more common stories. Not common in the sense that they tell of the everyday, regular occurrence, for many legends do tell of an amazing event or person; but rather, common in the sense that they do not have the spiritual dimension or resonance of myths. The defining characteristic of a legend is that people believe it is a true story. Legends can be about historical people or events. They can be about everyday occurrences or they can be about landmark events and people of historical importance.

Often, storytellers and writers have difficulty deciding whether to categorize a story as a myth, a legend, or a creation story. Some stories about the gods and the founding events of time and history people believe as true history. These stories contain qualities of several categories and could correctly reside in more than one category. In truth, the classification of stories is sometimes subjective, and many stories do contain qualities of more than one category.

The first story category in this book is that of essential legends. This is a category of my own classification, created for the purposes of this book. Several of the stories in this category represent more than one story type. I have separated them from their standard story categories and grouped them together as "essential" because of their collective importance in Mexican oral tradition. They share the characteristic of being likely to appear in more than one collection of Mexican tales, as they are well known to a wide range of people in the Mexican culture and represent significant aspects of Mexican oral tradition. I present these tales as legends because Mexican people believe the events described in these stories to have occurred in their history.

For example, the first story in the "Essential Legends" section tells the historically important legend of the founding of the Aztec city that eventually became Mexico City. But it could also be a myth because of the role an Aztec god plays in guiding people on their journey of discovery. Two other legends from this section, "The Legend of the Poinsettia" and "The Legend of the Two Volcanoes," could also be called *pourquoi* stories—"The Legend of the Poinsettia," because it explains why the plant has its red leaves; and "The Legend of the Two Volcanoes," because it tells how two volcanoes came into existence.

Pourquoi means "why" in French; therefore, *pourquoi* stories answer the questions "How?" and "Why?" Often *pourquoi* stories are creation tales about the first occurrence of a natural phenomenon or about how an object got its name. They can give reason and understanding to the origins of human practices and can provide comfort by explaining frightening natural events.

The next story category in this book is creation tales from indigenous pre-Hispanic Mexico. These stories are from a small variety of indigenous Mexican Indian groups and represent a sampling of Mexican Indian groups and their *pourquoi* tales. The stories in this section are proper *pourquoi* stories because they offer explanation for all sorts of natural occurrences—from the grand story of why the world exists to the simpler story about why an animal appears the way it does.

The Mexican Indian groups represented in the creation stories category include several groups that remain culturally active today. The Huichol live in the highlands of the Sierra Madre Mountains of western Mexico, where the states of Nayarit and Jalisco border each other. The Mazatec live in northeastern Oaxaca. The Yaqui live in the barren Mexican northwest. The Tarahumara live in the mountains of southwestern Chihuahua. Descendants of the Mexicas/Aztecs are the Nahua, who form Mexico's largest indigenous group. The Nahua live in several central Mexican states. Modern descendants of the Maya live on the Yucatán Peninsula.

The next category of stories is from the Spanish colonial era of Mexican history. Almost all of these stories exist in other versions on the Iberian Peninsula of southwestern Europe and trace their origins to Spain. Spain, during the time of the discovery and conquest of the New World, was a culture containing the influences of the Greek, Roman, Arab, and Jewish people who had lived on the Iberian Peninsula. The stories of medieval Europe, as well as those from the Orient and India, also existed in Spain.

The stories of Spain at this time reflected these rich cultural influences. The Spanish culture of the *conquistadores* and early settlers in the New World blended these diverse influences into a many-faceted collection of stories. During the Spanish colonial era in the history of Mexico, these stories became widely dispersed throughout New Spain and, later, independent Mexico. They would even travel as far north as the land that would one day become the American Southwest.

The first story type from the Spanish colonial era is the trickster tales of Pedro de Ordimalas. These stories are classic trickster tales because they humorously tell the story of a clever underdog living by his guile and wits. Tricksters are commonly likable rogues who outfox authority and rule in order to survive. In their own way, trickster tales are about justice, for by pitting the underdog against unjust authority, the story offers a vision of the world in which the "little guy" can be the hero of his own story. A second variation on the trickster motif has the trickster being the fool who is bested by his own cleverness and ends up worse off than before.

Pedro de Ordimalas tales exist in Spanish literature as far back as the sixteenth century. The great Spanish author Miguel de Cervantes even wrote a play, *Comedia Famosa de Pedro de Urdemalas* that portrays the exploits of this famous trickster.

The next story type from the Spanish colonial era is the classic folktale or fairy tale. Folktales and fairy tales can be interchangeable terms because they both refer to stories set in distant lands and times. The special characteristic of the fairy tale is that it occurs in an enchanted world where magical events are still possible. Often, these stories are called ordinary, wonder, or adventure tales. (They are called "ordinary," because in spite of their often fantastic story lines, so many of this type of story exist in any culture.) These are the classic stories of childhood. In the Western tradition, the fairy tales of the Grimm Brothers are the standard example of this type of story.

I have titled this section of the book "Tales of Transformation, Magic, and Adventure" because these qualities best describe the content of this section's stories. These are the traditional folktales or fairy tales that most clearly reveal their roots in European tales. These are the Spanish versions of classic stories of brave princes, beautiful princesses, heroic adventures, evil spells, magical helpers, enchanted objects, life-threatening danger, and true love.

Next in the category of Spanish colonial era stories are the *dos compadres* stories, which are some of the most delightful of all Mexican tales. *Dos compadres* stories are almost a genre in themselves in the Mexican oral tradition, as so many stories and versions are in existence. The foundation of a *dos compadres* story is based on two friends of opposite character types—usually, one rich and one poor—who have a conflict. A *dos compadres* story is about the constant arguments these two friends have to determine who is better than the other. Typically, the story is about how the poor man bests his rich friend and ends up the victor in both the argument and in life. The *dos compadres* stories usually contain a cautionary moral about the evils of greed. Also, the endings of these stories often have elements of the trickster tale in which the main character overcomes obstacles by his cunning spirit.

The final story type in the Spanish colonial era section of this book is the animal fable. The fable uses a very exact formula that includes talking animals as characters in a story that ends when a hidden truth or lesson is revealed. The animals in these adventure stories are portrayed with the same emotions, desires, and conflicts as humans. Animal fables are often characterized as "children's stories" (as children especially enjoy them), but they can be as entertaining and sophisticated as any other story type.

These stories often overlap with the *pourquoi* story category because they offer explanations for the ways of the animal world. For example, the fable "The Owl and the Painted Bird" doubles as a *pourquoi* story because of its explanation for the owl's hoot. And an example of a cross-cultural story would be "The Lion and the Cricket" because versions of it exist in many cultures of the world.

The small sampling of fables presented in this book are filled with the adventures and exploits of well-known animal characters that have delighted generations of Mexican children. The comic conflicts between the fox and the coyote in which the fox plays the coyote for a fool are among the most common animal fable stories in Mexican oral tradition. (It is interesting to note that in the Native American oral tradition, the coyote is often cast as the trickster hero, but in the Mexican oral tradition, the coyote is more often the buffoon of the story.)

The many stories presented in this book are a sampling of the greatness of the Mexican narrative oral tradition. From the pre-Conquest era to the Spanish colonial era, Mexico developed a vast repository of traditional stories. These stories have reached across generations to our own modern time to give us a clear sense of the Mexican spirit and soul. Through these stories, Mexico shares with the world its history, its traditions, and its dreams.

A GUIDE TO THE PRONUNCIATION OF AZTEC AND MAYAN NAMES

In Nahuatl, the accent always falls on the next-to-last syllable.

Ah Kin Xooc	Ahh-keen-shook	Mayan god
Chalchihtlicue	Chal-chee-oot-li-ky	The Lady of Jade Skirts
Cihuacoatl	Chi-wa-co-at-ell	Aztec goddess also known as Snake Skirt
Coatepec	Qua-te-pek	snake hill
Copil	Ko-peel	nephew of Huitzilopochtli
Cuetlaxochitl	Kweht-lah-soh-cheetl	the flower of purity
Huitzilopochtli	Hweet-sill-o-posht-lee	God of War
Ixtlaccihuatl	Eeks-tak-see-waa-tul	The sleeping woman
Mictlan	Micked-lan	Land of the dead
Mictlantecuhtli	Micked-lan-te-koot-lee	Lord God of the Land of the Dead
Nahuatl	Nah-wah-tul	Aztec language
Nanahuatzin	Na-na-oo-at-sin	Humble god who became the Sun
Nochtli	Noch-tlee	cactus
Ometeotl	O-meh-teh-tul	Creator Pair
Popocatepetl	Po-poca-tep-tul	The smoking mountain
Quetzalcoatl	Kwet-zall-co-at-ell	A plumed serpent; the creator god
Tamoanchan	Tam-o-an-chan	Land of miracles
Tecuciztecatl	Te-koo-sis-te-cat-ell	Proud god who became the Moon
Tenochtitlan	Ten-nooch-teet-lan	The capital city of the Aztecs
Tepeyac	Teh-peh-yak	Aztec religious site
Tezcatlipoca	Tex-cat-lee-poke-ah	Dark god known as Smoking Mirror
Tlaloc	Tla-lok	God of Rain
Tlaltecuhtli	Tla-lteh-quit-lee	great Earth monster
Tonacatepetl	Ton-a-cat-e-petal	Mountain of Sustenance
Tonatiuh	Ton-a-ti-u	The Fifth Sun
Tonantzin	Tone-nat-zeen	The protector of the Earth and corn

Color Plates

1

Color Plates 1 and 2 are examples of the carving skill and whimsical spirit of the Oaxacan carvers.

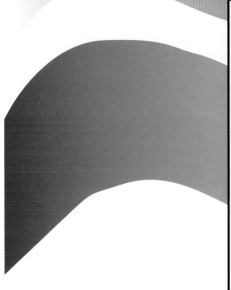

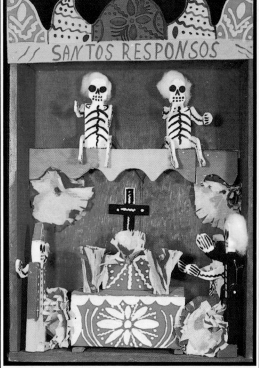

2

3

**Color Plates 3 through 6
show several examples of Huichol yarn art.**

4

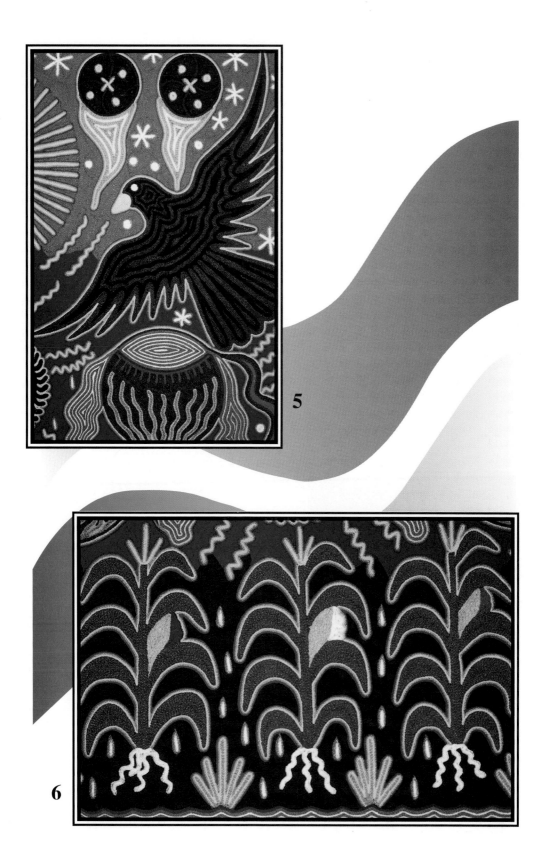

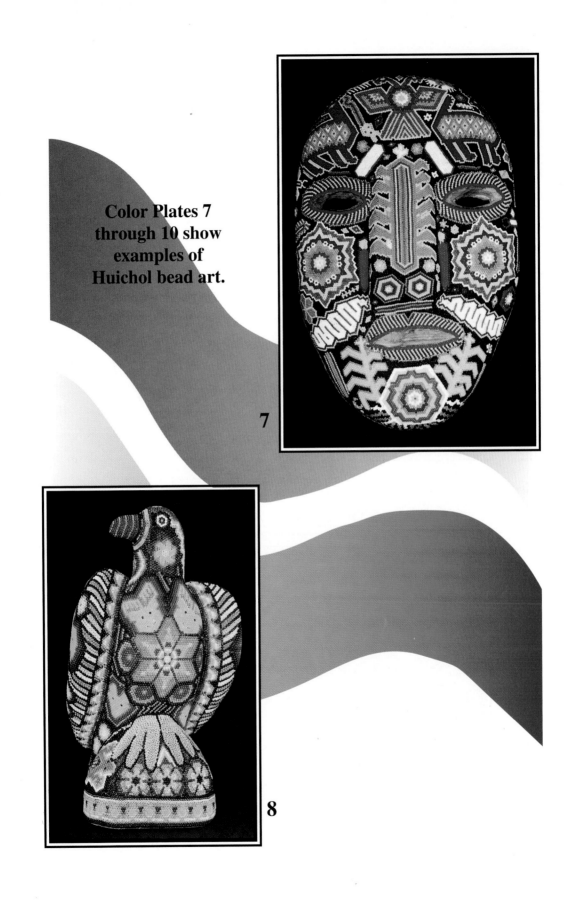

Color Plates 7
through 10 show
examples of
Huichol bead art.

7

8

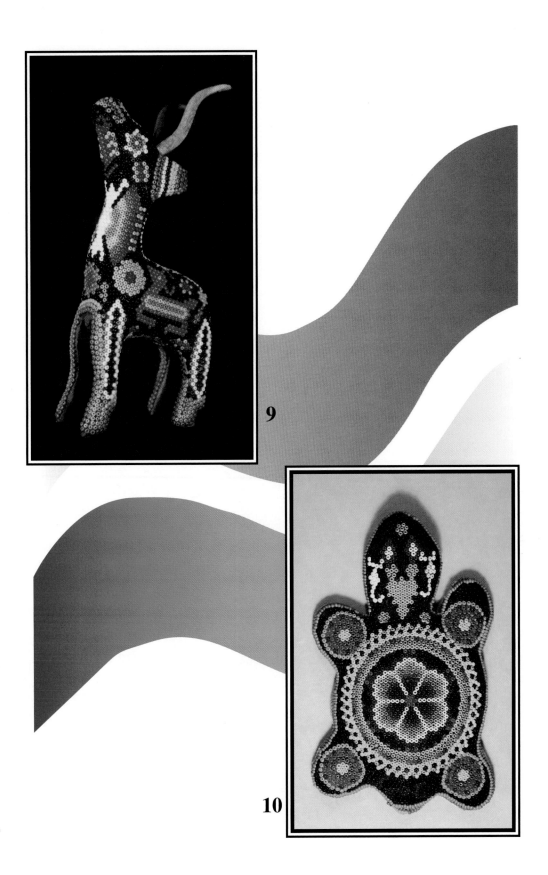

9

10

Color Plate 11 portrays a realistic-looking, fair-complected, European Spanish man's face mask. It is similar to the realistic style of masks worn in carnival dances.

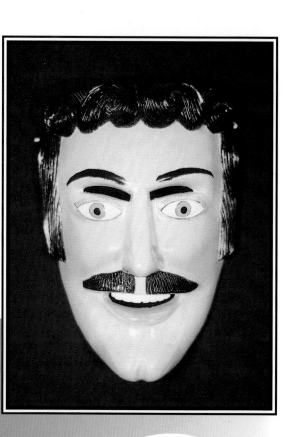

11

Color Plate 12 shows the mask for the Dance of *los Viejitos*. This mask, which is of a very traditional design, is worn by the dancers in the Dance of *los Viejitos*. See Color Plate 22 for a picture of the full male costume.

12

This mask is very similar in style to the *Vaquero* (Mexican cowboy) mask used in the *Vaquero* dance, an occupational dance representing the cowboy's capture of a bull. Donald Cordry (1980) describes the round mouth as indicating the *Vaquero*'s calling and whistling for the cattle.

13

Color Plate 14 shows a bat mask. The bat is a common figure on Mexican animal masks, with the bat often carved atop a human face.

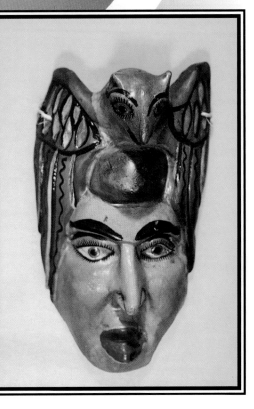

14

Color Plate 15 shows a realistic old man mask. It is similar to several types of old person Mexican masks, especially the mask of the hermit for the Christmas season *Pastorela* dance celebrating the birth of the Christ child.

15

Color Plate 16 shows another animal mask. It represents the tiger or jaguar. The mask is extremely dramatic in design, with real teeth (animal unknown), mirrored eyes, and animal hair. It is meant to be worn with a full body costume, completing the dancer's tiger or jaguar image.

16

Color Plate 17
shows a butterfly mask.
The protruding nose
represents the curved
proboscis of the
butterfly.

17

Color Plates 18 through
20 show playful masks
that are made for the
tourist trade and that are
not associated with any
traditional ceremonies or
dances. They are called
coco masks because they
are painted over coconut
shells. They are tiny,
inexpensive, and common
in tourist areas. They
come in a seemingly
infinite variety of styles.

18

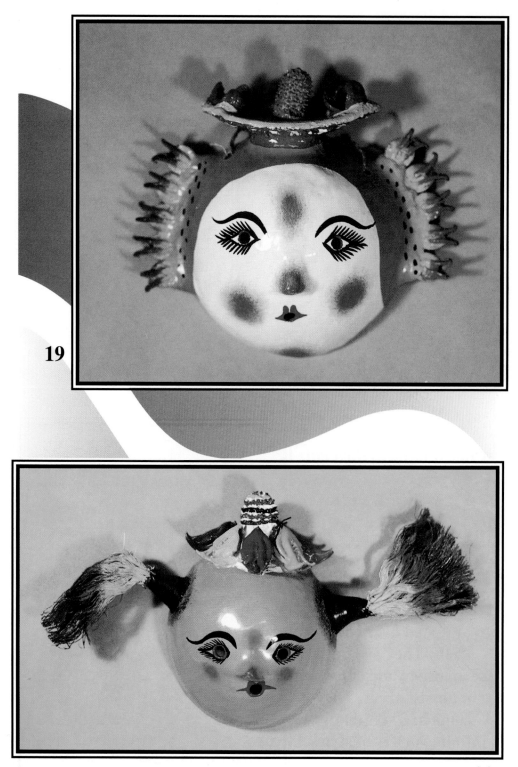

19

20

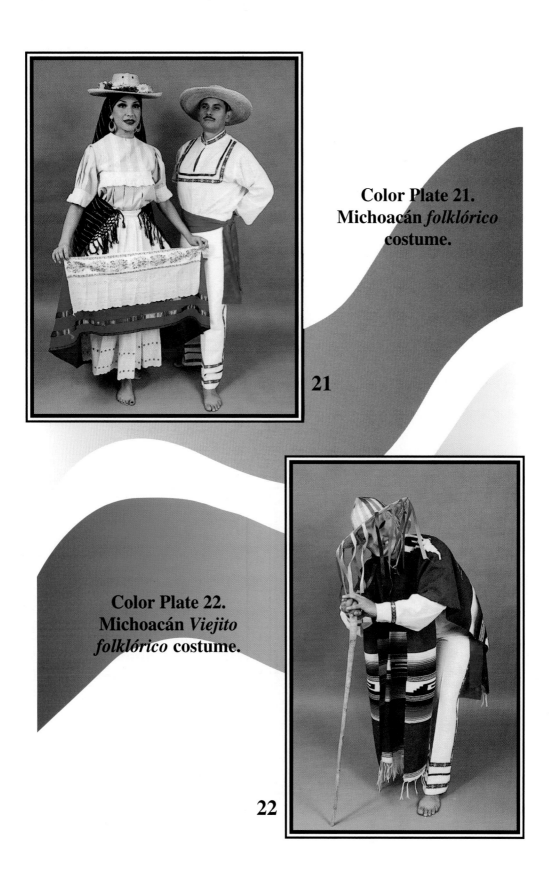

**Color Plate 21.
Michoacán *folklórico*
costume.**

21

**Color Plate 22.
Michoacán *Viejito*
folklórico costume.**

22

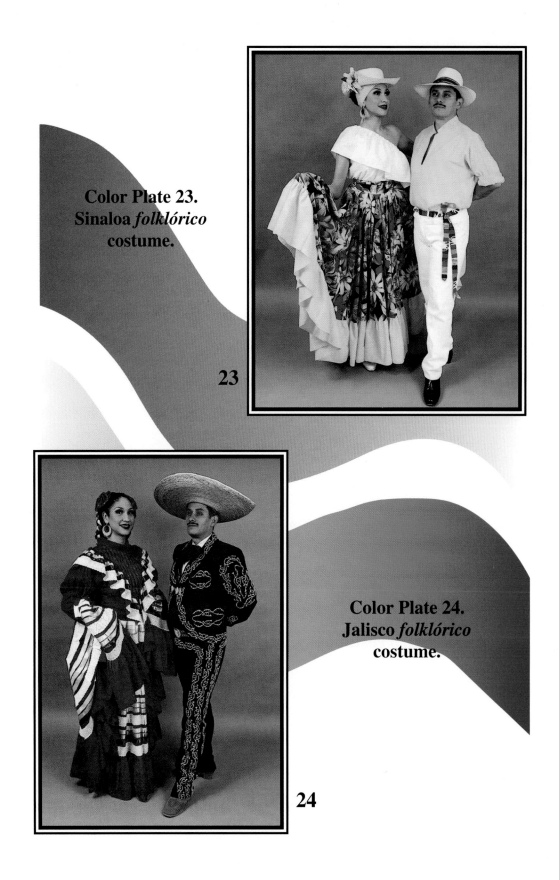

**Color Plate 23.
Sinaloa** *folklórico*
costume.

23

**Color Plate 24.
Jalisco** *folklórico*
costume.

24

**Color Plate 25.
Nayarit** *folklórico*
costume.

25

**Color Plate 26.
Veracruz** *folklórico*
costume.

26

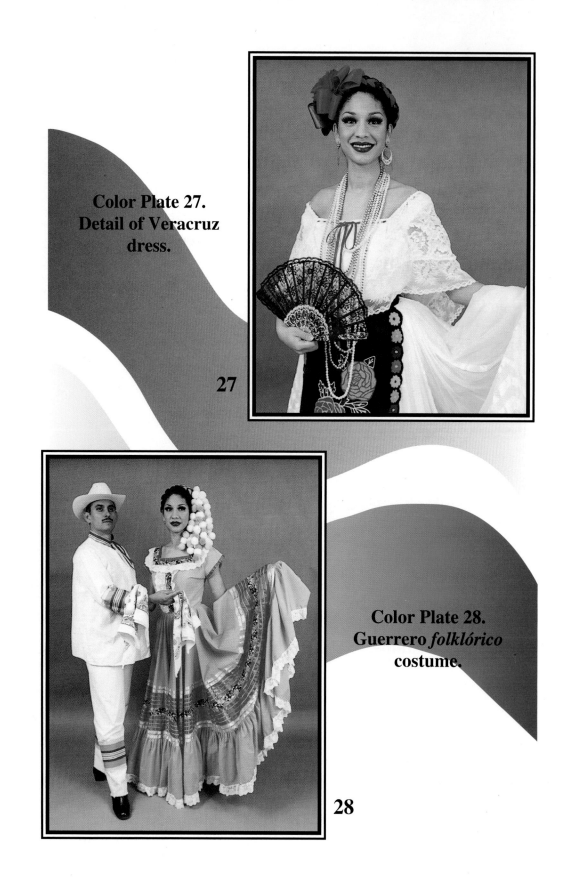

**Color Plate 27.
Detail of Veracruz
dress.**

27

**Color Plate 28.
Guerrero *folklórico*
costume.**

28

**Color Plate 29.
Yucatán *folklórico*
costume.**

29

**Color Plate 30.
Detail of Yucatán
huipil dress.**

30

ESSENTIAL LEGENDS

The Founding of Tenochtitlan—Mexico City

In the center of the Mexican flag is a striking image of an eagle with a snake in its mouth landing on a cactus. (See book cover.) This Mexican national image represents the legend of the founding of the Aztec capital city of Tenochtitlan, which lay on an island in Lake Texcoco in the Valley of Mexico. The modern capital of Mexico—Mexico City—is built on top of this ancient Aztec city of Tenochtitlan.

The land of Aztlan described in the legend is the homeland of the Aztec Indians. While its true location is unknown, scholars believe that Aztlan was an island in a lake located in northwest Mexico and that the nomadic Indians who eventually became the ruling Aztec people originated from this area.

The legend of the ancients tells of the founding of the great Aztec capital Tenochtitlan.

The Eagle on the Cactus

Many years ago, the Aztec people lived in a faraway land known as Aztlan, which means "the place of the heron." One of the seven Nahua tribes, they took their name from their legendary homeland, Aztlan.

The origin of the Aztec culture, according to the legend, can be traced to this tribe's emergence from seven underground caves known as Chicomostoc. With some knowledge of agriculture and hunting, the Aztecs lived a life of meager subsistence. They also listened to the voices of their gods as they spoke to them through priests.

One day, Huitzilopochtli, the God of War, spoke to the Aztecs through a hummingbird statue. He told them that they were to leave their homeland and become nomads, following a path to the south until they came to their promised land, in which they would prosper and rule. In the early twelfth century, the Aztec people obeyed the command of Huitzilopochtli and began their journey to the south.

For many years the Aztecs wandered, searching the skies for a sign from their god Huitzilopochtli that they had found their new homeland. They finally settled in Coatepec ("snake hill" in their Nahuatl language) near Tula, the Toltec capital city.

The Aztecs lived in Coatepec for many years until the followers of Huitzilopochtli decided that their god had not delivered the sign they awaited and that their journey should begin again. As they started their quest for a second time, their god Huitzilopochtli told them that they would no longer be called Aztecs. He gave them the new name of the Mexicas (meh-SHEE-kahs), followers of the god Mexi, which was another name belonging to Huitzilopochtli. They carried the clay idol image of their god Huitzilopochtli on their backs throughout their long journey. Many centuries later, their new name, Mexica, eventually became the name of the new country of Mexico.

It was at this time that the most important event of the legend occurred. Huitzilopochtli told the Mexicas that they would find their homeland when they saw an eagle with a serpent in its mouth landing on a spiny *nopal* cactus on an island in the middle of a lake.

The Mexicas searched for this god-given sign for many years. Finally, in the year 1325, the Mexicas came upon a set of uninhabited islands on Lake Texcoco in the Valley of Mexico. As they searched the islands, they had a vision of the eagle with a snake in its mouth landing on a *nopal* cactus on one of the islands in the lake. Their journey had ended when they discovered their destiny. The Mexicas, or Aztecs, built a magnificent city on the site of their vision. They named their city, Tenochtitlan, after their first ruler, Tenoch. The name Tenochtitlan means "place of the prickly pear cactus."

The Mexicas, or Aztecs, in a short two centuries had transformed themselves from a primitive nomadic people to the dominant culture in the Valley of Mexico—conquerers of all other nations in the region. Their city of Tenochtitlan was the ceremonial, religious, and political center of a vast empire that was unsurpassed in size, grandeur, and beauty until the arrival of the Spanish. The Spanish would in turn build their own capital, Mexico City, on top of Tenochtitlan.

According to the legend of the founding of Mexico City, the ancient Aztecs were a god-driven people who would found a great civilization stretching from the Pacific Ocean to the Gulf of Mexico, build a magnificent capital, and give their name to a modern nation. To this day, all who behold the Mexican flag are reminded of the miraculous sign of Huitzilopochtli and of his people who found their great destiny on an island in the middle of a lake.

BACKGROUND ABOUT NUESTRA SEÑORA DE GUADALUPE (OUR LADY OF GUADALUPE)

The story of Our Lady of Guadalupe is Mexico's most beloved religious legend. It tells the miraculous story of the apparition of the Virgin of Guadalupe to Juan Diego, a humble Aztec Indian, in 1531, just ten years after the Spanish conquest of the Aztecs. The image of the Virgin of Guadalupe, enveloped by celestial light and held aloft by a heavenly angel, is the most well known religious icon in Mexico.

This legend also is one of the clearest examples of the melding of indigenous and Christian belief systems in the New World. The Spanish missionaries, dedicated to the holy task of bringing Christianity to the indigenous populations, searched for ways to introduce the natives to Catholic religious thought. By building on existing native practices, the Spanish missionaries were successful in converting the native Indians to Christian beliefs.

The story of the Virgin of Guadalupe is an example of how this strategy worked. The legend

Figure 9 Our Lady of Guadalupe.

takes place on a hill named "Tepeyac." Tepeyac was the site of an Aztec shrine to their Mother Goddess Tonantzin, the protector of the earth and corn. The Spanish built a shrine to the Virgin of Guadalupe on this Aztec site. In addition, the original stories about the miraculous apparition had the Virgin looking like an Aztec princess and speaking the Aztec native language, Nahuatl. Before the conquest, the Aztecs had come to the shrine of Tonantzin seeking cures. After the conquest, they came to the same holy hill, only now seeking cures and salvation from the Virgin of Guadalupe. By establishing the site of veneration for the Virgin of Guadalupe on the Aztec hill of Tepeyac, the Spanish missionaries facilitated the conversion of Aztec Indians to Catholic Christianity.

The legend of the Virgin of Guadalupe quickly spread throughout Mexico and the Americas. In 1754 the Pope recognized the Virgin of Guadalupe as the Patroness of New Spain. She became the Patroness of Latin America in 1910, and in 1959 she became the Mother of the Americas.

In Mexico, December 12—the Feast Day of Our Lady of Guadalupe—marks the beginning of the Christmas season. It is also common for Mexican families to name a daughter Guadalupe and for that name to be shortened into the nickname Lupe. Today, the legend of the Virgin of Guadalupe is a Mexican truth representing the possibility of religious miracles in everyday life and the hope for heavenly intercession in human affairs.

Nuestra Señora de Guadalupe
Our Lady of Guadalupe

It had been 10 years since the last fierce battles between the Aztec warriors and the Spanish *conquistadores*. The Spanish had been victorious, and now the Aztec Indians were adjusting to the new ways the Spanish had brought to their land. Of the many lessons the Spanish missionaries labored to teach the Indians, the lessons about a new god—the Christian God—seemed most important. The Spanish missionaries were especially dedicated to teaching the Indians about a life lived according to the teaching of their Catholic God.

On a cold winter morning in December 1531, a poor Aztec Indian, whose Aztec name was Quauhtlatoatzin, was walking to church for his religious lessons. A Franciscan priest had recently converted him to Christianity, baptized him, and given him the Christian name of Juan Diego. Juan was going to meet with the village priest for his religious instruction. His own village did not have a church yet, so he had to walk to a larger neighboring village, Tlatelolco, just outside of Mexico City.

As he walked to the church, Juan Diego thought about all of the changes that had occurred in his life in the past 10 years. The priest had been teaching Juan Diego that the new Spanish ways were better for him and his family. Juan Diego especially enjoyed the stories the priest told about the religious miracles of the Church. Juan Diego knew the ancient stories of the powerful Aztec gods, and it seemed to him that this new Catholic religion also was a religion of miracles and powerful events.

In his everyday, poor and humble life, Juan Diego saw little chance for any miracle to enter his world. He knew that his world was a simple world of daily hard labor. In this way, the miracles of the new religion seemed as remote and unavailable to him as the gods of his old religion.

As he walked past the hill he knew as Tepeyac, Juan Diego imagined all of the times he had come to the hill to pray to the Aztec god Tonantzin. He had prayed to Tonantzin, god of the earth and corn, for a bountiful harvest. But those prayers and that time truly seemed a lifetime away for Juan Diego. For a man of Juan Diego's station in life, prayers more often than not went unanswered, and the only constants in his life were the love of his family and the hard work of the field.

As he passed the hill, Juan Diego suddenly felt a strange longing to climb to the crest of the hill. At first he dismissed the feeling as something akin to his sadness and longing for the ways of his former life. But he had learned to let go of those feelings. The priest had taught him that his old life was over and that the miracles of his new life awaited him. At first, Juan Diego had expected to see miracles right away. Soon, however, he realized that the miracles of the new Spanish god were as rare as the answered prayers of his old gods.

Juan Diego started to walk away from Tepeyac, but still the hill seemed to be calling out to him. He knew he would be late to see the priest but could not shake this sudden longing to climb to the top of the hill. This longing moved Juan Diego deeply and soon he found himself climbing the hill. It was as if he were being called by the hill and he was powerless to resist its call.

As he neared the crest, he could hear a beautiful melody, a melody played by the lightest tinkling of bells he had ever heard. The priest had mentioned many times the beauty of the music of heaven, and the sound of these tinkling bells was exactly how Juan Diego had imagined this music.

When Juan Diego reached the top of the hill, he was struck with an amazing vision. Before him was the most radiant woman he had ever seen or imagined. She was bathed in a shining light that outlined her whole body. The heavenly music he had heard seemed to be coming from within her. She was literally surrounded by light and music. Juan Diego did not know what to do, but he knew that this was the reason he had been drawn to the top of the hill. For a moment, he thought that he would finally witness one of his longed-for miracles. Could this be Tonantzin, come to answer his prayers after all these years? Or was it one of the priest's holy saints come to earth from heaven above?

Suddenly, the woman spoke. Amazingly, she spoke in Nahuatl, Juan Diego's native language. In the most soothing voice she said, "Juan Diego, I have come to seek your help. I am on a holy mission and have chosen you to deliver a message to the bishop."

Juan Diego could not believe what was happening before his eyes. Questions raced through his mind. Who is this beautiful woman? Why was he chosen to deliver the message? How did she know his name? Maybe this was the work of the devil the priest had told him about and he should run for his life.

As if she could read his mind, the woman answered all his silent questions. "Juan Diego, I am the Blessed Virgin Mary, the mother of the Lord Jesus Christ. I have watched your hard work on this earth, and because of your good and pure soul, I have chosen you to deliver my message to the bishop. Go and tell the bishop to build a church for me on the top of this hill. The church will be a reminder to people of my love for them and that I am always here to answer their prayers and to help them in their times of need. Go now; deliver my message."

Juan Diego could not believe what he was hearing. The priest had taught him about the Blessed Virgin Mary, but he never imagined that he would see her one day on this earth. Truly, a miracle had finally happened to him.

He ran as fast as he could all the way into the village and to the cathedral to deliver his message to Bishop Zumarraga. When he arrived, he rushed up to the cathedral door and knocked loudly. Two of the bishop's helpers answered the door. Out of breath from his run, Juan Diego spilled out his incredible story.

The two helpers laughed slightly and then answered, "Well, the Blessed Virgin Mary herself decided to appear to a poor Aztec Indian. What a miracle! And now the bishop is supposed to build a church on some Aztec hill." They then stopped laughing, and their voices became stern: "Now enough of your silly stories. The bishop is too busy with the important matters of the church to listen to such foolishness. Now go back to your village and confess to your priest this outlandish lie you have told us."

Juan Diego dejectedly returned to the hill of Tepeyac. He believed that he had witnessed a miracle and that the woman indeed was the Blessed Virgin Mary. He was ashamed and disappointed that he had failed in his mission. When he again saw the Blessed Virgin Mary he fell to his knees, crying, "Please forgive me. I have failed you. The bishop's helpers did not believe my story. They didn't believe that you would appear to a poor Indian like me."

The Blessed Virgin Mary smiled a small smile and in a gentle voice said to Juan Diego, "Do not doubt yourself. I, myself, have chosen you, and you have my holy protection in all that you do. Return to the bishop and tell him again of my request that he build a church to me on this hill."

A second time Juan Diego returned to the cathedral and knocked on its large doors. When the bishop's helpers saw that it was Juan Diego again, they became angry and spoke sharply to him: "Now did we not tell you to go away? Enough of this foolishness. Go away!"

Juan Diego persisted in telling them his story until one of the helpers was touched by his heartfelt sincerity. The helper said, "Perhaps there is some truth to some part of your story. Wait here while I deliver your story to the bishop. Now, he is a very busy man, and he might not have time to listen to any part of it. Come inside and wait here until I return."

Juan went inside the cathedral and patiently waited for the bishop's helper to return. He sat in a corner and thought of the Blessed Virgin and the beautiful music he had heard. As he looked around the cathedral, he imagined an even more beautiful church built for the Blessed Virgin.

Soon, the bishop's helper returned and sat beside Juan Diego. She put a hand on Juan Diego's hand and told him, "The bishop does not believe your story. He said that you must bring some proof of your story before he will listen to any more of it. I'm sorry. Perhaps you will learn your lesson and not bother the bishop anymore after this."

As Juan Diego walked back to the hill of Tepeyac, he thought of how he would tell the Blessed Virgin Mary that he had failed again. As he approached the hill, a cousin of Juan Diego ran frantically to Juan and delivered a crushing message. Juan Diego's uncle was dying and was not expected to last the night.

Now Juan truly believed that his lot on this earth was to suffer and fail. Discouraged, he climbed the hill and prepared to tell the Blessed Virgin Mary to seek a worthier messenger. When he beheld the celestial light surrounding the Blessed Virgin Mary and heard the heavenly bells and their soothing sounds, for a moment, his soul was comforted.

Even before he could speak, once again it appeared that the Blessed Virgin Mary could read his deepest thoughts. She spoke to him: "Juan Diego, do not despair. I came to this earth to bring you comfort and strength in your darkest hours. Know that I am always by your side. Even now as we speak, I am healing your uncle. He will see many more days and will live a long life. Now come with me. We will give your bishop the proof he seeks."

Juan Diego followed the Blessed Virgin Mary further up the hill to an area where wild bushes grew. But the wild flowers and bushes had long withered in the cold December air. All that greeted them was barren earth and empty branches.

With no apparent effort, the Blessed Virgin Mary rose and hovered above one of the empty bushes. Suddenly, the celestial light became as bright as a summer's day, and the heavenly bells rang out in a joyous melody. Juan Diego could almost smell the sweet fragrance of summer roses in full bloom. The Blessed Virgin Mary opened her arms around one of the bushes, and as she did, fresh rose petals—roses de Castilla—cascaded to the ground. She gathered them up and said to Juan Diego, "Take these to the bishop. Let these summer roses be the proof he seeks."

Juan Diego gathered up the roses in his *tilma* and ran down the hill in joyous delirium. He thought to himself: "She is the Blessed Virgin Mary, and this is the heavenly miracle the priest has told me about. Now the bishop will believe me."

For a third time, he knocked on the doors to the cathedral. The bishop's helper who had been so kind answered and, in astonishment, saw fresh, summer roses de Castilla fall from Juan Diego's *tilma*. She rushed to get the bishop, and soon they both came running out of the church. When Bishop Zumarraga saw the roses, he knew they were a gift from the Blessed Virgin Mary. As he reached to touch the roses they receded back into the *tilma* and became part of an apparition image of the Virgin in the fabric of the *tilma*. Bishop Zumarraga fell to his knees and cried out, "*Un milagro! Un milagro!* It is a miracle!" Then the bishop's helpers reached out to touch the roses and they too saw an image of the Blessed Virgin Mary inside Juan Diego's *tilma*.

Bishop Zumarraga believed Juan Diego's message and built a church dedicated to the Blessed Virgin Mary on the hill of Tepeyac. To this day, Juan Diego's *tilma* hangs in the church as a reminder of the miracle that came to this earth so many years ago. Now the Mexican people call the site Guadalupe, and supplicants come to the church to see the miraculous *tilma*. As they pray and gaze at the *tilma*, they remember the love of the Blessed Virgin and the promise of the Blessed Virgin Mary, Our Lady of Guadalupe, always to help and comfort people in their times of need.

Nuestra Señora de Guadalupe

La historia de Nuestra Señora de Guadalupe es la más venerada de las leyendas religiosas en México. Esta leyenda relata la milagrosa historia de la aparición de la Virgen de Guadalupe a Juan Diego, un humilde indio azteca, en 1531, poco después que los españoles conquistasen a los aztecas. La imagen de la Virgen de Guadalupe, revestida de luces celestiales y sostenida por una ángel celestial, es la imagen religiosa más conocida en México.

Esta leyenda es uno de los más claros ejemplos de la síntesis en el Nuevo Mundo de los sistemas de creencias indígenas y cristianos. Los misioneros españoles, dedicados a la santa tarea de traer el cristianismo a los pueblos nativos, buscaron la manera de introducir a los aborígenes en el pensamiento religioso católico. Al contruir sobre la prácticas nativas ya existentes, los misioneros españoles tuvieron éxito en la conversión de los nativos a las creencias cristianas. La historia de la Virgen de Guadalupe es un ejemplo de cómo funcionó esa estrategia. La leyenda se ubica en la colina llamada "Tepeyac". Tepeyac era el sitio de un santuario azteca dedicado a la Diosa Madre Tonantzín, protectora de la tierra y del maíz. Los españoles construyeron un santuario a la Virgen de Guadalupe en este sitio azteca. Además, las historias originales de la aparición de la Virgen presentaban a la Virgen como una princesa azteca y hablando en el idioma nativo de los aztecas, el nahuatl. Antes de la conquista, los aztecas iban al santuario de Tonantzín para buscar sanidad. Después de la conquista, iban a la misma colina sagrada, pero ahora para buscar la sanidad y la salvación impartidas por la Virgen de Guadalupe. Al establecer el sitio de veneración a la Virgen de Guadalupe en la colina azteca de Tepeyac, los misioneros españoles facilitaron la conversión de los indios aztecas al cristianismo católico.

La leyenda de la Virgen de Guadalupe se esparció rápidamente por todo México y las Américas. En 1754 el Papa reconoció a la Virgen de Guadalupe como la Patrona de Nueva España. La Virgen se transformó en la Patrona de América Latina en 1910, y en 1959 llegó a ser la Madre de las Américas.

En México, el 12 de diciembre, el Día de la Festividad de Nuestra Señora de Guadalupe, marca el inicio de la temporada de Navidad. También es común que las familias mexicanas le den el nombre "Guadalupe" a una de sus hijas, y que el nombre se acorte (como sobrenombre) a "Lupe". En la actualidad, la leyenda de la Virgen de Guadalupe es una verdad mexicana que representa la posibilidad de milagros religiosos en la vida diaria y la esperanza de intercesión celestial en los asuntos del hombre.

Ya habían pasado 10 años desde la última de las encarnizadas batallas entre los guerreros aztecas y los conquistadores españoles. Los españoles habían ganado, y ahora los indios aztecas se estaban acostumbrando al estilo de vida que los españoles habían traído a la tierra azteca. Entre las muchas lecciones que los misioneros españoles se esforzaron en enseñar a los indios, la lección del nuevo Dios, el Dios cristiano, parecía la más importante. Los misioneros españoles se dedicaron especialmente a enseñarles a los indios cómo vivir la vida según las enseñanzas del Dios católico.

Una fría mañana invernal en diciembre de 1531, un pobre indio azteca, cuyo nombre azteca era Quauhtlatoatzin, estaba yendo de camino a la iglesia para sus lecciones religiosas. Un sacerdote franciscano lo había convertido hacía poco al cristianismo, lo había bautizado, y le había dado el nombre cristiano de Juan Diego. Juan iba a encontrarse con el sacerdote de la aldea para recibir su instrucción religiosa. Su propia comunidad aldea todavía no tenía una iglesia, así que tenía que caminar hasta la vecina aldea de Tlatelolco, en las afueras de la Ciudad de México.

Al ir de camino a la iglesia, Juan Diego pensó en todos los cambios ocurridos en su vida durante los últimos diez años. El sacerdote le había enseñado a Juan Diego que las nuevas maneras de los españoles eran mejor para él y su familia. Juan Diego disfrutaba especialmente de las historias que los sacerdotes contaban sobre los milagros religiosos de la iglesia. Juan Diego conocía las antiguas historias de los poderosos dioses aztecas, y le parecía que la nueva religión católica era también una religión de milagros y de poderosos prodigios.

En su vida de todos los días, pobre y simple, Juan Diego veía pocas oportunidades de que un milagro entrase en su mundo. Sabía que su mundo era un mundo simple de duro trabajo diario. De esta manera, los milagros de la nueva religión parecían tan remotos y distantes para él como lo eran los milagros de su antigua religión.

Al caminar por la colina que él llamaba Tepeyac, Juan Diego pensó en todas las veces que él había venido a esa colina a orar a la deidad azteca Tonantzín. Le habia orado a Tonantzín, divinidad de la tierra y del maíz, pidiendo buenas cosechas. Pero aquellas oraciones y aquellos momentos parecían pertenecer a una vida muy alejada de Juan Diego. Para un hombre en el momento de la vida de Juan Diego, la mayoría de las oraciones no tenían respuesta. Lo único permanente en su vida era el amor por su familia y el duro trabajo en el campo.

Al pasar junto a la colina, Juan Diego fue súbitamente inundado por el extraño deseo de escalar hasta la cima de la colina. Al principio no le hizo caso al sentimiento y lo tomó como tristeza y nostalgia por su antigua manera de vivir. Pero él ya había aprendido a superar esos sentimientos. El sacerdote le había enseñado que su antigua manera de vivir ya había terminado y que le esperaban los milagros de su nueva vida. Pronto, sin embargo, comprendió que los milagros del nuevo Dios, el de los españoles eran tan infrecuentes como las respuestas de sus antiguos dioses a sus oraciones.

Juan Diego comenzó a alejarse de Tepeyac, pero todavía parecía que la colina lo llamaba. Sabía que llegaría tarde a ver al sacerdote, pero no pudo deshacerse del repentino deseo de subir a la cima de la montaña. Este deseo conmovió tran profundamente a Juan Diego que comenzó a subir a la colina. Parecía que la colina lo llamaba y que él era impotente para resistir el llamado.

Al acercarse a la cima, pudo escuchar una hermosa melodía, una melodía interpretada por la campanitas más suaves que él jamás había escuchado. El sacerdote había mencionado muchas veces la belleza de la música del cielo, y el sonido de estas campanitas era exáctamente como Juan Diego se había imaginado esa música.

Cuando Juan Diego llegó a la cima de la colina, le sorprendió una asombrosa visión. Ante él estaba la mujer más radiante que él jamás hubo visto o imaginado. Estaba bañada en una luz resplandeciente que delineaba todo su cuerpo. La música celestial que él había escuchado parecía provenir desde dentro de la mujer. Ella estaba totalmente rodeada de luz y música. Juan Diego no sabía qué hacer, pero supo que ésta era la razón que lo había atraído a la cima de la colina. Por un momento, pensó que finalmente presenciaría uno de los milagros que tanto ansiaba. ¿Sería ella Tonantzín, que venía a contestar sus oraciones después de tantos años? ¿O sería uno de los santos, de los que hablaba el sacerdote, que había venido a la tierra desde el cielo?

Súbitamente, la mujer habló. Sorprendentemente, habló en nahuatl, el idioma nativo de Juan Diego. Con una voz muy suave, dijo: "Juan Diego, he venido a pedir tu ayuda. Tengo una santa misión y te he elegido para que le lleves un mensaje al obispo".

Juan Diego no podía creer lo que estaba sucediendo ante sus incrédulos ojos. Las preguntas le llenaban la mente. ¿Quién era esta hermosa mujer? ¿Por qué era él el elegido para llevar el mensaje? ¿Cómo sabía ella su nombre? Quizá ésta era una obra del diablo del que hablaba el sacerdote y era el momento de salir corriendo para no perder la vida.

Como si pudiese leer la mente de Juan Diego, la mujer contestó a todas las preguntas hechas en silencio. "Juan Diego, yo soy la Bendita Virgen María, la madre del Señor Jesucristo. He observado tus duros trabajos en esta tierra, y por tu alma buena y pura, te he elegido para que lleves mi mensaje al obispo. Vé y dile al obispo que construya una iglesia para mí, en la cima de esta colina. La iglesia servirá para recordarles a las personas que los amo, y que siempre estaré aquí para contestar sus oraciones y para ayudarlas en tiempos de necesidad. Ahora vé, y entrega mi mensaje".

Juan Diego no podía creer lo que estaba oyendo. El sacerdote le había enseñado acerca de la Bendita Virgen María, pero nunca se había imaginado que la vería un día sobre la tierra. Verdaderamente un milagro había sucedido para él.

Corrió tan rápido como pudo hasta la aldea y hasta la catedral para entregar el mensaje al obispo Zumárraga. Cuando llegó, corrió hasta la puerta de la catedral y la golpeó ruidósamente. Dos de las ayudantes del obispo llegaron a la puerta. Sin aliento por la carrera, Juan Diego contó su increíble historia.

Las dos ayudantes se rieron discretamente y dijeron: "Bueno, la Bendita Virgen María en persona decidió aparecerse a un pobre indio azteca. ¡Qué milagro! Y ahora el obispo tiene que construir una iglesia en una colina azteca". Dejaron de reírse y con voz firme dijeron: "Basta de tus tontas historias. El obispo está muy ocupado con los temas importantes de la iglesia como para escuchar estas tonterías. Regresa a tu aldea y confiésale a tu sacerdote las estrafalarias mentiras que nos contaste".

Juan Diego regresó desanimado a la colina de Tepeyac. El creía que había presenciado un milagro y que la mujer era en verdad la Bendita Virgen María. Tenía vergüenza y estaba desilusionado que había fracasado en su misión. Cuando vio otra vez a la Bendita Virgen María, cayó de rodillas, llorando. "Perdóname. Te he fallado. Los ayudantes del obispo no creyeron mi historia. No creen que tú puedes aparecerte a un pobre indio como yo".

La Bendita Virgen María sonrío levemente y con una voz suave le dijo a Juan Diego: "No dudes de ti. Yo misma te he escogido y tú tienes mi santa protección en todo lo que hagas. Regresa al obispo y dile otra vez que yo pido que él construya una iglesia en mi honor en esta colina".

Por segunda vez Juan Diego volvió a la catedral y golpeó las inmensas puertas. Cuando las ayudantes del obispo vieron que era Juan Diego otra vez, se enojaron y le dijeron sin rodeos: "¿No te dijimos claramente que te marches? Basta de estas tonterías. ¡Lárgate!".

Juan Diego persistió en repitir su historia, hasta que una de las ayudantes fue conmovida por la sinceridad de su corazón. La ayudante dijo: "Quizá haya algo de verdad en parte de tu historia. Espera aquí mientras le cuento tu historia al obispo. Bueno, él es un hombre ocupado, y quizá no tenga tiempo para escuchar ni siquiera parte de la historia. Pasa y espera aquí hasta que yo regrese".

Juan entró en la catedral y esperó pacientemente el regreso de la ayudante del obispo. Se sentó en un rincón y pensó en la Bendita Virgen y en la hermosa música que había escuchado. Al contemplar la catedral, se imaginó que una iglesia aún más bella podría construirse para la Bendita Virgen.

Poco después la ayudante del obispo regresó y se sentó junto a Juan Diego. Puso una mano sobre la mano de Juan Diego y le dijo: "El obispo no cree tu historia. Dijo que debes traer alguna prueba antes de que él escuche más. Lo lamento. Quizás aprendas tu lección y ya no molestes al obispo después de esto".

Al caminar de regreso a la colina de Tepeyac, Juan Diego pensó en cómo le diría a la Bendita Virgen María que había fracasado nuevamente. Al acercarse a la colina, un primo de Juan Diego corrió frenéticamente hasta Juan y le dio un aplastante mensaje. El tío de Juan Diego se estaba muriendo y no se esperaba que pasara la noche.

Ahora sí Juan estaba convencido que su suerte en esta tierra era sufrir y fracasar. Desanimado, subió a la colina y se dispuso a decirle a la Bendita Virgen María que buscase un mensajero más meritorio. Cuando sintió la luces celestiales que rodeaban a la Bendita Virgen María y cuando escuchó las campanas celestiales y sus calmantes sonidos, por un momento, sintió consuelo en su alma.

Incluso, antes de que él hablase otra vez, parecía que la Bendita Virgen María podía leer sus pensamientos más profundos. La Virgen habló y le dijo: "Juan Diego, no te desesperes. He venido a esta tierra a traerte consuelo y fortaleza en tus horas más difíciles. Debes saber que siempre estoy a tu lado. En este momento mientras hablamos, estoy sanando a tu tío. Verá muchos días más y vivirá una larga vida. Ahora ven conmigo. Le daremos al obispo la prueba que pide".

Juan Diego siguió a la Bendita Virgen María más arriba de la colina, a una zona donde crecían flores silvestres. Pero tanto las flores como los pastizales estaban secos en el frío aire de diciembre. Todo lo que los recibió eran la tierra desnuda y las ramas vacías.

Sin esfuerzo aparente, la Bendita Virgen María se elevó y flotó por encima de uno de los arbustos. Súbitamente, la luz celestial se hizo tan brillante como un día de verano, y las campanas celestiales repiquetearon con una gozosa melodía. Juan Diego casi podía oler la dulce fragancia de las rosas de verano, plenamente florecidas. La Bendita Virgen María abrió sus brazos en torno a uno de los arbustos, y, al hacerlo, pétalos de rosas, de rosas de Castilla, se precipitaron hasta el suelo. Los reunió y le dijo a Juan Diego: "Llévale esto al obispo. Que las rosas sean la prueba que él quiere".

Juan Diego recogió las rosas en su tilma (o manta de algodón) y descendió de la colina con gozoso delirio. Pensó: "Ella es la Bendita Virgen María, y éste es el milagro celestial que el sacerdote me decía. Ahora el obispo me creerá".

Por tercera vez, golpeó las puertas de la catedral. La ayudante del obispo la que había sido amable con él, abrió las puertas y, con asombro, vio frescas y veraniegas rosas de Castilla caerse de la tilma de Juan Diego. Fue a llamar al obispo y los dos salieron corriendo fuera de la iglesia. Cuando el obispo Zumárraga vio las rosas, reconoció que eran un don de la Bendita Virgen María. Cuando se acercó para tocar las rosas, las rosas retrocedieron hasta adentro de la tilma y formaron parte de una imagen de la aparición de la Virgen en el tejido de la tilma. El Obispo Zumarraga cayó de rodillas y gritó: "¡Un milagro! ¡Un milagro!" Los ayudantes del obispo también trataron de tocar las rosas y también vieron la imagen de la Bendita Virgen María dentro de la tilma de Juan Diego.

Solo entonces el Obispo entonces creyó el mensaje de Juan Diego y construyó una iglesia dedicada a la Bendita Virgen María, en la colina de Tepeyac. Hasta el día de hoy la tilma de Juan Diego cuelga en la iglesia, como un recordatorio del milagro que sucedió en esta tierra hace tantos años. Ahora el pueblo mexicano llama a este lugar Guadalupe, y los suplicantes vienen a la iglesia para ver la tilma milagrosa. Al orar y al contemplar la tilma, recuerdan el amor de la Bendita Virgen y la promesa de la Bendita Virgen María, Nuestra Señora de Guadalupe, de siempre ayudar y consolar a su pueblo en momentos de necesidad.

BACKGROUND ABOUT LA LLORONA (THE WEEPING WOMAN)

The legend of *La Llorona*, The Weeping Woman, is one of Mexico's most powerful and enduring stories. This story actually exists in many variations throughout the Americas, extending northward into the United States Hispanic Southwest. Mexicans even sing a melancholy ballad about *La Llorona.*

The story is similar in plot to the Greek Media story of a woman who kills her two children in grim retaliation for her husband's betrayal. Of course, the story has a harsh moral in that *La Llorona* is destined to suffer for all eternity for her tragic misdeed. Her very name, The Weeping Woman, is descriptive of her consuming grief for her lost children.

The origins of the legend are lost in antiquity and contested by scholars and folklorists. One Mexican source is the Aztec stories about Cihuacoatl, a pre-Columbian goddess who ruled childbirth and death. Also known as Snake Skirt, she was the virgin mother of the Aztec God of war, Huitzilopochtli, who killed his own siblings. The Aztec stories of Cihuacoatl told of her nightly screams as she witnessed her children being killed.

Another Mexican source is the story of *La Malinche*, the Indian woman who was Hernán Cortés's interpreter and mistress. Named Doña Marina by the Spanish, she is a significant Mexican historical figure. Because of her invaluable skills as an interpreter of the native languages, Doña Marina had been instrumental in the eventual Spanish domination of the Aztec people.

Cortés first encountered Doña Marina when he received her as a gift from Tabascan nobles. She bore Cortés a son, and Cortés gave her to another Spanish soldier. As the legend goes, her abandonment by Cortés causes her to kill her son and cry out in grief, "*Ay, mi hijo!*" (Alas, my son!) as his spirit leaves his body.

This story is only a legend, however, for in truth she did not kill her son. Her association with the tragic story of *La Llorona* stems from Mexicans perceiving her as a traitor to her Indian people who gave birth to a *mestizo* child of mixed Spanish and Indian blood.

Other versions of the legend describe *La Llorona* as a seductive temptress leading men to an evil and sinful fate. In this legendary manifestation, she is the siren of feminine powers that no man can resist. Of course, this version of the legend tells of *La Llorona's* destructive power over a man's life and soul.

Each variation of the legend differs on the how and why of the children's death. Some versions have *La Llorona* deliberately killing the children in a mad fit of rage and jealousy, while others have the children accidentally drowning and *La Llorona* portrayed as a sad victim of cruel fate. Still others have *La Llorona* killing the children in order to be free to pursue her heart's desires. The common characteristics of all of the versions, however, are the drowning of the children and the eternal grief and suffering of *La Llorona.*

La Llorona
The Weeping Woman

According to the legend, there once was a beautiful Spanish maiden named Juanita who lived a life of peaceful harmony in her quiet village. Her days were filled with the carefree joys of a child: playing, laughing, and running free as the wind. Her home was of simple *adobe*. Although her family was poor, Juanita knew they were hardworking people of the land, and she loved her life.

As a young girl she spent many hours with her girlfriends imagining their lives when they grew up. The most common game they played was to imagine the man each would one day marry. Like the innocent children they were, they laughed and giggled as they described their knight in shining armor, their handsome man on the beautiful black horse, and their Spanish gentleman who would take them far away for a life of gentle luxury.

As Juanita grew up her beauty blossomed like a rose in the summer light. She soon left the idle games of her childhood and settled into the responsibilities of a young Spanish maiden. Her life now consisted of helping her mother with the womanly duties of caring for the house and the other, younger children. Her parents were proud of their daughter Juanita, and in their hearts they hoped that one day she would marry well and begin a family of her own.

In truth, Juanita carried the same hopes for herself. She had never forgotten the games of her childhood and still carried her dream of the Spanish gentleman close to her heart. The young men of the village began to notice Juanita's beauty and grace. Like frolicking young colts, they each tried to outdo the other in gaining a passing glance from Juanita. Juanita knew that one day her father would say yes to the family of one of these brash young men, and her hand would pass in marriage to one of them. Her only hope was that he would in some way measure up to her longed-for Spanish gentleman.

According to the legend, one day a Spanish gentleman moved to the village. His father had vast landholdings in the area, and he had come to take care of his family's interests. He was schooled in the manners and graces of the wealthy Spanish of Mexico City and immediately became the most prominent man in Juanita's simple village. When she first saw him, Juanita knew that the man of her dreams had come into her life.

As time passed, the Spanish gentleman became bored with the simple ways of the village. He missed the excitement of Mexico City and regretted that he had accepted his family's assignment in the village. So he found ways to bring some measure of excitement into his life by establishing harmless flirtations with the young women of the village. In the strict moral code of the time, families carefully guarded their young women from any occasion that would bring shame to the family's honor. But every family knew that the woman who married the Spanish gentleman would bring not only honor to her family but also wealth. So, in spite of their strict customs, the Spanish gentleman found ample opportunity to meet and exchange flirtations with the young women of the village.

It is at this point of the legend that the story begins to turn toward its tragic events. Whether it was cursed fate, bad luck, or dark destiny, Juanita and the Spanish gentleman soon found each other. For him, she was the flaming spark of excitement for which he had been longing. For Juanita, he was the Spanish gentleman come to true life.

The Spanish gentleman focused all of his idle energy on Juanita. Her beauty captivated him, and he courted her with all the gentlemanly manners of his station in life. In her heart Juanita knew that a man of his class would never marry someone like her, but her own longing for the Spanish gentleman of her dreams came to be her passion, and soon it was too late. Going against all that her family had instilled in her and against honor and common sense itself, her love-driven heart gave itself to the Spanish gentleman. To the shame of her family and the whole village, she had two children with the Spanish gentleman and lived with him as his common-law wife.

Her love for the Spanish gentleman and her great joy in her two children comforted Juanita during his long absences as he returned to Mexico City to tend to his family's business. She would ease her children's longing for their father by telling them stories of his important business in Mexico City. And each night, she would sing them to sleep with a lullaby of their father's eventual return.

One day, however, the Spanish gentleman returned to the village riding in a fine carriage, accompanied by a Spanish *señorita* who was dressed in a gown of the finest white Spanish lace. As Juanita saw him ride by their house, she knew that her world had come to an end. Her children saw their father ride by without stopping and ran after the carriage only to return home covered with its dust. That night, Juanita put her crying children to bed and promised them that their father would be home in the morning.

Late that night, Juanita went to the house where the Spanish gentleman was staying. She knocked on the door, and when a servant answered, she asked to see the Spanish gentleman. The servant returned and told her that the Spanish gentleman did not want to see her. She then told the servant to tell the Spanish gentleman that his children wanted to see him. The servant soon returned with a cruel message. He told Juanita that the Spanish gentleman had said that he was in town with his intended Spanish bride, a *señorita* approved by his family, and that the children she spoke of were not the legitimate heirs to his family's honor and wealth. The servant then closed the door in Juanita's face.

Juanita was struck with an anger that raged through her body. It came from the depth of her stricken heart. She was overcome with an immense sadness at the image of her children learning about their father's final words. In a blind fury, she raced home. When she saw her children sleeping the deep, peaceful sleep of childhood, she made up her mind that her children would never know the pain she had felt that night. She gently grabbed them up and wrapped them in their wool blankets. As they started to awaken, she assured them that everything was all right and that they should go back to sleep. Comforted by their mother's words and with dreams of seeing their father in the morning, they both fell back to sleep.

Juanita, guided by some unknown calling, stumbled to the river and in one valiant, crazed heave tossed her children into the river. As soon as they had left her arms, she realized her tragic mistake and threw herself into the river to save them. But the river raged with a deadly force, and the two beautiful children would never awaken from their eternal sleep.

Juanita climbed out of the river and wailed the most forlorn cry ever heard on this Earth: "Aaaaiiiiii, *mis hijos*!" ("My children!") The next day, the people of the village went down to the river to see what had caused the mournful wailing they had heard the night before. Juanita's family found her clothes on the river-bank, and they knew that the doomed, sinful love of Juanita and the Spanish gentleman had come to a tragic end.

From that day on, the people of the village will swear that on some nights, especially the dark and violent nights of summer storms, they can hear a weeping woman moaning by the riverbanks. They tightly close their window shutters in order to keep the woman's grief outside of their homes and away from their family and children. They tell the legend of *La Llorona* to all who will listen as a cautionary tale about how a bad love can bring grief, sadness, and tragedy to even the most beautiful of young women.

BACKGROUND ABOUT LA FLOR DE LA NOCHE BUENA (THE LEGEND OF THE POINSETTIA)

The popular decorative Christmas plant, the poinsettia, is at the center of a Mexican miracle legend, *La Flor de la Noche Buena*. The literal translation is "the Flower of the Good Night,"with the "Good Night" (*la Noche Buena*) meaning Christmas Eve. The legend tells the story of a girl with no gift for the baby Jesus at

Christmas Eve mass. By the end of the story, however, she has discovered the gift of true love, accomplished a miracle, and taught everyone the real meaning of Christmas. The story also describes how the poinsettia plant got its red leaves.

The Aztecs called the poinsettia plant *cuetlaxochitl*, the flower of purity. The plant is native to Mexico, where it can grow as tall as 10 feet, with leaves up to a foot long. Its most colorful period is during the Christmas season. The Spanish admired the poinsettia's colorful leaves and associated the plant with the Christmas season. They saw the green leaves as symbolic of the continuation of life and the red leaves as representative of the Blood of Christ. The indigenous Indians used the plant for medicinal uses, and because it grew so easily and abundantly, considered it a symbol of the "new life" gained by warriors killed in battle.

The plant is named after Dr. Joel R. Poinsett, the first United States ambassador to Mexico (from 1825 to 1830) and amateur botanist. Dr. Poinsett admired the colorful plant and called it "painted leaves." He sent cuttings of the plant to his greenhouse in South Carolina, and the plant soon became popular in the United States.

This version of *La Flor de La Noche Buena* takes place during the annual nine-day Mexican Christmas celebration of *Las Posadas*. *Las Posadas* translates as "the inns," and the community celebration is a reenactment of the journey of Mary and Joseph searching for lodging in Bethlehem. In the tradition of *Las Posadas*, for nine nights community members dramatize the roles of Joseph, Mary, angels, and shepherds. The procession travels from house to house as Joseph and Mary fail to find lodging for the first eight nights, only to be successful on the ninth night, Christmas Eve (*la Noche Buena*).

La Flor de la Noche Buena
The Legend of the Poinsettia

In a rural village in the remote land of Northern Mexico, the Martínez family was busy preparing for the annual celebration of *Las Posadas*. María, the youngest in the Martínez family, was watching her sister Theresa and brother Carlito get dressed in their angel costumes for the first day of the celebration. This evening would be the first night of the nine processions reenacting the journey of Joseph and Mary searching for lodging in Bethlehem.

As Theresa tried on her angel wings she admired their beauty. Looking in the mirror she sighed, "Oh, look how wonderful they are." Meanwhile, Carlito was struggling with his wings. They were too small to comfortably fit him. He loudly complained, "I can't get mine on. I think they're too small."

María was jealous that she was not allowed to be one of the angels. She felt that after all these years she was finally old enough to be one of the angels in the family processions. Eyeing Carlito's small and ill-fitting wings she volunteered, "Maybe they will fit me. I can be one of the angels this year!"

Theresa snapped back, "María, one day you will get to be one of the angels, but this year we get to be the angels. You will have to wait until you're a little bigger, just like I did."

María was crushed. With a full pout on her lips she cried, "That's not fair! I am old enough to be one of the angels. And Carlito, those wings don't even fit you. They're for a younger person like me."

Carlito tugged and pushed the tight wings into place, making sure he would be one of the angels, and answered back to María, "No. They are for a smaller person, not a younger person. There's a difference, you know. Anyway, Mama already said you could go with the singers. It wouldn't work if all the kids were angels."

Being the persistent girl she was, María would not take no for an answer. She looked jealously at both Theresa and Carlito in their angel wings. In frustration she yelled out, "But being a singer isn't any fun! The singers are all grown-ups. The kids just walk in the procession carrying candles. This was the year I wanted to be something special in the procession. I wanted to have the most special gift of all for baby Jesus when we got to the church."

Theresa tried to comfort María by telling her, "Maybe next year you can be an angel. And besides, you can still have a special present for baby Jesus. You'll be the best candle holder of all."

María still refused to be comforted. She wanted to be an angel, and no amount of kind words would take away her disappointment. She sulked away from Theresa and Carlito and sat down by herself.

Finally, it was time to leave for the first night of *Las Posadas*. Excited to be angels, Theresa and Carlito rushed out of their house to catch up with the procession. María trudged along behind them, with her head hanging down and her feet kicking up dry dust along the road.

On the third night of *Las Posadas*, the Martínez family was busily preparing for the night's procession. The father had taken on the special job of making the star *piñata*, which represents the Star of Bethlehem, that would be broken during the night's celebration. As he carefully applied the colorful layers of paper strips to the clay pot, he exclaimed with joy, "This is a great *piñata*! When I was a small boy, we always just had little *piñatas*. Nowadays, the *piñatas* are so much bigger. Everyone told me, 'Make it extra big.' So I did. And the ladies from the church took a collection, and we were able to buy all of these candies and nuts to put in it. Now you kids, it's your job to fill it. And don't take too long, because we need to get ready for tonight's procession."

Proudly watching their father make the *piñata*, and then helping stuff it full of candy and nuts, Theresa and Carlito could not help but be excited about the night's procession. It had been so much fun being angels, and now they were part of another special event of *Las Posadas*.

But even with all of the fun of making and filling the *piñata*, María continued to mope. Finally, the mother could no longer stand María's sulking. Holding María in her warm and caring arms, she said to María, "I hope you don't mope all through this procession like you did last night."

Theresa shook María playfully and said, "Oh, she's still sulking because she can't be an angel this year."

María defended herself by answering: "I'm not sulking. I just thought it would be a special gift to baby Jesus if I could be an angel in the procession. Theresa and Carlito get to be angels. I just walk along carrying a dumb, old candle. There's nothing special about that."

The mother looked at María sternly and in an authoritarian voice told her, "María, just being in the procession is a good enough gift. Baby Jesus sees you walking in the procession."

María would not be pacified, however. With tears in her eyes she answered her mother, "Even Papa gets to do something special. He made the *piñata* and gets to be *el diablo* telling people not to let Joseph and Mary stay for the night."

Quickly, Theresa corrected María: "But remember how many years Papa wanted to play *el diablo*? Even Papa had to wait his turn. You didn't see Papa moping around all night and ruining the celebration for everyone."

María cried back, "I'm not sulking! I just want to be something special for baby Jesus. I'm the only one not doing anything special!"

Before the argument could get any worse, the father stood up with the *piñata* and said, "Good. Now it's ready. Let's give it a test before we take it out." He held the *piñata* up in the air and let each of the children take a few playful swings at it, carefully snatching it out of reach each time. Holding the *piñata* in his arms, he then said, "Good. It's working. Time for us to go. And let's be careful with the *piñata*! We don't want it breaking early."

As the family excitedly hurried out of the house, María grabbed her candle and slowly walked after them. She took her place in the procession line with her candle held at her side.

By the ninth night of *Las Posadas*, María had finally accepted that she was not going to be an angel. Although they had not turned out like she had wanted them to, she had enjoyed the celebrations of the past eight nights. She was even looking forward to the ninth night, *la Noche Buena*. The family was in high spirits and were happily planning the night's activities. The procession would stop at their house on the way to the church, so they had spent all day preparing small baskets of sweets, sandwiches, cookies, and fruited punch for the other families in the village.

After they had helped to prepare the food, Theresa and Carlito busily began wrapping their presents for baby Jesus. It was the tradition of the village that the children would bring to the church presents for baby Jesus on *la Noche Buena* to celebrate his birth.

Theresa and Carlito were both making *papel picado*, colorful decorations made of cut paper, with paper they had left over from the day of the dead celebrations (the celebrations of the day the souls of the dead visit their families). María was clumsily trying to make an *ojo de dios*, a god's eye, with crossed sticks and yarn. She had seen the older children make them, but her tiny fingers were too small to hold the sticks and yarn at the same time and eventually her god's eye fell apart.

As she looked at the pile of sticks and yarn jumbled on the floor, she felt her lower lip start to quiver as she valiantly tried to hold back the tears. She looked at her family, each happily busy with the night's preparations and said, "See what I mean? It seems like everybody does something special for baby Jesus except for me. Theresa and Carlito both got to be angels. Papa made the *piñata*. Mama makes special food for everybody. I didn't do anything special. I really wanted to give baby Jesus a special gift this year."

The father took María into his arms and rocked her and soothingly whispered in her ear, "You know, one day you'll bring the most special gift of all to baby Jesus. You're just too small right now. Maybe next year will be your year. But right now, we all have to get ready for the procession, and then we will go to the church. This year, I'll let you sit up front with the big kids."

María tried to be comforted by her father's loving words but was still disappointed that she didn't have a special gift for baby Jesus. She looked up at her father and told him, "But I'm sad I'm not going to have my own special present for baby Jesus. You have always told me that the spirit of *la Noche Buena* is about giving presents—not just getting presents. And now that I'm old enough to go to church with the big kids, I want to bring the most special present in the whole world for baby Jesus."

Her father gave her a big hug and told her, "Like I said, one day you'll have the most special present of all. But now, let's get ready. I hear the singers, and soon it'll be time for church."

As the evening passed, María tried to be happy and to have fun with all of the other children. But deep inside she was sad. Like a typical child who is full of innocent wishes, she hoped that the day her father had spoken of—the day she would have the most special gift—would happen that night.

After the families had made the final stop of the procession at the Martínez house, everyone went to the church for midnight mass. At the beginning of the mass, the priest stood up and said, "Welcome to the most holy night of the year: *la Noche Buena.* Before we begin the holy mass, let's have the children bring up their presents for the baby Jesus."

Theresa and Carlito each took their carefully wrapped present of *papel picado* up to the altar. Their father looked around and asked, "Where is María? She was right behind us in the procession. Theresa, do you know where your sister is?"

Theresa shook her head and answered, "I thought she was with you."

Carlito then spoke up, "She told me she couldn't come without a present for baby Jesus."

The father became worried and asked Carlito, "She didn't go back home, did she?"

Sensing his father's concern, Carlito remembered, "I don't think so. She just took off right as we went past the field.

As the father prepared to leave the church to look for her, María came dashing into the church, carrying something behind her. She had a bright, beaming look on her face as she explained, "I couldn't come to midnight mass with nothing. I love baby Jesus too much. So I went in the field to wait until mass was over.

When I walked by these plants, they turned this beautiful red color. So I brought them as a present for baby Jesus."

From behind her back she pulled out a plant that had leaves of bright red mixed in with its deep green leaves. She proudly walked up to the priest and handed him the colorful red and green plant.

The priest carefully examined the plant and asked María, "Where did you get this plant with red leaves? This plant grows wild in the field and is most abundant at this time of year. But its leaves are never red. They are always green."

With a wide smile on her face, María answered the priest: "They turned red when I walked by them thinking about a present for baby Jesus. They were so beautiful that I brought one for my special present."

Just then some other children came running into the church. They stumbled over one another, as each tried to be first with the exciting news. Finally, one of the children spoke clearly to the priest, "You should see it. The whole field is filled with red plants. Just like the one María has. Come and see them. They're beautiful!"

As everyone from the church emptied out into the field, they beheld the most beautiful plants of red and green. Everyone shouted in excitement about the *milagro* (miracle) of the red leaves and about how María had truly given baby Jesus the most special present of the day.

And from that time on, the poinsettia has given us its red leaves on *la Noche Buena* to remind us that the best gift of all is a heart full of love.

BACKGROUND ABOUT LA CHINA POBLANA

One of Mexico's most charming legends is the story of *la China Poblana*, the Chinese girl from Puebla. The costume of *la China Poblana* is the national costume for Mexican women, in honor of the legendary princess who used her good fortune and bright, generous spirit to do good works for people less fortunate than her. The Mexican people have come to admire these saintly characteristics, and for this reason, Mexico has adopted *la China Poblana* as a reflection of the Mexican national character.

The costume for a *China Poblana* is beautiful in its splendor and folk identification. The basic costume consists of a full red and green skirt richly embroidered with sequins in designs of flowers and fanciful geometric patterns worn with a white embroidered blouse. Traditionally, *la China Poblana* wears her hair in braids down her back or wrapped atop her head and decorated with bright ribbons. The costume may also include a *rebozo*, a silk shawl worn by the majority of Mexican women. The *rebozo* is crossed around her waist, then over her back, then draped over her shoulders in front.

The costume also appears in *el Jarabe Tapatío*, also known as the Mexican Hat Dance, which is the best known and most popular of Mexican dances. Also recognized as the national dance of Mexico, *el Jarabe Tapatío* is a dance representing the courtship of a young maiden by a gallant young man. The young man, the *Charro* (a horseman from Jalisco), courts the maiden, the *China Poblana*, through the dance. The woman in the dance wears the costume of *la China Poblana*.

Several explanations exist about the origins of the *China Poblana* costume. In one version of this legend, a Chinese princess was brought to Acapulco as a slave. She was then sold to a wealthy family in Puebla, who adopted her as a daughter. She had a gentle disposition and became known for her virtue and charity. When she died, all the young women of Puebla wished to be like her, and so they adopted her style of dress—a simple red skirt, white blouse, and *rebozo*. In her memory they named this style of dress after her—*China* for Chinese, and *poblana* for Puebla.

Figure 10
A basic *China Poblana* costume.

Scholars, however, have dismissed the Chinese princess as the source of this legend. Mela Sedillo (1935), in *Mexican and New Mexican Folkdances*, refers to Andulucía and its Arabian influence as the origin of the *China Poblana* costume. Chloë Sayer (1985), in her book *Mexican Costume*, also refers to the Spanish peasant styles from Andalucía and Lagartera in the province of Toledo as the source for the *China Poblana* style.

Francis Toor (1947), in *A Treasury of Mexican Folkways*, points to two other possible origins of the *China Poblana* costume. She explains that the *China Poblana* style could have originated with gaily dressed girls who sold drinks on plazas. Another possibility presented by Toor is that the word *China* refers to a "maid servant," a class of domestic helpers who dressed in clothing similar to *la China Poblana*.

But the following legend is much more engaging than any of the scholars' explanations and is the popularly believed origin of the costume.

La China Poblana

Many years ago (in 1684 to be exact) in faraway China there lived the Mongol Princess Mirrah, descended from Humayum, the proud Mongol ruler and founder of a grand Mongol dynasty. The Princess Mirrah lived a life of ease and luxury as a member of the royal family. Her education was thorough and aimed at preparing her for a life of service to her people. Her education served her well, for of all of the young women of the Mongol court, Princess Mirrah was the wisest, kindest, and most considerate.

As part of her life of privilege, the Princess Mirrah was fortunate to travel. One fateful trip took her to Manila. The trip was dangerous because at that time pirates roamed the seas attacking and looting ships for their cargoes and wealth. According to the legend, pirates attacked and captured Princess Mirrah's ship. The pirates stole her away and immediately took her fine silken clothes and valuable jewels for themselves and dressed her in the clothes of a common slave. The pirates intended to sell her off as a slave in order to make an even greater gain from their treachery.

According to the legend, a viceroy of New Spain had solicited the services of the governor of Manila to acquire well-groomed and respectful servants to assist his ministers in the national palace. The governor of Manila knew that pirates often put up for sale slaves captured on the high seas. It was this twist of fate that eventually led to the pirates selling Princess Mirrah to the viceroy of New Spain. The viceroy, in turn, sold Princess Mirrah to a slave merchant for transport to New Spain. In no time, Princess Mirrah had found herself torn from her homeland, reduced to the life of a servant, and sailing on a boat from Manila to Acapulco.

When she arrived in Acapulco, the slave ship captain sold her as a servant to Captain Miguel de Sosa and his wife Doña Margarita de Chávez. Captain Sosa was a respected and wealthy merchant from Puebla. He and his wife immediately recognized that their new servant was well educated and extremely well mannered. They also discovered that she possessed a pure and joyful spirit in spite of her hardships. Eventually, they educated her in their Christian religion and had her baptized with the name of Catarina de San Juan, after a young nun and daughter of a friend who had recently died. They then freed her and gave her money to begin a life on her own.

Catarina adjusted quickly to her new life. Her noble heritage and gentle spirit had strengthened and sustained her through all of her hardships. She dedicated herself to a life of service and good deeds, as she had been raised and educated to do. She gave away most of her own wealth and became active in the charitable work of her church. Her life was an exemplary one of charitable and religious service.

She herself dressed in the simplest fashion. In the colder months she wore a goatskin suit. In the warmer months she wore a plain, red flannel skirt, a white blouse, and a *rebozo* draped around her shoulders. Her hair was always wrapped simply with bright ribbons. The people of Puebla came to associate this plain dress of a red skirt, white blouse, and *rebozo* with Catarina and her good work.

The people of Puebla greatly admired Catarina's humble and giving nature. Her natural beauty complimented the beauty of her spirit. They affectionately nicknamed her "*la China*," the Chinese girl. Soon, the maidservants of the noblemen's houses began to imitate her dress as a symbol of their admiration of Catarina.

When Catarina died, the people of Puebla deeply mourned her death and remembered her virtuous life and the great good she had brought to Puebla. They felt themselves fortunate that such a saintly woman as Catarina had come into their lives.

In honor of her memory, the women of Puebla adopted her style of dress. In time, the legend of Catarina spread, and women in other places adopted the dress of *la China Poblana*, the Chinese girl from Puebla.

La China Poblana

Una de las leyendas mexicanas más encantadoras es la historia de la China Poblana, la muchacha china de Puebla. El vestido de la China Poblana es el vestido nacional de la mujer mexicana, en honor a la legendaria princesa quien usó su buena fortuna y su espíritu brillante y generoso para hacer obras de bien para los menos afortunados. Los mexicanos admiran esas santas características, y, por eso, México adoptó a la China Poblana como una reflezo del carácter nacional mexicano.

El vestido de una China Poblana es hermoso en su esplendor y en su identificación popular. El vestido básico consiste en una falda roja y verde bordada con lentejuelas formando flores e imaginativos diseños geométricos, junto con una blusa blanca bordada. Tradicionalmente, la China Poblana lleva el pelo trenzado en la espalda o recogido sobre la cabeza y decorado con cintas brillantes. El vestido puede incluir un rebozo, un chal usado por la mayoría de las mujeres mexicanas. El rebozo, un chal de seda, se cruza alrededor de la cintura, luego sobre la espalda, y finalmente se pasa sobre los hombros y se deja caer al frente.

El vestido también aparece en el Jarabe Tapatío, también conocido como el baile mexicano del sombrero, que es una de las danzas mexicanas mejor conocidas y más populares. También reconocida como la danza nacional de México, el Jarabe Tapatío es una danza que representa el galanteo de una joven señorita con un galante joven. El joven, el Charro (el jinete de Jalisco) corteja a la señorita, la China Poblana, por medio de la danza. La mujer en la danza viste el traje de la China Poblana.

Existen varias explicaciones sobre los orígenes del vestido de la China Poblana. En una de las versiones de la leyenda, una princesa china fue traída a Acapulco como esclava. Más tarde fue vendida a una familia acaudalada en Puebla, quien la adoptó como hija. Tenía un carácter gentil y se la conocía por su virtud y caridad. Cuando murió, todas las mujeres de Puebla querían ser como ella, y adoptaron su estilo de vestirse, una simple falda roja, blusa blanca y rebozo. En su memoria llamaron a este estilo de vestirse con el nombre de la mujer, China, por venir de la China, y Poblana por ser de Puebla.

Los estudiosos, sin embargo, desestimaron la Princesa China como la fuente de la leyenda. Mela Sedillo (1935), en *Mexican and New Mexican Folkdances (Danzas populares de México y Nuevo México)*, hace referencia a Andalucía y a sus influencias árabes como el origen de la China Poblana. Chloë Sayer (1985), en su libro *Mexican Costume (Vestimentas mexicanas)*, también hace referencia a Andalucía y Lagartera en la provincia de Toledo como la fuente del estilo de la China Poblana.

Francis Toor (1947), en *A Treasury of Mexican Folkways (Un tesoro del floclore mexicano)*, indica otros dos posibles orígenes para el vestido de la China

Poblana. La autora explica que el estilo de la China Poblana se pudo haber originado con la muchachas alegremente vestidas que servían bebidas en las plazas. Otra posibilidad que Toor presenta es que la palabra "china" se refiera a "sirvienta", una clase de ayudantes domésticos que se vestían de una manera parecida a la China Poblana.

Pero la leyenda que se relata a continuación tiene más atractivo que las explicaciones de los estudiosos y es la que popularmente se acepta como el origen del vestido.

Hace muchos años, en 1648 para ser exactos, en la lejana China, vivía la Princesa de los mongoles, Mirrah, descendiente de Humayum, el orgulloso gobernador y fundador de una mongólica gran dinastía de mongólica. La Princesa Mirrah vivía una vida fácil y lujosa, como miembro de la familia real. Su educación era extensa, con la meta de preparla para una vida al servicio a su pueblo. Su educación le había servido, porque, de todas las jovencitas en la corte de Mongolia, la Princesa Mirrah era la más sabia, la más amable, y la más considerada.

Como parte de su vida de privilegio, la Princesa Mirrah tenía la fortuna de viajar. Un desafortunado viaje la llevó a Manila. El viaje era peligroso porque en esa época los piratas navegaban los mares, atacando y despojando a los barcos de su carga y de las cosas de valor. Según la leyenda, los piratas atacaron y capturaron el barco de la Princesa Mirrah. Los piratas apartaron a Mirrah, le quitaron sus vestidos de seda y sus joyas, y la vistieron con los vestido de una esclava común. Los piratas trataban de venderla como esclava para obtener una ganancia mayor.

Según la leyenda, el virrey de Nueva España había solicitado los servicios del gobernador de Manila para adquirir algunos sirvientes bien parecidos y respetuosos que ayudasen a los ministros en el palacio nacional. El gobernador de Manila sabía que los piratas, a menudo vendían los esclavos capturados en el mar. Por una de esas cosas del destino, los piratas le vendieron la Princesa Mirrah al virrey de Nueva España. El Virrey, a su vez, vendió la Princesa Mirrah a un traficante de esclavos para que la trajese a Nueva España. En poco tiempo, la Princesa Mirrah se encontró alejada de su tierra, reducida a la vida de esclava y navegando desde Manila a Acapulco.

Cuando la Princesa llegó a Acapulco, el capitán del barco de esclavos la vendió al Capitán Miguel de Sosa y a su esposa Doña Margarita de Chávez. El Capitán Sosa era un respetado y acaudalado comerciante de Puebla. El y su esposa inmediatamente reconocieron que su nueva sirvienta era muy educada, y de muy buenos modales. También descubrieron que poseía un espíritu puro y alegre, a pesar de sus tribulaciones. Eventualmente la educaron en la religión cristiana y la bautizaron con el nombre de Catarina de San Juan, por el nombre de una joven monja, hija de un amigo, que había fallecido recientemente. Entonces le dieron la libertad y dinero, para que comenzase una vida por sí misma.

Catarina se adaptó rápidamente a su nueva vida. Su nobleza y su espíritu gentil la había fortalecido y sostenido durante todas sus tribulaciones. Se dedicó a una vida de servicio y obras de bien, como se había criado y educardo a hacerlo. Donó gran parte de su fortuna y se mantuvo activa en las obras de caridad de su iglesia. Su vida era un ejemplo de caridad y servicio religioso.

Ella misma se vestía de manera simple. En los fríos meses de invierno se ponía pieles de cabra. En los cálidos meses del verano se vestía con una falda roja de franela, una blusa blanca y un rebozo sobre los hombros. Su cabello siempre estaba recogido con cintas brillantes. La gente de Puebla asoció este vestido de falda roja, blusa blanca y rebozo con Catarina y sus buenas obras.

La gente de Puebla admiraba la naturaleza humilde y generosa de Catarina. Su belleza natural complementaba la belleza de su espíritu. Con afecto la llamaban "la China". En poco tiempo, las sirvientas de las casas de los nobles comenzaron a imitar esa forma de vestir como un símbolo de su admiración por Catarina.

Cuando Catarina murió, la gente de Puebla lloró profundamente su muerte y recordó su virtuosa vida y el gran bien que había traído a Puebla. Se sintieron afortunados que una mujer tan santa como Catarina hubiese formado parte de sus vidas.

En honor de su memoria, las mujeres de Puebla adoptaron ese estilo de vestido. Con el tiempo, la leyenda de Catarina se esparció, y las mujeres de otros lugares adoptaron el vestido de la China Poblana.

BACKGROUND ABOUT THE LEGEND OF THE TWO VOLCANOES

Southeast of Mexico City lie the two most famous volcanoes in Mexico. A beautiful and tragically romantic legend tells of the origin of the two volcanoes. One of the volcanoes is Popocatepetl, which means "smoking mountain." Eleven miles away is Ixtlaccihuatl, "the sleeping woman." This volcano has three peaks that remind people of a giant woman reclining to sleep. The volcanoes are so impressively large that their snowy peaks can be seen three states away.

Several legends concern the origin of the volcanoes. One of the legends, an ancient Nahua Indian story, tells of two lovers, the son of the sun and the daughter of the moon, leaving the heavens and coming to Earth. On Earth, they discover and enjoy such beauty and peaceful harmony that they decide to give up their heavenly and eternal existence and spend the rest of their days on their earthly paradise. They both eventually die on Earth, and their bodies are transformed into the two volcanoes.

The following story, however, is the more common version of the legend. This version has a definite Romeo and Juliet quality to its narrative.

The Legend of the Two Volcanoes

According to ancient legend, the two beautiful volcanoes that adorn the Valley of Mexico with their towering and snowy peaks were once two lovers. One of the lovers, Ixtlaccihuatl, was the daughter of a powerful Aztec emperor. She had fallen in love with Popocatepetl, one of her father's bravest soldiers. He, in turn, was deeply in love with her. Their deepest desire was that they would live their lives together and that their love would never be separated.

The emperor had ruled for many years, and in his old age, his enemies began to wage war on him in order to gain control of his lands and wealth. The emperor called upon his bravest soldiers to defend their land. Of course, Popocatepetl answered the call and dedicated himself to winning the war for his emperor. On the day he left for battle, Ixtlaccihuatl swore her eternal love for him and promised that she would wait in eternity for his return.

The war raged on for years, and Ixtlaccihuatl often heard stories of fierce and cruel battles. She always listened to them fearing for the life of her beloved Popocatepetl. One day, a soldier approached her and announced that he had news of Popocatepetl. The soldier was one of her father's enemies in disguise who secretly longed to have Ixtlaccihuatl for himself.

When she heard that the soldier carried news of her cherished Popocatepetl, she invited the soldier to tell his story. The soldier told Ixtlaccihuatl that Popocatepetl had been killed in battle and that his body was lost at war. The evil soldier tricked Ixtlaccihuatl, hoping that she would turn her love to him.

Instead, stricken with grief, Ixtlaccihuatl fell sick with a mysterious illness. All the incantations, magic potions, and salves of the priests could not cure Ixtlaccihuatl, for in truth she was dying of a broken heart.

Ixtlaccihuatl climbed to the top of a mountain that rose high above the Valley of Mexico, and there she lay upon the ground. A winter storm covered the mountain, and its fierce wind attacked Ixtlaccihuatl. Immune to its dangers she refused to leave the mountaintop. Instead, she lay down and wept with grief for Popocatepetl.

Snow fell on Ixtlaccihuatl until she was covered with a blanket of deep, white snow. The snow fell for many days and nights until finally the muffled crying of Ixtlaccihuatl could be heard no more. The people of the Valley of Mexico realized that Ixtlaccihuatl had fallen into an eternal sleep and that the snowcapped mountain peak was Ixtlaccihuatl, waiting in peaceful rest for Popocatepetl to join her.

Eventually, the battle to protect the emperor's land ended, and the warriors returned home. One of the returning warriors was Popocatepetl. When he arrived home and asked for Ixtlaccihuatl, the people of the Valley of Mexico told him that she had been deceived by an evil soldier who had told her that Popocatepetl was dead.

With great sadness, they pointed to the snowy-peaked mountain and told Popocatepetl of her final, heartbroken days. Popocatepetl immediately climbed the mountain and fell to his knees, weeping for his lost love Ixtlaccihuatl. Nothing on this Earth could soften his grief. He built a great pyramid next to the body of Ixtlaccihuatl, and on it he lit a torch as an everlasting symbol of their love. He held the bright torch aloft until snow began to fall, and soon he too was covered in an eternal snowy blanket. The snow never extinguished the torch, and it still shines as eternal as the love of Ixtlaccihuatl and Popocatepetl.

To this day, when the people of the Valley of Mexico gaze upon the two volcanoes, they call one Popocatepetl, the smoking mountain, and the other Ixtlaccihuatl, the sleeping woman. The end of the legend tells that the deepest desire of Ixtlaccihuatl and Popocatepetl came true, for they are eternally united in their love, and their love will never be separated.

La leyenda de los dos volcanes

Al sureste de la ciudad de México se encuentran los dos volcanes más famosos de México. Una leyenda hermosa y trágicamente romántica cuenta el origen de estos volcanes. Uno de los volcanes es el Popocatépetl, que significa "montaña humeante". A once millas (17,5 kms) se ubica el Ixtlaccihuatl, "la mujer durmiente". Este volcán tiene tres picos que recuerdan a la gente a una mujer reclinada para dormir. Los volcanes son tan impresionantemente grandes que sus cimas se ven desde tres estados de distancia.

Varias leyendas hablan del origen de los volcanes. Una de las leyendas, una antigua historia Nahua, dice que dos amantes, el hijo del sol y la hija de la luna, dejaron los lugares celestiales y vinieron a la tierra. En la tierra descubrieron y disfrutaron de tal hermosura y de la pacífica armonía, que decidieron renunciar a su existencia celestial y eterna y pasaron el resto de sus días en su paraíso terrenal. Eventualmente los dos murieron en la tierra y sus cuerpos se transformaron en los dos volcanes.

La siguiente historia, sin embargo, es la versión más común de la leyenda. Esta versión tiene, sin duda, la calidad narrativa de Romeo y Julieta.

Según la antigua leyenda, los dos hermosos volcanes que adornan el valle de México con sus majestuosas cimas nevadas, una vez fueron dos amantes. Uno de los amantes, Ixtlaccihuatl, era la hija de un poderoso emperador azteca. Ella se había enamorado de Popocatépetl, uno de los más valientes soldados de su padre. El, a su vez, se había enamorado profundamente de ella. Su más profundo deseo era pasar el resto de sus vidas juntos y que nunca se terminase su amor.

El emperador había reinado por muchos años, y a su avanzada edad, sus enemigos comenzaron a combatirlo para ganar control de sus tierras y sus riquezas. El emperador llamó a sus soldados más valientes para que defendiesen la tierra. Por supuesto, Popocatépetl respondió al llamado y se dedicó a ganar la guerra para su emperador. El día que salió para la batalla, Ixtlaccihuatl le juró eterno amor y le prometió que se pasaría la eternidad esperando su regreso.

La guerra continuó durante años e Ixtlaccihuatl, a menudo, escuchaba las historias de las feroces y crueles batallas. Siempre las escuchaba temiendo por la vida de su amado Popocatépetl. Un día, un soldado se le acercó y le anunció que tenía noticias de Popocatépetl. El soldado era uno de los enemigos de su padre que se había disfrazado, y que deseaba tener a Ixtlaccihuatl para él.

Cuando Ixtlaccihuatl escuchó que el soldado tenía noticias de su querido Popocatépetl, lo invitó a relatar la historia. El soldado le dijo a Ixtlaccihuatl que Popocatépetl había muerto en combate y que su cuerpo se había perdido en el mar. El mal soldado engañó a Ixtlaccihuatl, esperando que ella dirigiese su amor hacia él.

Pero por el contrario, llena de dolor, Ixtlaccihuatl se enfermó con una enfermedad misteriosa. Todos los encantamientos, pociones mágicas y ungüentos de los sacerdotes no pudieron curar a Ixtlaccihuatl, pues en verdad ella sufría de un corazón desgarrado.

Ixtlaccihuatl subio hasta la cima de la montaña que se elevaba muy por encima del valle de México, y allí se recostó en el suelo. Una tormenta de invierno cubrió la montaña, y los fuertes vientos atacaron a Ixtlaccihuatl. Inmune a sus peligros, ella rehusó abandonar la cima de la montaña. Por el contrario, se recostó y lloró de dolor por Popocatépetl.

La nieve cayó sobre Ixtlaccihuatl hasta que quedó cubierta por una profunda capa de nieve. La nieve continuó cayendo durante muchos días y noches, hasta que el llanto amortiguado de Ixtlaccihuatl ya no se escuchaba. La gente del valle de México comprendió que Ixtlaccihuatl estaba sumida en el sueño eterno y la montaña cubierta de nieve era Ixtlaccihuatl, esperando en pacífico reposo que Popocatépetl se uniese a ella.

Eventualmente, la batalla para proteger la tierra del emperador terminó y los guerreros volvieron a sus hogares. Uno de los guerreros que retornó fue Popocatépetl. Cuando llegó a su hogar y preguntó por Ixtlaccihuatl, la gente del valle de México le dijo que ella había sido engañada por un soldado malvado que le había dicho que Popocatépetl estaba muerto.

Con gran tristeza, señalaron a la montaña nevada y le contaron a Popocatépetl los días finales y angustiados de Ixtlaccihuatl. Popocatépetl inmediatamente subió a la montaña y se arrodilló, llorando por el amor perdido de Ixtlaccihuatl. Nada en el mundo podía aliviar su pesar. Construyó una pirámide junto al cuerpo de Ixtlaccihuatl, y encendió una antorcha como un símbolo imperecedero de su amor. Sostuvo la antorcha en alto hasta que comenzó a caer la nieve. En poco tiempo, él también quedó cubierto con una eterna capa de nieve. La nieve nunca extinguió la antorcha, que todavía brilla tan eterna como el amor de Ixtlaccihuatl y Popocatépetl.

Hasta este día, cuando la gente del valle de México contempla los dos volcanes, a uno lo llaman Popocatépetl, la montaña humeante, y al otro Ixtlaccihuatl, la mujer durmiente. El final de la leyenda dice que el profundo deseo de Ixtlaccihuatl y Popocatépetl se hizo realidad, pues están eternamente unidos en su amor, y su amor nunca terminará.

CREATION STORIES FROM INDIGENOUS MEXICO

BACKGROUND ABOUT THE FIVE SUNS

The Aztec people had a complex culture, with a demanding religion at its center. Their cosmology included many gods, each of whom ruled supreme in a different aspect of Aztec life. The Aztec people viewed themselves as a chosen people, responsible for the sustenance of their gods and the continuation of life on Earth. Religious ritual controlled their daily life, and their mythology reminded them of their religious responsibilities.

The Aztec creation myth not only recounted the creation of their world but also had profound religious significance for them. Their creation myth contained the fundamental aspects of their cosmology (their concept of the universe and their place in it) and provided the Aztecs with the cosmic principles by which they ordered their life on Earth.

The magnificent Aztec Sun Stone provides a visual representation of the Aztec creation story. In 1790, workers excavating beneath the Zocalo, the central plaza of Mexico City, unearthed a monumental stone sculpture—the Aztec Sun Stone. The stone measures 12 feet in diameter and weighs 24 metric tons. Miraculously, the stone had escaped the Spanish destruction of all Aztec artifacts in the years immediately following the conquest. The Sun Stone is not a functioning calendar as it is so often misrepresented.

An examination of the inner circle of the Sun Stone reveals its representation of the Aztec creation myth of The Five Suns, the five creation epochs. The center image of the circle is the fifth epoch and represents present-day Earth, Tlaltecuhtli. Some interpretations of this image name it Tonatiuh, the Fifth Sun. The four surrounding glyphs represent the four ancient epochs, each of which ended in the destruction of the Earth:

- 4 Jaguar (The First Sun): The Earth is destroyed by jaguars.
- 4 Wind (The Second Sun): The Earth is destroyed by wind.
- 4 Rain (The Third Sun): The Earth is destroyed by a rain of fire.
- 4 Water (The Fourth Sun): The Earth is destroyed by a flood.

Each epoch of the Aztec creation myth ends on a day identified by the number 4 and a specific name. The Aztec calendar was a complex mechanism identifying days by combining a series of numbers from 1 to 13 in numeric order with another series of 20 separate signs. By combining both series the Aztecs created a ritual calendar with precisely named days. Each named day at the end of each mythical epoch represents a precise day in the Aztec calendar. Of additional significance is that the number 4 is of primary importance in Aztec ritual.

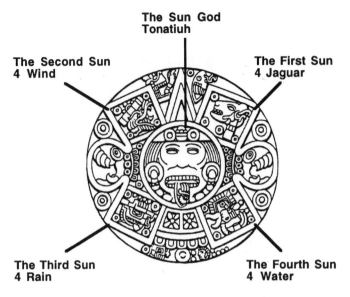

The Sun God
Tonatiuh

The Second Sun
4 Wind

The First Sun
4 Jaguar

The Third Sun
4 Rain

The Fourth Sun
4 Water

Figure 11 The center image of the Aztec Sun Stone
showing the five Suns, or epochs, of the Earth.

The story of the Fifth Sun tells of the cosmic battle for supremacy between two of the Aztec people's primary gods, Quetzalcoatl and Tezcatlipoca. Quetzalcoatl, the plumed serpent, is the God of Civilization, or the Creator God. He is also the God of Enlightenment and Learning. Tezcatlipoca is the supreme divinity of the Aztec people. He is called Smoking Mirror, or God of Darkness and Light. This dark god of the night is the God of Fate, both beneficial and destructive. The Aztec emperors prayed to Tezcatlipoca that he might bless their reign.

According to the Aztec creation myth of The Five Suns, the world has had five incarnations. In each of its first four incarnations, the Earth ended in destruction, only to be reborn. We now live in the time of the fifth incarnation, or the Fifth Sun.

The Creation of the World

An Aztec Myth

The story begins with the Creator Pair, called the Ometeotl, or the Lord and Lady of Duality, at the beginning of time and space, giving birth to two gods, Tezcatlipoca and Quetzalcoatl. The epic story of the battle for supremacy between Quetzalcoatl and Tezcatlipoca through these five incarnations tells the history of the Aztec world.

During the time of the First Sun, giants roamed the Earth, eating roots and acorns, and Tezcatlipoca ruled supreme. He took it upon himself the honor of carrying the Sun on its daily journey through the heavens, lighting the sky above and the Earth below. With great pride, he daily led the Sun in its fiery, celestial path.

Quetzalcoatl was jealous of Tezcatlipoca and his great honor. In a terrible fit of anger he climbed into the sky and gave Tezcatlipoca a mighty blow. The blow stunned Tezcatlipoca, and he fell tumbling from the sky. As he crashed to Earth, Tezcatlipoca transformed himself into his sacred animal spirit, the jaguar. As the jaguar, he destroyed all living creatures on the Earth. The time of the First Sun of the Earth came to an end, and darkness covered the Earth. The Aztecs marked this day of the Earth's first destruction with the name 4 Jaguar.

Quetzalcoatl now reigned supreme. It was his divine honor to lead the Sun on its daily journey to defeat the powers of darkness on the Earth. The Earth existed again for a second time—the time of the Second Sun. During this time, the Earth was populated with monkeys who existed on pine nuts.

Now, it was Tezcatlipoca's turn to be jealous. He was determined to regain his dominance over Quetzalcoatl. It was Tezcatlipoca this time who rose into the sky and delivered a smashing blow to Quetzalcoatl. Quetzalcoatl could not survive the blow and came roaring to Earth with such force that a great windstorm destroyed all living creatures. For the second time, the age of the Sun had ended with the destruction of the Earth. The Aztecs called this day 4 Wind.

The gods were angry at this destructive battle between Quetzalcoatl and Tezcatlipoca. They decided that another god should have the honor of carrying the Sun across the sky. They chose the rain god Tlaloc. Tlaloc ruled supreme during this third creation of the Earth. His fall of nourishing waters brought back life to the Earth, covering it with rivers, lakes, and oceans.

This time, both Quetzalcoatl and Tezcatlipoca began to plot against Tlaloc. Together they attacked Tlaloc and caused a fierce rain of celestial fire to fall on the Earth. The time of the Third Sun ended in the destruction of the Earth by scorching fire. The Aztecs marked the end of this third age of the Sun with the name 4 Rain.

Once again, the gods intervened to recreate the Earth. During this time of the Fourth Sun, Tlaloc's sister, the god Chalchiuhtlicue, or the Lady of Jade Skirts, carried the Sun across the skies.

As before, however, Quetzalcoatl and Tezcatlipoca sought control and struck down Chalchiuhtlicue. As Chalchiuhtlicue, the Goddess of Water, fell to the Earth, the sky opened up with a deluge of heavenly waters. A great flood covered the Earth and destroyed it for a fourth time. The Aztecs marked this day with the name 4 Water.

After the fourth destruction of the Earth, Quetzalcoatl and Tezcatlipoca felt remorse for their battles. Tezcatlipoca and Quetzalcoatl looked down upon the darkened and flooded Earth and knew that their time of battle must come to an end if there was to be another Sun. They abandoned their fierce fighting and together created the Earth for a fifth time. The Fifth Sun, the sun of motion, is the sun of our present age. According to this Aztec myth, the age of the Fifth Sun will one day end in a cataclysm of earthquakes.

Other myths tell of how Tezcatlipoca and Quetzalcoatl formed the Earth, bringing life and vegetation back to it. The myth of The Five Suns, however, remains the primary Aztec creation story of our present-day Earth.

Los cinco soles
La creación del mundo

Un mito azteca

El pueblo azteca tenía una cultura compleja, cuyo centro era una rigurosa religión. Su cosmología incluía muchos dioses, cada uno de los cuales reinaba supremo en una aspecto distinto de la vida azteca. Los aztecas se veían a sí mismos como el pueblo elegido, responsable por la subsistencia de sus dioses y por la continuación de la vida en la Tierra. Los rituales religiosos controlaban la vida diaria de los aztecas, y su mitología les hacía recordar sus reponsabilidades religiosas.

El mito de la creación de los aztecas no solamente contaba la creación de su mundo, sino también tenía un profundo significado religioso para ellos. El mito azteca de la creación contenía los aspectos fundamentales de su cosmología (su concepto del universo y su lugar en ese universo), y proveía a los aztecas de los principios cósmicos por los cuales ordenaban su vida en la Tierra.

La magnífica Piedra Azteca del Sol provee una representación visual de la historia azteca de la creación. En 1790, trabajadores excavando debajo del Zócalo, la plaza central de la Ciudad de México, desenterraron una monumental escultura de piedra, la Piedra Azteca del Sol. La piedra mide 12 pies (4 metros) de diámetro, y pesa 24 toneladas. Milagrosamente, la piedra evitó ser destruída por los españoles, quienes destruyeron todos los artefactos aztecas en los años que siguieron inmediatamente a la conquista. A pesar de que muchas veces así se la presenta, la Piedra del Sol no es un calendario funcional.

Un exámen del círculo interior de la Piedra del Sol revela la representación del mito azteca de la creación de los Cinco Soles, las cinco épocas de la creación. La imagen central del círculo es la quinta época y representa la Tierra actual, *Tlaltecuhtli*. Algunas interpretaciones de esta imagen la llaman *Tonatiuh*, el Quinto Sol. Los cuatro glifos de alrededor representan cuatro épocas antiguas, cada una de las cuales concluyó con la destrucción de la Tierra:

- 4 Jaguar (El Primer Sol): La Tierra es destruída por jaguares.
- 4 Viento (El Segundo Sol): La Tierra es destruída por el viento.
- 4 Lluvia (El Tercer Sol): La Tierra es destruída por una lluvia de fuego.
- 4 Agua (El Cuarto Sol): La Tierra es destruída por un diluvio.

Cada época del mito azteca de la creación termina en un día identificado por el número 4 y un nombre específico. El calendario azteca era un complejo mecanismo que identificaba a los días por medio de una combinación de números del 1 al 13 en orden numérico junto con otra serie de 20 símbolos. Al combinar ambas series los aztecas crearon un calendario ritual cuyos días tenían nombres precisos. Cada día nombrado al final de cada época mítica representa un día preciso en el calendario azteca. Otro hecho significativo es que el número 4 es de primordial importancia en el ritual azteca.

La historia del Quinto Sol relata la batalla cósmica por la supremacía entre dos de los dioses primordiales de los aztecas, Quetzalcoatl y Tezcatlipoca. Quetzalcoatl, la serpiente emplumada, es el dios de la civilización o el dios creador. También es el dios de la iluminación espiritual y el aprendizaje. Tezcatlipoca es la deidad suprema de los aztecas. Se lo llama el Espejo Humeante, o dios de las tinieblas y la luz. Este tenebroso dios de la noche es el dios del destino, tanto beneficioso como destructivo. Los emperadores aztecas rezaban a Tezcatlipoca pidiéndole que bendijese sus reinados.

Según el mito azteca de la creación de los Cinco Soles, el mundo ha tenido cinco encarnaciones. En cada una de sus cuatro primeras encarnaciones, la Tierra terminó en destrucción, solamente para renacer. Ahora vivimos en el tiempo de la quinta encarnación, o el Quinto Sol.

La historia comienza con la Pareja Creadora, llamada Ometeotl, o el Señor y la Señora de la Dualidad, quienes, en el comienzo del tiempo y el espacio, dan nacimiento a dos dioses, Tezcatlipoca y Quetzalcoatl. La épica historia de la batallas por la supremacía entre Quetzalcoatl y Tezcatlipoca a través de estas cinco encarnaciones relata la historia del mundo azteca.

Durante el tiempo del Primer Sol, los gigantes recorrían la tierra, comiendo raíces y semillas, y Tezcatlipoca reinaba supremo. El se adjudicó a sí mismo el honor de cargar el Sol durante su diario viaje por los cielos, iluminando el cielo arriba y la tierra abajo. Con gran orgullo, cada día Tezcatlipoca conducía al Sol por su ígneo sendero celestial.

Quetzalcoatl se puso celoso de Tezcatlipoca y de su gran honor. En un terrible acto de ira, Quetzalcoatl subió a los cielos y golpeó ferozmente a Tezcatlipoca. El golpe paralizó a Tezcatlipoca, quien cayó del cielo. Al chocar contra la tierra, Tezcatlipoca se transformó en el espíritu de su animal sagrado, el jaguar. Como el jaguar, Tezcatlipoca destruyó todas las criaturas vivientes de la Tierra. El tiempo del Primer Sol de la Tierra llegó al final, y las tinieblas cubrieron la tierra. Los aztecas marcaron este día de la primera destrucción de la tierra con el nombre 4. Jaguar.

Quetzalcoatl ahora reinaba supremo. Era su divino honor conducir al Sol en su diario viaje para derrotar los poderes de las tinieblas en la Tierra. La Tierra existía otra vez por segunda vez, el tiempo del Segundo Sol. Durante este tiempo, la Tierra estaba poblada por monos que subsistían con nueces de pinos.

Era ahora el turno de Tezcatlipoca para estar celoso. Tomó la determinación de reconquistar su dominio ahora en manos de Quetzalcoatl. Fue Tezcatlipoca quien esta vez ascendió al cielo y golpeó fuertemente a Quetzalcoatl. Quetzalcoatl no sobrevivió al golpe, y se precipitó hacia la Tierra con tanta fuerza que una gran tormenta de viento destruyó todas las criaturas. Por segunda vez, la época del Sol había terminado con la destrucción de la tierra. Los aztecas llamaron este día 4. Viento.

Los dioses se enojaron con la destructiva batalla entre Quetzalcoatl y Tezcatlipoca. Los dioses decidieron que otro dios tendría el honor de llevar al Sol a través del cielo. Eligieron a Tlaloc, dios de la lluvia. Tlaloc reinó supremo durante esta tercera creación de la Tierra. Su lluvia de aguas nutrientes devolvió la vida a la Tierra, y la cubrió con ríos, lagos, y océanos.

Esta vez, tanto Quetzalcoatl como Tezcatlipoca comenzaron a conspirar contra Tlaloc. Juntos atacaron a Tlaloc y causaron que una lluvia de fuego celestial cayese sobre la Tierra. El tiempo del Tercer Sol terminó con la destrucción de la tierra por medio de fuego abrasador. Los aztecas marcaron el final de la tercera edad del Sol con el nombre 4. Lluvia.

Una vez más, los dioses intervinieron para recrear la tierra. Durante este tiempo del Cuarto Sol, la hermana de Tlaloc, la diosa Chalchiuhtlicue, o diosa de las Faldas de Jade, llevó al Sol a través del cielo.

Como antes, sin embargo, Quetzalcoatl y Tezcatlipoca querían el control y derribaron a Chalchiuhtlicue. Cuando Chalchiuhtlicue, la diosa del agua, cayó sobre la tierra, los cielos se abrieron con un diluvio de aguas celestiales. Una gran inundación cubrió la Tierra y la destruyó por cuarta vez. Los aztecas marcaron este día con el nombre 4. Agua.

Tras la cuarta destrucción de la Tierra, Quetzalcoatl y Tezcatlipoca se arrepintieron de sus batallas. Tezcatlipoca y Quetzalcoatl miraron la tenebrosa e inundada tierra y reconocieron que la hora de batallar debía terminar si querían que hubiese otro Sol. Los dos dioses abandonaron sus encarnizadas batallas y juntos crearon la Tierra por Quinta vez. El Quinto Sol, el sol del movimiento, es el sol de nuestra edad actual. Según el mito de los aztecas, la época del Quinto Sol terminará un día con un cataclismo de terremotos.

Otros mitos relatan cómo Tezcatlipoca y Quetzalcoatl formaron la tierra, repoblándola con seres vivos y con vegetación. El mito de los Cinco Soles, sin embargo, permanece como la primordial historia azteca de la creación de nuestra Tierra actual.

The Flowing Waters
The Creation of the Earth

An Aztec Myth

According to the stories of *los ancianos*, after Quetzalcoatl and Tezcatlipoca finally abandoned their fierce battles that had destroyed the Earth, they decided to cooperate in creating a new time. This new creation epoch would be called the time of the Fifth Sun.

In the aftermath of Quetzalcoatl and Tezcatlipoca's fourth and final cosmic battle, the sky had opened up in torrential downpours, and the Earth lay flooded with all its life drowned. Quetzalcoatl and Tezcatlipoca gazed upon the destructive results of their battle for supremacy and realized that they would have to build the Earth anew. While examining the flooded Earth, they saw the great Earth monster Tlaltecuhtli. Tlaltecuhtli was riding the seas searching for flesh to devour. With jaws of sharp teeth on all of the joints of her body, her fierceness was great.

Quetzalcoatl and Tezcatlipoca decided that they could not create a new Earth as long as Tlaltecuhtli threatened the seas. So they descended to the seas and transformed themselves into two giant serpents. Wrapping themselves around Tlaltecuhtli, they tore her into two pieces. The upper half of her body became a new sky, and the bottom half formed a new Earth.

The gods were once again angered with the violent actions of Quetzalcoatl and Tezcatlipoca. In order to bring honor to the mutilated Tlaltecuhtli, the gods decreed that her dismembered parts would be used to form all aspects of the new world.

Her spiny crocodilian back became the towering mountain ridges of the world. Her hair became the trees and shrubs that fill the earthly forest. Her skin made the grasses and small flowers that cover the vast ground. Great rivers to sustain life on Earth flowed from her mouth. And from her eyes formed small pools and ponds.

For a fifth time, the Earth existed anew. The time of the Fifth Sun—the time of our world—had begun.

Into the Fire
The Creation of the Sun and the Moon

An Aztec Myth

According to Aztec myth, after the final battle between Quetzalcoatl and Tezcatlipoca came the time of the Fifth Sun. The terrible ages of the Earth's destruction had passed, but darkness remained on the Earth. The Earth did not know the warm and sustaining light of the Sun.

The gods gathered in the heavens and conferred on how they would bring light to the darkened Earth. After a lengthy consultation, they decided that one of them would sacrifice his life to bring light to the Earth. They built a tremendous, roaring fire and waited for one of the gods to come forth and give his life so that the Sun might exist again.

The gods called out, "Who among us will give their life for the life of the Sun? Who among us is most brave to face the flames of the fire? Who among us is most worthy for this noble sacrifice?"

One of the gods stepped forward. He was Tecuciztecatl, a rich and proud god. Tecuciztecatl approached the fierce fire and delivered a lengthy speech about how he alone, among all the gods, was most worthy for this noble sacrifice. He told the assembled gods, "Only I am most worthy. Because of my wealth and noble character only I am worthy of this supreme sacrifice. I challenge another god to come forth to test their courage against my own." He then laid his royal robes aside and gave incense, gold, and quetzal feathers as offerings for his journey to the other side of life. He then knelt to pray by the fire.

Another god, Nanahuatzin, stepped forward. Nanahuatzin was a poor, humble god. He spoke to the gods, saying, "I offer my deepest prayers that I will have courage when the flames roar up to end my life. I am willing to give my life so that the Earth may know again the warmth of the Sun." He then knelt to pray by the fire. He had no royal clothing or fine gifts to offer. He, however, prayed that his life would be worthy of the sacrifice to give life to the Sun.

For four days and nights, the two gods prayed and did penance to be worthy of the sacrifice. At the end of the time of prayer, Tecuciztecatl was first to approach the fire. He circled the sacrificial pyre, feeling the heat of the flames. The fire roared up and seared Tecuciztecatl with its hot flames. Tecuciztecatl's courage failed him, and he backed away from the fire, frightened by its fierceness.

Then Nanahuatzin approached the fire. In a moment of bold courage, he leapt into the flames. Time and the cosmos stopped at the moment of Nanahuatzin's sacrificial leap into the fire. The gods waited, wondering if the sacrifice of Nanahuatzin would be worthy to give life to the Sun.

After what seemed an eternity, the flames roared, and out of the east began to rise a golden sun. It was Nanahuatzin, transformed into the Fifth Sun.

Tecuciztecatl was so ashamed by his failure of will and his display of cowardice that he suddenly leapt into the fire. A tremendous explosion of light and sound followed, and another, second sun began to rise out of the fire. It was Tecuciztecatl also transformed into a glowing sun.

The gods were angered that Tecuciztecatl would try to steal the glory of Nanahuatzin. The gods said, "While there can be two bright lights in the earthly sky, one should not shine as brightly as the other. Only Nanahuatzin deserves to be supreme. Nanahuatzin was first to courageously leap into the fire and to hold fast at the fury of the flames. The glory of being the Sun shall belong for all eternity to Nanahuatzin. This light of Tecuciztecatl shall be less bright than Nanahuatzin's, and it shall rise second, following the sun of Nanahuatzin for all its days."

One of the gods then arose and threw a rabbit into the face of Tecuciztecatl. This blow caused the sun of Tecuciztecatl to darken and become dimmer than Nanahuatzin's bright sun and transformed Tecuciztecatl into the Moon.

To this day, when the descendants of the Aztecs look up at the dark night sky and gaze upon the pale Moon, they see a rabbit clearly marked on the Moon's face. They also watch daily as the Sun rises first in its bright glory in the eastern sky, to be followed later by the much dimmer Moon.

The Trail of Stars
How the Milky Way Came To Be

An Aztec Myth

The time after the creation of the Fifth Sun, the gods Quetzalcoatl and Tezcatlipoca had transformed the remains of the Earth monster Tlaltecuhtli into the Earth's plant life, mountains, and bodies of water, as well as its sky. But still the sky was dark and hung close to the Earth.

Quetzalcoatl observed the dark night and said, "I am the cause of this destruction. Just as I have labored to make a new Earth and sky, so must I make the sky have its brilliance again." Tezcatlipoca answered, "We are the supreme gods. Let us continue the work of making a new sky."

Quetzalcoatl and Tezcatlipoca each went to the farthest corners of the Earth. Planting their feet firmly in the ground, they stretched their arms up toward the sky. They then began to grow upward, like two tall, powerful oak trees. These two giant trees lifted the sky higher and higher until, once again, the sky was in its rightful place, high above the Earth like a protective blanket of dark velvet.

Quetzalcoatl and Tezcatlipoca were proud of their work of raising the sky high above the Earth. Together they walked from one end of the sky to the other admiring their work. With each step they took, their feet left a trail of stars behind them.

To this day, on especially dark nights, we can still look up into the starry skies and see the trail of stars that marks the celestial path of Quetzalcoatl and Tezcatlipoca. We know this trail of stars by its modern name, the Milky Way.

The Broken Bones
The Creation of People

An Aztec Myth

During the time of the creation of the Fifth Sun, the gods had almost completed their work of making a new world. Quetzalcoatl and Tezcatlipoca had formed a new Earth and sky and had marked their creation of the night sky with a starry path we call the Milky Way. And Nanahuatzin and Tecuciztecatl had sacrificed themselves to create the Sun and the Moon.

But the Earth was void of human life. Quetzalcoatl wanted the Earth to be alive with the spirit of the human people. He remembered the other worlds before he had destroyed them. He remembered the joy of human life on the Earth. He knew that human life would only return to the Earth in one way. He alone would have to descend into the darkness—to the land of the dead—and bring back the bones of the humans who had died in the destruction of the previous worlds. These bones would build the beginnings of a new world of human life.

Quetzalcoatl descended into the land of the dead, which was called the Land of Mictlan. The Lord of Mictlan was Mictlantecuhtli. Mictlantecuhtli was a devious and dangerous god, ruling supreme over his underworld kingdom. He knew why Quetzalcoatl had ventured into Mictlan.

When Quetzalcoatl approached the Lord of Mictlan's throne, Mictlantecuhtli asked him, "Quetzalcoatl, why does your heart wander so far from the Earth and its blue skies? The Land of Mictlan has nothing for you."

Quetzalcoatl answered, "Lord God Mictlantecuhtli, I have come to ask you for the bones of the humans who have lived and died in the worlds before the time of the Fifth Sun. I want my new world to know again human life. You are the keeper of these bones." Then he asked, "May I have them?"

Mictlantecuhtli did not want to give up the bones, but he knew that Quetzalcoatl was a powerful and clever god and that he would have to be careful. Cautiously, he gave Quetzalcoatl a challenge. He told Quetzalcoatl, "Take this conch shell. Travel across the Land of Mictlan four times, each time sounding the conch shell. Do this simple task, and the bones are yours."

Quetzalcoatl knew that the Lord God Mictlantecuhtli would never give him a "simple task," but he also knew that this was the only way he could ever get the bones he wanted. Quetzalcoatl placed his lips on the conch shell and gave it a mighty blow. No sound came from the conch shell, no matter how hard Quetzalcoatl blew. He investigated the conch shell and discovered that Mictlantecuhtli had given him a conch shell that had been blocked solid, so that it could never make a sound. As Quetzalcoatl struggled to make a sound on the conch shell, Mictlantecuhtli laughed at the trick he had played on him.

Quetzalcoatl looked around Mictlan and saw some worms burrowing into the dark ground. Quetzalcoatl called to the worms and asked for their help. The worms knew that Quetzalcoatl had brought life back to the fifth world, so they agreed to help him. The worms burrowed into the conch shell, opening a passageway for air. Next, Quetzalcoatl asked the bees of Mictlan to fly through the open passages of the conch shell. When the bees did this, their buzzing sound could be heard coming out of the conch shell. Quetzalcoatl then took the conch shell, blew into it, and listened as the Land of Mictlan filled with its reverberating buzzing sound.

Mictlantecuhtli knew that Quetzalcoatl had outsmarted him, but he was not about to give in yet. He told Quetzalcoatl, "You have accomplished my simple task. The bones are yours on one condition: The bones shall give life to a new race of people on your world, but when those lives come to an end, the people must return to me and the Land of Mictlan."

Quetzalcoatl agreed to this condition, but in his heart, he was lying to the Lord God of the Dead. He wanted his new people to have eternal life. He took the bones and began to leave Mictlan.

Mictlantecuhtli realized that Quetzalcoatl had lied to him about his people returning to Mictlan. He immediately sent the quail birds to bring back the bones of the dead. Quetzalcoatl heard the birds approaching and knew that Mictlantecuhtli was trying to retrieve his bones. As he ran to escape from Mictlan, Quetzalcoatl tripped and dropped all of the bones, causing them to break into many different sizes. This is the reason people are of all different sizes.

The quail birds flew down to the bones and pecked on them until fine fracture lines covered each one. It is because of this damage that people are too weak to live forever. In this way, the request of the Lord God of the Dead holds true. One day, we must all return to the land of the dead.

Quetzalcoatl gathered up the broken and weakened bones and finally escaped from the Land of Mictlan. He took the bones to the land of the gods—a land of miracles called Tamoanchan. There the gods ground the bones into a fine powder and placed them into a ceremonial bowl. For four nights, the gods prayed over the bones. On the fourth night, the gods stood over the ceremonial bowl and pierced their skin. The blood of the gods mixed with the powdered bones and, in four days, the first man rose out of the bowl. Four days later, the first woman rose out of the bowl.

Quetzalcoatl's bold journey to the land of the dead had given the human race another chance for life. The blood of the gods and the bones of humans ancestors had combined to create a new race of people to live on the Earth.

Food from the Gods
How Maize Came to the People

An Aztec Myth

After Quetzalcoatl and the other gods had created a new race of people to walk the Earth, they realized that the people had no food to eat. Knowing that the people would need food for sustenance, or else they would perish again, all of the gods scattered and searched for food for the new people.

Quetzalcoatl immediately began an intense search for food. Not long after he had begun his journey, he noticed a red ant carrying a seed of *maize*, the corn that was destined to become the sacred food of the Aztec people. Quetzalcoatl approached the ant and asked, "Where did you get that grain of *maize*? That seed would make a perfect food for the new race of people."

The ant ignored Quetzalcoatl and kept walking. Again, Quetzalcoatl addressed the red ant: "Perhaps you did not understand my question. Please tell me where you got the grain of *maize*."

Again, the red ant ignored Quetzalcoatl and kept on its path. The red ant's arrogant manner finally angered Quetzalcoatl. He stood before the red ant, blocking its path, and said, "I am Quetzalcoatl, Lord God of the Wind, the creator and destroyer of worlds. I demand that you tell me where you found the grain of *maize*."

This time the red ant realized who Quetzalcoatl was. He also knew that Quetzalcoatl could be a fierce god who could send a fierce wind to destroy the red ant. Finally, the red ant said, "I got this grain of *maize* from inside Tonacatepetl, the Mountain of Sustenance. Follow me and I shall lead you to it."

Quetzalcoatl followed the red ant to Tonacatepetl and watched the red ant go into a small crack in the side of the mountain. Quetzalcoatl was much too large to fit through the small hole, so he transformed himself into a black ant and followed the red ant into the mountain.

Inside a vast mountain cavern, Quetzalcoatl saw giant stacks of grain reaching as high as the ceiling of the mountain cavern. Quetzalcoatl said to himself, "There are enough grains of *maize* here to feed a whole race of people." He then gathered a few grains and carefully left the mountain cavern by the same small crack through which he had entered it.

He took the grains of *maize* to the gods and said, "These are grains of *maize*, and in a mountain cavern, there is enough grain to feed our new people." He then told the gods the story of the red ant and Tonacatepetl, the Mountain of Sustenance.

The gods responded, "The great god Quetzalcoatl has found food for his people, but how are we to get to the caverns of grain?" Quetzalcoatl told the gods, "I know a way for us to have the riches of the caverns of grain, but I will need the help of other gods."

Four gods spoke up and said they would help Quetzalcoatl. These were the four directional gods: the blue, white, yellow, and red Tlalocs.

First, Quetzalcoatl went to Tonacatepetl and threw a sling around its great girth. He struggled to move the mountain, but it was too large and too heavy for one god to move. The four directional gods then attacked the mountain and split it wide open.

The moment the mountainsides cracked open, the *maize* seeds scattered in all directions. The gods gathered the grains of *maize*, along with other grains of beans and edible plants. Finally, the gods had secured a source of food for the new people. In this way, *maize* became the sacred, god-given food of the Aztec people.

Because of their efforts to gather the *maize* and other grains, the Tlaloc gods became known as the gods of nourishing rains and abundant crops. Quetzalcoatl became the Creator God for the Aztec people because of the central part he played in the creation of almost all aspects of their world.

Alimento de los Dioses
Cómo el maíz llegó a la gente

Un mito azteca

Después que Quetzalcoatl y otros dioese crearon una nueva raza de personas que caminaban sobre la Tierra, los dioses comprendieron que esta gente no tenía alimentos para comer. Sabiendo que las personas necesitan alimento para subsistir, pues de lo contrario perecerían otra vez, todos los dioses se dispersaron para buscar alimento para las nuevas personas.

Quetzalcoatl comenzó inmediatamente una intensa búsqueda de alimento. No mucho después de haber comenzado su viaje, vio una hormiga roja llevando una semilla de maíz, destinado a convertirse en el alimento sagrado de los aztecas. Quetzalcoatl se acercó a la hormiga y le preguntó: "¿Dónde obtuviste ese grano de maíz? Esa semilla sería un alimento perfecto para la nueva raza de gente".

La hormiga ignoró a Quetzalcoatl y siguió caminando. Otra vez, Quetzalcoatl habló a la hormiga: "Quizás no entendiste mi pregunta. Por favor, dime dónde conseguiste el grano de maíz".

Una vez más, la hormiga roja ignoró a Quetzalcoatl y continuó por su sendero. La actitud arrogante de la hormiga roja finalmente hizo enojar a Quetzalcoatl. El se paró frente a la hormiga, interrumpiéndole el paso, y le dijo: "Yo soy Quetzalcoatl, Señor Dios del Viento, creador y destructor de los mundos. Demando que me digas dónde encontraste el grano de maíz".

Esta vez la hormiga roja se dio cuenta quién era Quetzalcoatl. Comprendió que Quetzalcoatl era un dios temible, quien podría enviar un temible viento para destruir a la hormiga roja. Finalmente, la hormiga roja dijo: "Obtuve este grano de maíz del interior de Tonacatepetl, la Montaña del Sustento. Sígueme y te conduciré allí".

Quetzalcoatl siguió a la hormiga roja hasta Tonacatepetl y miró a la hormiga roja entre en una pequeña grieta a un lado de la montaña. Quetzalcoatl era muy grande como para entrar en la pequeña apertura, así que se transformó en una hormiga negra y siguió a la hormiga roja al interior de la montaña.

Dentro de una inmensa caverna en la montaña, Quetzalcoatl vio gigantescas pilas de grano que llegaban casi hasta el techo de la cueva en la montaña. Quetzalcoatl se dijo: "Hay suficientes granos de maíz para alimentar a todo el nuevo pueblo". Reunió entonces unos pocos granos y cuidadosamente salió de la montaña usando la misma pequeña grieta por donde había entrado.

Quetzalcoatl llevó los granos de maíz a los dioses y les dijo : "Estos son granos de maíz, y en una cueva en la montaña hay suficientes granos para alimentar al nuevo pueblo". Quetzalcoatl contó entonces la historia de la hormiga roja y de la Tonacatepetl, la Montaña del Sustento.

"El gran dios Quetzalcoatl encontró alimento para su gente, pero ¿cómo llegaremos a las cavernas del grano?", preguntaron los dioses. "Conozco una manera de obtener las riquezas de la caverna de granos, pero necesitaré la ayuda de los otros dioses", dijo Quetzalcoatl.

Cuatro dioses hablaron y dijeron que ayudarían a Quetzalcoatl. Eran los cuatro dioses direccionales, los Tlalocs azul, blanco, amarillo y rojo.

Primero, Quetzalcoatl fue hasta Tonacatepetl y lanzó una cuerda alrededor de la montaña. Quetzalcoatl trató de mover la montaña, pero era muy grande y muy pesada para ser movida por un solo dios. Los cuatro dioses direccionales atacaron entonces a la montaña y la partieron, abriéndola.

En el momento que las laderas de la montaña se abrieron, las semillas de maíz se desparramaron en todas direcciones. Los dioses reunieron los granos de maíz, junto con los granos de otras plantas y frijoles comestibles. Finalmente, los dioses tenían una fuente segura de alimento para el nuevo pueblo. De esta manera, el maíz se convirtió en el alimento sagrado, dado por los dioses, del pueblo azteca.

Debido a sus esfuerzos para conseguir el maíz los dioses Tlaloc fueron reconocidos como los dioses de las lluvias nutrientes y de las cosechas abundantes. Quetzalcoatl se convirtió en el dios creador del pueblo azteca debido a su papel central en la creación de casi cada aspecto de este mundo.

Music from the Gods
How Music Came to the World

An Aztec Myth

After people had returned to walk the Earth and Quetzalcoatl had brought the sacred *maize* to them, Tezcatlipoca, Smoking Mirror, came to Earth. This god was pleased that lush vegetation covered the Earth, giving it a beautiful fragrance wherever he traveled. The flowers of the valley displayed the colors of the rainbow in all directions and as far as the eye could see. The Earth was truly covered in beauty.

Tezcatlipoca noticed, however, that the human people seemed to lack an inner joy. Even the beauties of the Earth could not make their hearts sing with the joy of life. It was then that Tezcatlipoca realized what was missing. After the mighty battles with Quetzalcoatl and the time of reconciliation that resulted in the reconstruction of the Earth and the coming of the Fifth Sun, the Earth was still empty of music.

In no corner of the Earth did people greet the morning sun with a joyous song. In no corner of the Earth did people pray to the gods with the songs of prayer. In no corner of the Earth did people play the instruments of music to bring peace and soothing comfort to their world.

The world of the gods was filled with the magic and beauty of music. The heavenly musicians were the givers of bliss, daily filling the heavens with their gifts of music and song. Tezcatlipoca knew that the people of the Earth needed music to complete their world.

He also knew that the Lord of the Sun would not let the heavenly musicians leave the House of the Sun. Only one god could take on the task of bringing music to the Earth. That god was Quetzalcoatl, who had given life and food to his people.

Tezcatlipoca called to his brother Quetzalcoatl and spoke to him. After leading Quetzalcoatl on a pilgrimage of the Earth searching for music and finding none, he told him, "Quetzalcoatl, the people do not have the beauty of music in their lives. They live in a sad silence that is not good for their souls. Go to the House of the Sun and ask him for musicians to come to Earth, bringing with them the gift of music."

Quetzalcoatl knew that the Earth was still not complete, and as he had so many times before, he wished for his people to have all of the riches of life. He then told Tezcatlipoca, "I will go to the House of the Sun and ask for the musicians and their music. It is a long journey, however. The House of the Sun is a great distance away, and it is so high in the sky that a bridge will be necessary to reach it."

Tezcatlipoca answered him: "I will send my helpers of the sea to make a bridge for you, and I will use my sacred powers to assist you and them in this great journey. Go to the sea and call for the whale, the sea turtle, and the sea cow. They will help you."

Quetzalcoatl began his long journey. He first traveled to the edge of the sea and called for the whale, the sea turtle, and the sea cow. First the whale arrived and allowed Quetzalcoatl to mount his immense back. The whale then raced to the end of the world, and with a tremendous leap, carried Quetzalcoatl high into the sky.

When the whale had exhausted his great energy, Quetzalcoatl called out, "Sea turtle, come to my assistance. I am traveling to the House of the Sun to bring music to the Earth, and the whale is finished with his part of the journey."

As if by some powerful magic spell, the sea turtle appeared and carried Quetzalcoatl higher in the sky on its sturdy back. The skies became hotter and hotter as they approached the House of the Sun. The sea turtle was used to the cool waters of the ocean seas and began to weaken from the heat. Quetzalcoatl told the sea turtle, "Your part of the journey has come to an end. Thank you, sea turtle, for your assistance. The sea cow will be the final link of the bridge to the House of the Sun."

The sea cow appeared just then and carried Quetzalcoatl on the final part of the journey. When he arrived at the House of the Sun, Quetzalcoatl called back, "Thank you, whale, sea turtle, and sea cow. Because of your help I am now at the House of the Sun, ready to begin my sacred task of bringing music to the Earth."

The Lord of the Sun had been watching Quetzalcoatl as he rode the backs of the sea animals to the House of the Sun. He knew why Quetzalcoatl had come to his land, and he did not want any of his musicians to take away the beautiful music he loved so much. As Quetzalcoatl approached, the Lord of the Sun called to the musicians and said, "Stop playing your music. When Quetzalcoatl arrives, be as still as frozen statues. Most importantly, do not listen to anything Quetzalcoatl says to you. You are the musicians of the House of the Sun, and you will remain the musicians of the House of the Sun."

Quetzalcoatl noticed that as soon as he came near the House of the Sun, the music abruptly stopped. As he entered through the gates of the house, he saw many statues of musicians scattered throughout the grounds. He knew that the Lord of the Sun had cast a spell on the musicians. Quetzalcoatl approached each statue and said, "The Earth is without music. I have come to take you there, so you can bring music and joy to the people. Please awaken from this spell and come with me."

None of the statues moved. Quetzalcoatl became angry that the Lord of the Sun would want to keep music only for himself. He rose up in a fury and unleashed a hurricane of wind throughout the Land of the Sun. The statues knew of Quetzalcoatl's power to destroy worlds. Afraid of what might happen to them if Quetzalcoatl blew the winds with his full powers, one by one, the musicians came out of the spell and awoke. One of them said, "We will come with you to Earth, but we must leave quickly before the Lord of the Sun discovers that we have disobeyed his command."

Quetzalcoatl cradled the musicians, being careful not to harm their melodies, and brought them to Earth. He scattered the musicians throughout the world and commanded them to give their gift of music to the human people.

The musicians played such beautiful melodies and sang such joyful songs that the spirits of the human people immediately soared. The sky filled with rainbows. Birds began to echo the melodies and created songs of their own. Gentle breezes carried the music to all corners of the world. Music had become the special gift of the gods to the human people.

The musicians were happy because they could look up in the sky and still see the Sun and feel the heat of their heavenly home. And the Lord of the Sun was no longer angry about the loss of his musicians, because the earthly winds carried the music to the heights of the sky where he could still enjoy his heavenly music.

Music had come to the Earth and its people. The musicians had filled the silence with beauty. Soon, as the birds of the sky had done, the people learned to make their own music. At that time, the heavenly musicians returned to the House of the Sun. From that time on, both the heavens and the Earth were filled with the music of the heavens.

Música de los Dioses
Cómo la música llegó al mundo

Un mito azteca

Después que la gente volvió a caminar sobre la Tierra y que Quetzalcoatl les dio al maíz sagrado, Tezcatlipoca, Espejo Humeante, vino a la tierra. Este dios se complació con la exuberante vegetación que cubría la tierra, dándole una hermosa fragancia por dondequiera que él viajaba. Las flores del valle mostraban los colores del arco iris en todas direcciones, y hasta donde alcanzaba la vista. La Tierra estaba realmente cubierta de belleza.

Tezcatlipoca notó, sin embargo, que la gente humana parecía carecer de gozo interior. Ni siquiera las bellezas de la Tierra hacían que los corazones de las personas cantadesen con el gozo de vivir. En ese momento Tezcatlipoca se dio cuenta lo que faltaba. Después de las poderosas batallas con Quetzalcoatl y en la época de reconciliación que resultó en la reconstrucción de la Tierra y la llegada del Quinto Sol, la Tierra todavía carecía de música.

En ningún rincón de la Tierra la gente saludaba al sol matutino con una canción de gozo. En ningún rincón de la Tierra la gente rezaba a los dioses con cánticos de oración. En ningún rincón de la Tierra la gente tocaba instrumentos musicales para traer paz y aliviante consuelo a su mundo.

El mundo de los dioses estaba lleno con la magia y la belleza de la música. Los músicos celestiales eran quienes daban la felicidad, llenando cada día los cielos con sus dones de música y canciones. Tezcatlipoca reconoció que la gente de la Tierra necesitaba de la música para completar su mundo.

También reconoció que el Señor del Sol no podría permitir que los músicos celestiales abandonasen la Casa del Sol. Solamente un dios podría afrontar la tarea de traer la música a la Tierra. Ese dios era Quetzalcoatl, quien le había dado la vida y el alimento a su pueblo.

Tezcatlipoca llamó a su hermano y le habló. Tras peregrinar con Quetzalcoatl por la Tierra buscando música y sin hallarla, él le dijo: "Quetzalcoatl, la gente carece de la belleza de la música en sus vidas. Viven en un silencio triste que no es bueno para sus almas. Vé a la Casa del Sol y pídeles que los músicos vengan a la Tierra, trayendo con ellos el don de la música".

Quetzalcoatl reconoció que la Tierra todavía no estaba completa, y como lo había hecho tantas veces antes, quiso que su pueblo tuviese todas las riquezas de la vida. Le dijo entonces a Tezcatlipoca: "Iré a la Casa del Sol y pediré los músicos y su música. Sin embargo, es un largo viaje. La Casa del Sol está a una gran distancia, y tan alto en el cielo que será necesario un puente para llegar allí".

Tezcatlipoca le respondió: "Enviaré a mis ayudantes del mar a que construyan un puente para ti, y usaré mis poderes sagrados para ayudarte a ti y también a ellos, en este gran viaje. Vé al mar y llama a la ballena, la tortuga marina, y el manatí (o vaca marina). Ellos te ayudarán".

Quetzalcoatl comenzó su largo viaje. Primero llegó a la orilla del mar, y llamó a la ballena, la tortuga y el manatí. La ballena llegó primero y dejó que Quetzalcoatl se montase en su inmensa lomo. La ballena entonces fue a la carrera hasta el fin del mundo, y con un tremendo salto, llevó a Quetzalcoatl hasta el alto cielo.

Cuando la ballena hubo consumido toda su gran energía, Quetzalcoatl gritó: "Tortuga marina, ven a ayudarme. Estoy viajando a la Casa del Sol para traer música a la Tierra y la ballena ha terminado su parte del viaje".

Como por arte de poderosa magia, la tortuga marina apareció y llevó a Quetzalcoatl aún más alto en el cielo, sobre su dura concha. Los cielos eran cada vez más calurosos cuando más se acercaban a la Casa del Sol. La tortuga marina estaba acostumbrada a las aguas frías de los mares oceánicos, y el calor comenzó a debilitarla. Quetzalcoatl le dijo a la tortuga: "Tu parte del viaje ha concluído. Gracias, tortuga marina, por tu ayuda. El manatí será el eslabón final del puente a la Casa del Sol".

El manatí apareció justo en ese momento y llevó a Quetzalcoatl en la parte final del viaje. Cuando llegaron a la Casa del Sol, Quetzalcoatl habló otra vez: "Gracias, ballena, tortuga marina y manatí. Gracias a vuestra ayuda estoy ahora en la Casa del Sol, listo para comenzar mi sagrada tarea de llevar la música a la Tierra".

El Señor del Sol había estado observando a Quetzalcoatl mientras éste viajaba hacia la Casa del Sol sobre los animales marinos. El sabía por qué Quetzalcoatl había llegado a su dominio, y no quería que ninguno de sus músicos se llevase la bella música que a él tanto le gustaba. Mientras Quetzalcoatl se acercaba, el Señor del Sol llamó a los músicos y les dijo: "Dejen de tocar su música. Cuando Quetzalcoatl llegue, quédense tan quietos como estatuas congeladas. Más importante, no escuchen nada de lo que Quetzalcoatl les diga. Ustedes son los músicos de la Casa del Sol, y ustedes deben seguir siendo los músicos de la Casa del Sol".

Quetzalcoatl notó que tan pronto como se acercó a la Casa del Sol, la música se interrumpió abruptamente. Cuando él atravesó las puertas de la casa, vio muchas estatuas de músicos en los jardines. Se dio cuenta de que el Señor del Sol había lanzado un hechizo sobre los músicos. Quetzalcoatl se acercó a cada estatua y dijo: "La Tierra carece de música. He venido a llevarte conmigo, para que puedas llevar tu música y tu gozo a la gente. Por favor, despiértate de este hechizo y ven conmigo".

Ninguna de las estatuas se movió. Quetzalcoatl se enojó de que el Señor del Sol quisiese guardar la música solamente para él. Quetzalcoatl se levantó enfurecido y desató un huracán de viento en la Tierra del Sol. Las estatuas ya conocían el poder de Quetzalcoatl para destruir mundos. Temerosos de lo que les podría pasar si Quetzalcoatl desataba sus vientos con todo su poder, uno por uno, los músicos se deshicieron del hechizo y despertaron. Uno de ellos dijo: "Iremos contigo a la Tierra, pero debemos partir rápidamente, antes que el Señor del Sol descubra que hemos desobedecido su mandato".

Quetzalcoatl protegió a los músico, siendo cuidadoso de no dañar sus melodías, y los trajo a la Tierra. Los esparció a través del mundo y les ordenó que ofreciesen su don musical a las personas humanas.

Los músicos tocaron melodías tan bellas y cantaron canciones tan bellas que los espíritus de los seres humanos inmediatamente se elevaron. El cielo se llenó con arco iris. Los pájaros comenzaron a repetir las melodías y crearon sus propias canciones. Las suaves brisas llevaron la música a todos los rincones del mundo. La música se transformó en el don especial de los dioses para los seres humanos.

Los músicos se sintieron felices porque podían mirar al cielo y ver al Sol, y sentir el calor de su hogar celestial. Y el Señor del Sol ya no estaba enojado por la pérdida de sus músicos, porque los vientos terrenales llevaban la música hasta las alturas del cielo, donde él podía aún disfrutar la música celestial.

La música había llegado a la tierra y a sus habitantes. Los músicos llenaron el silencio con belleza. Pronto, como lo habían hecho las aves del cielo, la gente aprendió a componer su propia música. En ese momento, los músicos celestiales volvieron a la Casa del Sol. Desde ese momento, tanto los cielos como la tierra están llenos de música celestial.

El Nopal
How the Cactus Came to the World

An Aztec Myth

The story of *El Nopal*, the *nopal* cactus, is one of Mexico's most important stories. The history of the Aztec people, and of Mexico, is critically linked to this beautiful plant. According to the ancient story, the Aztecs migrated from their sacred homeland, Aztlan, in search of a new home, where they would build a new capital city. Their god Huitzilopochtli had commanded them to search until they discovered an eagle with a snake in its mouth perched on a *nopal* cactus on an island in a lake. This image would be their sign that they had discovered the site for their new capital. Of course, the Aztecs did discover the island with the eagle on the cactus and built their city, Tenochtitlan, which eventually became Mexico City, upon it. This story is so central to the history of Mexico that the image of an eagle landing on a cactus became the sole symbol on the Mexican flag.

The Aztecs told a story about how this cactus came to be on the lake. The story begins with the Aztec god Huitzilopochtli commanding the Aztecs to leave their homeland and journey to the south until they found the island in the lake with the eagle on the cactus. The Aztecs' journey lasted many centuries and was filled with great difficulty.

Eventually, the Aztecs arrived in the Valley of Mexico, where they came upon Lake Texcoco. The lake was filled with several islands, but none of them contained the image of the eagle for which they had searched so long. Discouraged, the Aztecs settled on one of the islands and decided to wait for a sign from their gods.

The land surrounding the islands was inhabited by many other tribes of people who were accustomed to a peaceful existence. The Aztecs, however, were subject to the severe and uncompromising demands of their great God of War, Huitzilopochtli. One of his demands was human sacrifice. In order to find prisoners for religious sacrifice, the Aztecs waged war on their neighbors.

In a land to the north lived Huitzilopochtli's sister, his brother-in-law, and his nephew, Copil. They lived in a peaceful tribe, where Copil prospered and grew to be an intelligent and valiant young man.

One day, Copil told his mother, "When I grow up, I'm going to conquer my uncle Huitzilopochtli so he will not be the cause of so much death and sacrifice in this world."

His mother warned him: "Your uncle is the most powerful God of War. It would be very dangerous to do what you say." Copil agreed with his mother, but he felt dedicated to doing something to protect a peaceful way of life.

Copil gathered a small army and led them to the shores of Lake Texcoco. As he approached the island of the Aztecs, he ordered his men to camp for the night. Huitzilopochtli learned about Copil's plans from his many spies who constantly roamed the Aztec land looking for trouble. Huitzilopochtli commanded these spies to kill Copil and bring him his heart for sacrifice.

The spies did as commanded. Huitzilopochtli then ordered them to bury Copil's heart on an island in Lake Texcoco. The spies buried the heart among some wild plants on a large island in the middle of the lake.

The next day, the spies discovered a beautiful green plant with magnificent red flowers growing from the spot where Copil's heart was buried. When the Aztecs came to witness this miraculous site, they watched in awe as an eagle swooped from the sky and landed on the cactus. In the eagle's mouth was a snake.

The Aztecs knew that this dramatic sight was the fulfillment of their prophecy. They had received the sign from their god that they had discovered their final destination. Upon this island they built the capital city of their great empire—the city that would one day become Mexico City.

To this day, the image of the cactus on the Mexican flag is a reminder of the brave and noble sacrifice Copil made to give birth not only to a new city but also to a new nation.

The Murmur of the River
How Music Came to the World

A Mayan Myth

According to ancient Mayan myth, the Earth was without music at the beginning of time. The people of the Earth spent their nights and days without music, never knowing the joy of the heart's song. The gods knew that their creation of Earth and people would forever be unfinished if the people never had music in their hearts. Music would help the people of the Earth to remain joyful throughout the hardships of life.

The Mayan gods gathered under the Tree of Life to hold a council about how to bring music to their creatures on Earth. One of the gods, Ah Kin Xooc, the god most familiar with life on Earth, had noticed that the Earth was constantly alive with sound. As he looked around at the gods gathered under the Tree of Life, he realized that all of the gods had taken part in the creation of the Earth and had given their sounds to its life. He then realized a way to bring music to the people of the Earth.

Ah Kin Xooc asked each of the gods to give him a sound: The God of Water gave him the murmur of the river and the tapping of the rain; the God of Wind gave him the whisper of the wind; the God of Corn gave him the rustle of the corn leaves; the God of the Ocean gave him the crashing of the waves; the God of Winter gave him the cracking of ice; the God of the Mountains gave him the creaking of the trees; the God of the Birds gave him the chirping of the morning birds; the God of Fire gave him the crackling of the embers; and the God of Night gave him the echoes of the darkness.

Ah Kin Xooc took all of these sounds and swallowed them, securely placing them in his throat. He then descended to the Earth. Ah Kin Xooc went to its center, the sacred place from which the Earth's own heartbeat originated, opened his mouth, and let all the sounds of the gods fly out. These sounds mixed with the essence of life coming from the Earth's beating heart. As the sounds rose to the Earth's surface, they transformed into sounds never before heard in the world.

People of the Earth heard for the first time the sound of lament, the sound of complaint, the sound of truth, the sound of forgiveness, and the sound of joy. The people knew that these sounds were the most important sounds ever heard on Earth. Their profound beauty brought both joy and sadness to the hearts of the people. The people imitated these sounds, and soon they were inventing their own. They gave voice to these sounds and made instruments that could also make the sounds.

Before he returned to the heavens, Ah Kin Xooc taught his sounds to all the people of the Earth. The sounds became the music of the people of Earth. The songs were the most beautiful sounds heard on Earth, for they had come from the gods themselves.

El murmullo del río
Cómo la música llegó al mundo

Un mito maya

Según un antiguo mito maya, la Tierra carecía de música al principio del tiempo. La gente de la tierra pasaba sus noches y sus días sin música, sin conocer jamás el gozo de una canción en el corazón. Los dioses sabían que la creación de la tierra y de la gente quedaría incompleta para siempre si la gente no tenía música en sus corazones. La música ayudaría a las personas de la Tierra a permanecer gozosos en medio de las dificultades de la vida.

Los dioses mayas se reunieron debajo del Arbol de la Vida y tuvieron una junta sobre cómo traer la música a las criaturas de la tierra. Uno de los dioses, Ah Kin Xooc, el dios más familiarizado con la vida en la Tierra, notó que ésta estaba constantemente llena de sonidos. Al mirar a los dioses reunidos en el Arbol de la Vida, comprendió que todos los dioses habían participado de la creación de la tierra, y habían dado sus sonidos a la vida terrestre. El dios se dio cuenta entonces que había una manera de traer la música a la tierra.

Ah Kin Xooc pidió a cada dios que le diesen un sonido. El Dios del Agua le dio el murmullo del río y el repiqueteo de la lluvia. El Dios del Viento le dio el susurro del viento. El Dios del Maíz le dio el crujido de las hojas de maíz. El Dios del Océano le dio el golpear de las olas. El Dios del Invierno le dio el sonido del hielo al quebrarse. El Dios de las Montañas le dio el rechinar de los árboles. El Dios de los Pájaros le dio el gorjeo de las aves matinales. El Dios del Fuego le dio el crepitar de las brasas. Y el Dios de la Noche le dio los ecos de las tinieblas.

Ah Kin Xooc tomó todos estos sonidos y se los tragó, asegurándoselos en su garganta. El descendió entonces a la Tierra. Ah Kin Xooc fue al centro de la Tierra, el lugar sagrado donde se había originado el palpitar de la Tierra. Allí abrió su boca, y dejó que los sonidos de los dioses volaran. Los sonidos se mezclaron con la esencia de la vida que venía del latiente corazón de la Tierra. Cuando los sonidos llegaron a la superficie de la, se transformaron en sonidos que nunca antes se habían escuchado en el mundo.

La gente de la Tierra escuchó por primera vez el sonido del lamento, el sonido de la queja, el sonido de la verdad, el sonido del perdón, y el sonido del gozo. La gente supo que estos sonidos eran los sonidos más importantes jamás escuchados sobre la Tierra. La profunda belleza de estos sonidos trajo tanto gozo como tristeza a los corazones de las personas. La gente imitó estos sonidos, y pronto comenzó a inventar los suyos propios. Las personas hicieron sonidos con sus voces, y fabricaron instrumentos para hacer esos sonidos.

Antes de regresar al cielo, Ah Kin Xooc enseñó sus sonidos a toda la gente de la tierra. Los sonidos se transformaron en la música de las personas de la tierra. Las canciones fueron los sonidos más hermosos escuchados sobre la tierra, pues venían de los mismos dioses.

The Possum's Tail
How Fire Came to the World

A Mazatec Myth

Many years ago, in the time of the ancients, the stars lit the night sky with their fiery brilliance. On the darkest nights, the sky would be filled with a billion points of light, each one aglow with the explosions of a ball of fire one million years old.

But nighttime was also a time of cold darkness on the Earth, when the ancients would sit shivering, awaiting a new morning and the rising of the warm Sun. The ancients had not yet tamed fire, so they had it neither to keep them warm nor to cook their food.

Every so often, a star would explode with such fierceness that it would shoot out a ball of fire, which would streak across the sky. Occasionally, in the magic time, the darkest part of the night, one of the balls of fire would penetrate the Earth's atmosphere and crash to the ground.

When the ancients saw these balls of fire streaking across the sky, they believed that they were messages from the star gods—messages too complex for the ancients to understand. In some tribes, special priests possessed the sacred calling to explain the meaning of these shooting stars to their people. Ancient stories even told of priests who could learn the secrets of the universe from balls of fire that they found.

One story of the ancients tells of a night when an old woman was out searching the skies for shooting stars. Suddenly, the sky lit aflame as hundreds of the balls streaked above her. The old woman followed an especially bright ball and marked the place in the sky where it entered the circle of the Earth. She kept her eyes fixed on it as it made its explosive crash into the Earth. She walked across mountain and desert until she eventually found that ball of fire, still aflame with the fires of the cosmos.

The old woman took the ball of fire home with her. She kept it aflame, and in turn, it gave her nightly warmth.

Soon, the people discovered that the old woman had fire. They asked her to share it with them, but she refused. She would not share a single ember of the fire with anyone.

The people longed for the old woman's fire. They made several attempts to steal it, but the old woman was ferocious and carefully guarded it.

One day, a possum came to the people and said, "I will go to the old lady and bring back fire for all to share."

The people laughed and told the possum, "You are just a little possum. We have already tried to steal the fire and have failed. How would you be able to do something that even the people of the Earth cannot do?"

The possum answered, "I am small but clever. Wait, and I shall return with the fire."

When evening came, the possum could see that the old woman had the fire in her house. He went to the door of the old woman's house and knocked on it. When the old woman came to the door, the possum said to her, "Good evening, old woman. I am weary and cold from my travels." Then he asked: "Would you please let me rest a few moments inside your house, away from the darkness and the cold of the night?"

The old woman looked at the possum and believed that he was truly cold. She told him, "Yes, you may enter—but only for a few moments. And do not go near the fire."

The possum thanked the old lady for her kindness and entered the house. He felt the warmth of the fire but could not get close to it because the old woman kept him in her gaze.

After a while, the old woman said, "That is enough. You must leave now."

When she turned her back to open the door, the possum leaped into the fire. He stuck his tail into the hottest part of it and then ran out the open door, past the surprised old lady.

The possum ran across the world, his tail aflame, sharing fire with all of the people of the Earth. To this day, the possum walks around with a bald tail, reminding all of that night so long ago when he brought the gift of fire to the people of the world.

The Gift of the Toad
Why People Use Sticks to Make Fire

A Yaqui Myth

The Yaqui Indians tell the story of the time when no fire could be found in the entire world. This was also the time when the division had not yet happened between the animal world and the world of people. All living creatures shared the same cold world—a world without fire.

The living creatures had heard stories of a land far away where fire warmed the houses and cooked the food. They had also heard of a great God of Fire who ruled supreme and closely guarded his fire, lest he lose a single flame of it.

The living creatures gathered in council under the dark night sky. They told the old stories about the fire in a faraway land. They tried to imagine a land with the heat and warmth of fire. They also frightened themselves with stories about the God of Fire—a god who threw thunderbolts of lightning in his anger.

During the council, many animals stood up and said that it would be a great idea for one of them to go to the Land of Fire, steal the fire, and bring it back to their world. Not a single one, however, volunteered for the dangerous duty.

Finally, one animal, the toad, stood and said he would go to the Land of Fire and bring back fire for the living creatures. He knew that the God of Fire lived under the sea and that no other animal could survive a battle there. Only the toad could enter the waters and remain alive.

So, the toad departed for the Land of Fire. The other living creatures bid him farewell and wished him good fortune. They all prayed that not only would the toad return safely but that he would return with the sacred fire.

As the toad approached the Land of Fire, the God of Fire sensed his arrival. He knew that the toad was on a mission to steal his fire. Incensed, he hurled thundering bolts of lightning at the toad in an attempt to kill him. The bolts drove through the waters and crashed into the land. They churned up the waters and created a maelstrom of flashing light and raging water.

The toad, however, remained safe deep under the waters. He entered the Land of Fire, and while the God of Fire was busy tossing his gigantic lightning bolts through the turbulent waters, he stole the flames of fire.

Suddenly, the waters were filled with hundreds of toads. The toad's children had arrived to help him bring fire back to the living creatures.

The toad gave some fire to each of his many children. They all swam away from the Land of Fire, blazing a trail in the water with the flames of fire in their mouths. The God of Fire tried to stop the toads, but there were too many of them. He eventually tired of the battle and accepted that now the living creatures would also have fire.

When the toad returned to the land of the living creatures, he gave to them the fire. The creatures put the fire into sticks and rocks and transported them to the four corners of the world. The brave toad and his children had brought fire to the world.

To this day, the Yaqui Indians create fire by twirling a stick against a rock until a flame bursts alive. They too have heard the story of how the toad brought fire to the world and that fire is in the sticks and rocks of this world.

Badger Names the Sun
Why the Badger Lives Underground

A Yaqui Myth

At the beginning of time, all of the Earth's creatures gathered in order to give names to the different parts of the world. The work of naming these parts was to be one of the earliest and most important accomplishments of the creatures.

But when it came time to name the Sun, the creatures of the world found themselves confused. Because the world was still new, and the Sun had only recently been created, no one knew whether it was a man or a woman. The creatures deliberated for days but could not come up with an answer.

One morning, as the Sun was boosting itself into the sky for its daily journey across the heavens, the badger came out of his hole in the ground where he lived. The Sun seemed to also be coming out of a hole in the ground. It then lifted above the waters of the ocean and brought light to the whole world. The badger scooted over to the place where the creatures of the world were having their discussion. When he entered the circle of discussion, he spoke up in a loud voice and said, "The Sun comes out of a hole in the ground, just like I do. And I know that the Sun is a man, just like I am."

All the creatures of the world cheered and yelled with excitement because their question about the Sun had been answered. Now they could give the Sun a name and finish up the business of naming all the parts of the world.

But they cheered so wildly and loudly that the badger thought he had done or said something wrong and that all the animals of the world were angry with him. So, he quickly scurried away. But the creatures wanted to congratulate the badger, and they began to chase him. The badger then popped back down into his hole.

To this day, the badger rarely ventures outside his hole because he thinks the creatures of the world are angry with him for causing such a commotion so long ago. The badger is perfectly content to live a peaceful existence under the ground.

The Bridge of Many Colors
The First Rainbow

A Zapotec Myth

Many years ago, during the time when the world was still fresh and new and the gods were still creating all the beauty of the Earth, the God of Lightning ruled supreme in the sky. The people of the Earth lived in darkness at this time, and the only light they knew was the flash of the God of Lightning's lightning bolts that he threw about in anger or playfulness.

The God of Lightning ruled from a royal throne in the heavens. At his feet were four immense clay pots, each securely capped with a large lid. At the side of each clay pot stood a younger lightning god, alertly guarding the pot.

Each of the pots held one of the powerful sky elements the God of Lightning used to control the weather on the Earth. In one were all the clouds of the sky. In another was the water of the heavenly rain. In the third were the solid rocks of water—the damaging hail of the thunderstorm. In the fourth pot was the wind—both the gentle spring breeze and the fierce winter storm gale.

One day, the God of Lightning decided it was time to play with his clay pots. He commanded one of the guards, "Open the pot of clouds. Let the skies be covered with their white softness today."

The guard opened the pot of clouds, and immediately the skies were filled with immense, billowing clouds. The guards were so excited to see the clouds flying free in the sky that they began to run among them, tossing them back and forth in a playful game. The more they played, the more the clouds gathered together. Soon, the clouds had transformed their billowy softness into giant, threatening storm clouds, tossed about by the guards until they released cracking booms of thunder. Each time one of the clouds collided in thunder, one of the guards would let loose a bolt of lightning.

To the people on Earth, these games of the gods of lightning appeared as thunderstorms, which had grown more frightening with each crash of thunder and lightning. The people gazed in awe and amazement at the heavenly display of sound and light, but soon, the violence of the storm scared them. Then the people grew thirsty. They prayed to the gods to stop the violent storms and allow the heavens to let loose their nourishing and refreshing waters.

The God of Lightning heard the people's prayers and called to another guard, "Open the pot of water. The people pray for relief. Let the waters flow down to the Earth."

The guard opened the pot of water and stood back as cascades of water gushed out and flowed over the pot's rim. The waters fell down to Earth in a torrent of rain.

At first, the people were thankful to have their prayers answered, and they dashed about in the open rain quenching their thirst. Soon, they had filled their water pots and wished for the rains to end. The lightning gods, however, were enjoying the rain too much to notice the people's pleas. The rains continued to flow until they became drowning floods to the people on Earth. The people knew that the gods were not hearing their prayers, so they decided to send some messengers to the heavens to ask the God of Lightning directly to stop the flooding of the Earth.

When the messengers arrived in the heavens, they were amazed to see the riches and splendor of the heavens. They dashed about like children in a new playground, examining all the wonders of the heavens. They forgot all about their mission to ask the gods to release the Earth from the torrential floods.

The messengers were especially intrigued by the four beautiful clay pots that sat at the foot of the throne of the God of Lightning. They respectfully asked the God of Lightning, "Oh great God of Lightning, please show us the wonders of these clay pots. We pray to you to show us the mysteries of your world."

The God of Lightning heard their prayers and commanded, "Open the third pot. Let the people of the Earth witness my mighty power."

Out of the pot jumped a maelstrom of hail, pelting the people of the Earth with sharp rocks of hard water. The people screamed in pain and begged, "Please, God of Lightning, stop the hail. It will soon destroy us and the plants of the Earth."

The gods of lightning had released thundering storm clouds, crashing waves of flooding waters, and now, pelting hail. The gods were lost in a frenzy of storm energy and did not hear the prayers of the people. The lightning gods tossed their bolts of lightning until the dark Earth sky lit up with the brilliance of exploding firecrackers.

The people of the Earth knew that their world would soon be destroyed unless the cataclysmic storm unleashed by the gods of lightning stopped. The people prayed to the greatest god—The God of Heaven—and asked, "Great God of Heaven, hear our prayers. Stop the games of the gods of lightning. Bring peace back to the Earth and its people."

The God of Heaven heard their prayers and came out of his palace in the sky. When he saw the destruction the games of the gods of lightning were causing, he lifted his scepter and commanded to the guard of the wind pot, "Uncover the pot of wind. Let the wind loose in the heavens to blow the storm clouds away and to bring peace back to the skies."

The guard of the pot of wind uncovered the pot and let loose the heavenly winds. As the winds flew out of the pot, the God of Heaven commanded them to blow the clouds away until the God of the Sun could come out.

The winds did as commanded and blew the clouds out of the skies until the bright light of the God of the Sun broke through from the East and lit the world below. For the first time, the people of the Earth saw the light of the Sun.

The God of Lightning saw that the God of the Sun was more powerful than he was, for the God of the Sun could illuminate the vast expanse of the whole sky with one sweep of his light. He humbly commanded the guards: "Guards of the Lightning, put the lids back on the clay pots. The time of the destroying storms is over, and now it is the time of the peaceful Sun."

The God of Lightning saw that the people of the Earth were overjoyed that their world was lit with the rays of the Sun instead of the frightening bolts of lightning. He also saw that under the light of the Sun, all things on the Earth prospered and grew into greater life.

In order to show his respect for the peaceful and nourishing ways of the God of the Sun, the God of Lightning had his guards build a bridge—an arc stretching from one end of the sky to the other that linked the world of the heavens with the world of the Earth. It was his gift to the people of the Earth to make amends for his destructive storms. The bridge would allow the people of the Earth to have a direct path to the heavens when their time on Earth had come to an end.

This bridge captured the light of the Sun and reflected it back to the Earth as a bridge of many colors. To this day, the people of the Earth know that after a violent storm, the gods will send them this bridge of many colors to remind them that peace and tranquility will always return to the Earth.

El puente multicolor
El primer arco iris

Un mito zapoteca

Hace muchos años, en una época cuando el mundo era fresco y nuevo, y los dioses todavía estaban creando la belleza de la Tierra, el Dios del Relámpago reinaba supremo en el cielo. La gente de la tierra vivía en tinieblas en ese momento, y la única luz que conocía era el resplandor de los relámpagos que el Dios del Relámpago lanzaba cuando estaba enojado o para divertirse.

El Dios del Relámpago reinaba desde su trono real en los cielos. A sus pies habían cuatro inmensas vasijas de arcilla, cada una cerrada con una gran tapa. A los lados de cada vasija había un jóven dios del relámpago, custodiando alertamente la vasija.

Cada vasija contenía uno de los poderosos elementos del cielo que el Dios del Relámpago usaba para controlar el clima de la Tierra. En una estaban todas las nubes del cielo. En otra estaba el agua de la lluvia celestial. En la tercera estaban las sólidas piedras de agua, es decir, el destructor granizo de las tormentas. En la cuarta estaba el viento, tanto la suave brisa de la primavera como el fuerte vendaval de la tormenta invernal.

Un día, el Dios del Relámpago decidió que era hora de jugar con sus vasijas de arcilla. Le dijo a uno de los guardianes: "Abre la vasija de las nubes. Que los cielos hoy se cubran con su blanca suavidad".

El guardián abrió la vasija de las nubes, e inmediatamente el cielo se llenó de inmensas y ondulantes nubes. Los guardias se animaron tanto al ver las nubes volar libremente en el cielo, que comenzaron a correr entre ellos, lanzándolas una y otra vez, en un divertido juego. Cuando más jugaban, más nubes se juntaban. En poco tiempo las nubes habían transformado su ondulante suavidad en inmensas y amenazadoras nubes de tormenta, a las que los guardias continuaron arrojando de un lado a otro, hasta que las nubes comenzaron a resonar con estruendosos truenos. Cada vez que las nubes chocaban y tronaban, uno de los guardianas lanzaba un relámpago.

Para la gente de la Tierra, estos juegos de los dioses del relámpago aparecían como tormentas eléctricas, que crecían cada vez más amenazadoras con cada choque de trueno y relámpago. La gente admiraba con temor y asombro a la divina exhibición de sonidos y luces, pero pronto, la violencia de la tomenta les causó temor. La gente comenzó a tener sed. Pidieron a los dioses que detuviesen las violentas tormentas y que permitiesen a los cielos descargar sus nutritivas y refrescantes aguas.

El Dios del Relámpago escuchó las oraciones de las personas y llamó a otro guardian. "Guardian del Agua, abre la vasija con el agua. La gente reza pidiendo alivio. Dejan que las aguas fluyan a la Tierra".

El guardián abrió la vasija con el agua y se apartó, a la vez que cascadas de agua emanaron y rebosaron el borde de la vasija. Las aguas cayeron sobre la Tierra como torrentes de lluvia.

Al principio, la gente estaba agradecida porque sus oraciones habían sido contestadas, y salieron bajo la lluvia a calmar su sed. En poco tiempo, habían llenado sus vasijas con agua y querían que la lluvia terminase. Los dioses del relámpago, sin embargo, estaban disfrutando tanto de la lluvia que ni notaron las súplicas de las personas. Las lluvias continuaron cayendo hasta que se convirtieron en inundaciones que ahogaron a las personas de la Tierra. La gente se dio cuenta que los dioses no estaban escuchando sus oraciones, así que decidieron enviara algunos mensajeros al cielo, y pedir directamente al Dios del Relámpago que detuviese las inundaciones sobre la Tierra.

Cuando los mensajeros llegaron a los cielos, se asombraron al ver las riquezas y el esplendor de los cielos. Comenzaron a corretear como niños en una nueva plaza de juegos, examinando todas las maravillas de los cielos. Se olvidaron por completo de su misión de pedirles a los dioses que detuviesen las torrenciales inundaciones en la Tierra.

Los mensajeros se sintieron especialmente intrigados por la cuarta de las hermosas vasijas de arcilla que estaban al pie del trono del Dios del Relámpago. Respetuosamente le preguntaron al Dios del Relámpago: "Oh Gran Dios del Relámpago, por favor muéstranos las maravillas de estas vasijas de arcilla. Te rogamos que nos muestres los misterios de tu mundo".

El Dios del Relámpago escuchó las oraciones y ordenó: "Abrid la tercera vasija. Que la gente de la Tierra sea testigo de mi inmenso poder".

De la vasija saltó un torbellino de granizo, que golpeó a los habitantes de la Tierra con agudas rocas de agua solidificada. La gente gritó en dolor y suplicó: "Por favor, Dios del Relámpago, detén el granizo. En poco tiempo nos destruirá y también a las plantas de la Tierra".

Los dioses del relámpago habían liberado las nubes de tormenta y sus truenos, las aplastantes aguas del diluvio, y ahora, el torrencial granizo. Los dioses estaban perdidos en un frenesí de tormentosa energía y no escucharon las oraciones de la gente. Los dioses del relámpago arrojaron sus rayos de luz hasta que la oscura tierra se iluminó con el resplandor de los explosivos petardos.

La gente de la tierra sabía que en poco tiempo perecerían a menos que la cataclísmica tormenta desatada por los dioses del relámpago se detuviese. La gente oró al más grande de los dioses, el Señor del Cielo, y pidió: " Gran Señor del

Cielo, escucha nuestras oraciones. Detén los juegos de los dioses del relámpago. Devuelve la paz a la Tierra y a sus habitantes".

El Dios del Cielo escuchó las oraciones y salió de su palacio celestial. Cuando vio la destrucción que los juegos de los dioses del relámpago habían causado, levantó su cetro y ordenó al guardián de la vasija con el viento: "Remueve la tapa de la vasija. Deja al viento en libertad en los cielos, para que sople las nubes de tormenta y devuelva la paz a los cielos".

El guardián de la vasija con el viento removió la tapa de la vasija y dejó libres a los vientos celestiales. Al salir los vientos de la vasija, el Señor del Cielo les ordenó soplar las nubes hasta que el Dios del Sol pudiese ser visto.

Los vientos hicieron lo que se les ordenó y soplaron las nubes, removiéndolas del cielo hasta que la brillante luz del Señor del Sol resplandeció en el este e iluminó el mundo de abajo. Por primera vez, la gente de la tierra vio la luz del Sol.

El Dios del Relámpago vio que el Dios del Sol era más poderoso de lo que él era, porque el Dios del Sol podía iluminar la vasta expansión de todo el cielo con un solo golpe de su luz. Humildemente le dijo a sus guardianes: "Guardianes del Relámpago, poned las tapas en las vasijas de arcilla. El tiempo de nuestras destructivas tormentas ha terminado. Ahora es el momento del pacífico Sol".

El Dios del Relámpago vio que la gente de la tierra se regocijaba en sobremanera porque su mundo estaba iluminado por el Sol en vez de los terribles rayos y relámpagos. También vio que bajo la luz del Sol todas las cosas en la Tierra prosperaban y crecían en una vida más grande.

Para mostrar su respeto hacia la manera pacífica y nutritiva del Dios del Sol, el Dios del Relámpago hizo que sus guardianes construyesen un puente, un arco que iba de un extremo al otro del cielo, y que conectaba el mundo de los cielos con el mundo de la Tierra. Era un regalo para la gente de la Tierra, para dar una compensación por sus destructivas tormentas. El puente permitiría a la gente de la Tierra tener un sendero directo hasta los cielos, cuando su tiempo en la Tierra llegase al final.

Este puente capturó la luz del Sol y la reflejó hacia la tierra como un puente multicolor. Hasta este día, la gente de la Tierra sabe que después de una violenta tormenta, los dioses enviarán este puente multicolor para recordarles que la paz y la tranquilidad siempre retornarán a la tierra.

Song to Three Stars
Why Coyote Howls to the Sky

A Tarahumara Myth

Many years ago, when the Earth was still filled with magic beings and powerful forces roamed its lands, there lived an evil wizard in the land of the Sierra Madre in northern Mexico. This evil wizard had captured three beautiful maidens. The maidens were gentle young women with skin as light as the pale moon and eyes as dark as obsidian.

From the moment the Sun broke over the mountains of the Sierra Madre until the moon lit the Earth below with its cold light, the maidens were forced to do the wizard's work. This included his hunting, which was a particularly horrid task for the maidens, for in their gentle ways, they could not bring themselves to kill any living creature. Whenever they returned from hunting empty-handed, the wizard would severely punish them by whipping them with the spiny needles of the cactus and releasing wasps to sting them.

The maidens spent their troubled days and nights fearful of what the wizard would do to them next. They plotted ways to escape, but the wizard always discovered their plots and punished them even more.

One night, the maidens heard a voice calling to them from the mountain forest. The voiced called out, "Maidens, do not fear. The gods of the spirits of the forest will protect you. Escape to the heart of the forest and you will be safe."

The maidens knew that this would be their one chance for escape. The wizard was gone and did not know about the voice from the forest. The eldest maiden called back, "Forest spirit, please do not forsake us. We are answering your call. Guide us to you."

The forest voice continued to call to the maidens. His voice was like a beacon in the dark night, guiding them to the heart of the forest.

When the Sun rose over the rim of the Sierra Madre Mountains and lit the Earth in all its splendor, the maidens found themselves in a mountain valley more beautiful than they had ever seen. Butterflies flitted around their heads. The air was sweetened with the perfume of mountain flowers. The birds filled the skies with their morning songs. Fish playfully leaped in the roaring mountain streams. Hummingbirds flew in the sky, darting and diving here and there. The maidens knew that they were in a special place and that the voice of the forest spirit had led them to a safe place.

When the wizard returned the next morning, he discovered that the maidens had fled. He called out in anger, but he heard no response. He concocted an evil potion, and in the smoke of the fire he saw the maidens playing in the heart of the forest. He immediately knew where they were and set out to recapture them.

The maidens were resting under the shade of a large tree when a bird flew up to them in great agitation. The bird chirped out, "The wizard has discovered your place of hiding. He is coming here right now. You must flee for your lives!"

The maidens heard the wizard approaching and they ran faster than the deer through the forest. As they ran they could hear the wizard calling to them, "Maidens, do not run. There is no escape from my powers. Give up and return with me. You are mine for all eternity. There is no escape."

Just as the maidens began to fear that the wizard was right, the voice of the forest spirit called to them, "Maidens. Run toward my voice. I will save you from the evil wizard. Come to me, and I will raise you up into the sky far from the powers of the wizard."

The maidens felt their feet lifting off the ground. Sustained by a divine strength, they floated high above the Earth, where they gazed down on its mountains and streams. They danced in the air of the sky just as they had danced in the flowers of the Earth.

The wizard was furious that the maidens were escaping, and he cast a spell on his arrows. He then shot three of the arrows into the sky, aiming them at the hearts of the maidens. Because of the spell he had put on the arrows, they were too powerful for the magic of the forest voice and they pierced the maidens' hearts.

The voice of the forest spirit called to the heavenly gods, "Take the souls of the maidens. They are free of the evils of the Earth. Protect them and let them shine on the Earth as a sign of all that is good in the world."

The gods embraced the spirits of the maidens and transformed them into three bright stars in the night sky. The three stars shine in the winter sky as part of the constellation Orion.

The gods then punished the wizard for his evil. They transformed him into a coyote. For all eternity the coyote is destined to howl in sadness at the night sky. He laments his evil ways and weeps mournfully for the death of the three beautiful maidens. His howling songs of sorrow pierce the night air and remind all of the just punishment those who live an evil life will receive.

The Comet and the Tiger
Why the Tiger Has Black Spots

A Mexica Myth

Many years ago, in the time before man walked on this Earth, all of the animals and plants lived lives of happiness. The world was surrounded by a lasting peace, and no single animal had dominion over another.

One tiger was especially at peace with the world. This tiger was golden colored—his fur was the color of the Sun. The tiger's hide was unmarked, smooth, and beautiful. And the tiger was not ferocious, in fact, his temperament was peaceful. He would never eat other animals, rather his diet consisted of fruits and vegetation. In truth, the tiger was very contented, and he spent his days majestically walking throughout the land, composed like a prince.

When evening came, the tiger would go to the Hill of the Stars and recline under his favorite tree. He would rest his head on his paws and spend hours and hours contemplating the heavens above. Because of his nightly meditations on the night sky, all of the other animals considered the tiger to be a dreamer.

The tiger possessed a great knowledge of the sky and loved best the Moon and the stars. Such was his knowledge of the sky that, of all the animals, only he knew the locations of the Southern Cross, the Great Bear, Orion, and Seven Sisters. To all the animals, this dreamer was the most in love with the inhabitants of the starry night.

One night, while he was spending his customary evening gazing at the night sky, the tiger noticed a comet he had never seen before. The beautiful comet was large and bright, sending its light throughout the sky the tiger knew so well.

For several nights, the tiger observed the new comet. To the tiger, the comet was an intruder, shining too brightly in his beloved night sky. So brightly, in fact, that the tiger believed its brilliance almost surpassed the light of the grand *señora* of the night sky, the Moon herself. The tiger loved the Moon and resented the comet—an intruder—for trying to outshine the "queen" of the night sky.

Then one evening, the tiger heard the voice of the planet Venus. The planet had noticed that the comet troubled the tiger. Venus told the tiger, "Dear tiger, do not object to the presence of the new comet. She is a proud and beautiful stranger in our world." The tiger listened to the words of the planet Venus, but he still believed that he should dislike the intruder.

While out watching the sky one night, the tiger once again spied the comet. He called out to her: "Intruder, I want you to know that I love the Moon and all of her children, the stars. From birth I have watched the night sky for her beautiful light. Now you are here as an intruder. I want to know what you are doing here."

The comet was offended by the brash question of the tiger. She responded, "Who are you to speak to me in such a manner? It is the privilege of the gods to contemplate my beauty. And listen well, you insignificant dweller of the mountain: Never speak to me like that again."

Now the tiger was angry. He furiously told the comet, "*Señora* Moon and her children the stars are friends of mine. I have spent many nights conversing with them, and I give them all of my admiration. Now, I command you to abandon your starry wanderings through the night sky and the giving of light to the land, an honor that should only belong to the Moon and her children.

The comet also became furious and answered the tiger, "You should know, poor tiger, that just as I can be beautiful, I can be dangerous. My appearance in the sky foretells the death of a prince, a king, or a warrior. I can be the sign of famine and war. Because of this, you are obliged to show me respect."

The tiger fearlessly answered, "I will never respect you! You are not the queen of the sky. You are a perverse intrusion."

The comet angrily told the tiger, "Stupid tiger. I am the star that throws arrows of fire." She then reached into her fiery tail and threw down arrows of fire to strike the tiger. The arrows struck the tiger all over his body.

A roar of pain came from the Hill of Stars and swept throughout the land. The tiger's beautiful fur had been charred from the comet's arrows. From this time on, the tiger's once beautiful and unmarked hide is covered with dark spots, a reminder of his unfortunate encounter with a comet so many years ago.

The Rain of Five Years
The Story of the Creation of the World

A Huichol Myth

At the beginning of time, when the world was still new, a Huichol man lived on the Earth and toiled in its soil. Every day he would rise and greet the Sun with a prayer to the five sacred directions: north, south, east, and west and above and below. The Aztecs considered above and below, or heaven and earth, to be the central, or fifth, direction. After he had greeted the Sun, he would begin his day's work of clearing the land for planting. From the Sun's first bright rays in the east to its last dim rays in the west, he cut down trees and moved rocks and boulders.

His hard work was extremely frustrating, however, because every morning he returned to his field, the trees he had cut down the day before would be standing again in their original places. When this first started happening, he thought that he had simply forgotten where he had been cutting trees. Soon, however, it was evident to him that some magical power was replacing the trees. He secretly kept watch on his field, determined to discover the cause of the strange occurrence.

He began to carefully watch his field, and on the fifth day of vigilance, he saw a woman rise out of the middle of the clearing. With a wave of her staff, she caused the fallen trees to stand upright again as if they had never been cut down.

The Huichol man was bewildered by the woman's presence in the field. He did not know that she was the Goddess of the Earth, who had the power to make all living plants and trees rise up and grow out of the ground. He saw her point her staff to the five sacred directions and watched in amazement as trees sprung up in all five directions.

He approached the Goddess of the Earth and asked her, "Are you the person who has been causing the trees I have cut down to stand upright again?"

She told him, "Yes I am. I have been causing the trees to live and grow again as a warning to you. All of your work is in vain, because a great flood is coming in five days. I have come to help you prepare for the creation of a new world."

The Huichol man asked her, "What must I do to survive the flood, and what will become of my world?"

The Goddess of the Earth answered, "Your world will end. A terrible wind will come in five days, and along with it, destroying waters that will flood the Earth. You will survive, however, if you do exactly as I tell you. First, you must make a box big enough for you to lie in. You must then gather the grains for the new world. These must be five grains of corn of each color and five beans of each color. You must also take fire, as well as wood to feed the fire. Finally, you must take a female dog with you. All of these items must fit in the box with you."

The Huichol man did as he was commanded. He built the box out of the sturdiest wood he could find. Then he carefully gathered the grains of corn and the beans and laid them in the box. Next, he placed fire in the box and sufficient wood to keep the flame alive. Finally, he found a female dog and put her in the box. Then he lowered himself into the box.

The Goddess of the Earth shut the top of the box and sealed it with tree sap and pitch. When the box was watertight, she sat on top of the box with a bird perched on her shoulder and waited for the waters to come.

When the wind and waters came, they flooded the Earth and killed all of its living creatures. The Goddess of the Earth rode the box on the waves of the flooding waters for one year in each of the four directions: east, north, south and west. In the fifth year of the flood, the waters had risen even higher, and the whole Earth was flooded. Finally, at the end of the fifth year, the waters receded, and the box came to rest on dry land.

As the box landed, the Goddess of the Earth raised herself above the box and transformed into the wind, flying away to the five sacred directions. As the goddess left, the bird that had been on her shoulder flew high into the sky and dove back to the Earth, parting the waters with its beak to create the oceans and the continents. The Huichol man climbed out of his box, and with the provisions he had carried with him and the female dog, he set off to find new land to work.

When he had found his new land, he planted the grains of corn and the beans. Soon his crops were abundant, and food had returned to the Earth. With the fire, he was able to cook the food he had grown.

Every evening when the Huichol man returned home from his day's work on the land, he would find a stack of fresh *tortillas* waiting for him. He was bewildered because no other living creature was on the Earth besides himself.

One day, he returned home immediately after he had left for his fields and looked inside the house to see if he could discover the secret of the *tortillas*. As he peered in the window, he saw the dog take off her skin and transform into a woman. She then ground the corn on a *metate* and used the corn flour to make *tortillas*.

The Huichol man rushed into the house, grabbed the dog's skin, and threw it into the fire. When her dog's skin burned up, the woman was destined to remain a woman for the rest of her days.

The Huichol man and the woman became the first family on the new Earth. They had many children, and these children became the new families of the Earth. In this way, the world was created anew after the flood, and people returned to the Earth to enjoy its great beauties.

STORIES FROM SPANISH
COLONIAL MEXICO

Pedro and the Money Tree

One of the many stories of Pedro de Ordimalas tells of the time long ago when Pedro was out of money and down on his luck. Now, this situation was nothing new for Pedro, for most of the time he was out of money and down on his luck. But Pedro lived by his wits, and he knew that soon something would happen to change his fortune for a little while.

Things were so bad for Pedro this time, however, that he had made a desperate decision. He would try to find work. Unfortunately, no matter where he looked or asked for work, there was nothing for him to do. Of course, it didn't help that everyone knew about Pedro's many tricks and didn't trust him. In fact, most of the people who lived in that part of the country knew to be very careful when dealing with Pedro.

Soon, it became obvious to Pedro that he was going to have to come up with some special plan if he was going to find a way out of his troubles. But what type of plan? He thought and thought until he finally devised a quite clever plan.

Pedro took out his moneybag and looked inside to see how many coins remained. His search of the meager bag didn't reveal much—just a few dirty gold coins—the last of all of Pedro's money on this Earth. But they were sufficient for Pedro's plan.

He first took the coins to the river and washed them until they sparked like new. Then he drilled a hole in all of the coins and tied a string to each one. For the last part of his plan, he went to a road leading out of town and found a mesquite tree that would work for his plan. He climbed into the tree and carefully hung all of his newly washed and shined gold coins on the tree's limbs. Then he descended the tree and began to act as if he were cultivating and tending the ground around the tree. He busied himself with raking the dirt and watering the roots just like any farmer would a prize plant. All that was left for his plan to be successful was the arrival of some greedy victims.

It wasn't long before two travelers passed by the tree on their way out of town. The travelers had stayed for several days, and their loud and brash manners had offended many in the town. In fact, most of the townspeople were quite happy to see the travelers leave for good.

Pedro y el Árbol de Dinero

Una de las muchas historias de Pedro de Ordimalas cuenta de aquella vez, hace mucho tiempo, cuando Pedro no tenía dinero y andaba escaso de suerte. Ahora bien, esta situación no era nada nuevo para Pedro, porque la mayor parte del tiempo no tenía dinero y andaba escaso de suerte. Pero Pedro vivía gracias a sus artimañas, y sabía que pronto algo sucedería que cambiaría su fortuna por algún tiempo.

Esta vez las cosas estaban tan mal para Pedro, así, que él tomó una desesperada descisión. Trataría de buscar trabajo. Desafortundamente, sin importar dónde Pedro buscó o preguntó por trabajo, no había nada para que él hiciese. Por supuesto, no ayudaba mucho que todos conocían de los numerosos trucos de Pedro, y que desconfiaban de él. De hecho, la mayoría de las personas en aquella zona del país aprendieron a ser muy cuidadosos al tratar con Pedro.

Pronto le resultó evidente a Pedro que necesitaría algún plan especial si quería salir de sus problemas. Pero, ¿qué clase de plan? Pensó y pensó, hasta que finalmente desarrolló un plan muy astuto.

Pedro sacó su monedero y se fijó cuántas monedas le quedaban. Su inspección de la mísera bolsa no reveló mucho, solamente unas pocas y sucias monedas de oro, lo último de todo el dinero de Pedro en esta tierra. Pero era suficiente para el plan de Pedro.

Primero llevó las monedas al río y las lavó hasta que relucían como nuevas. Luego perforó un orificio en cada moneda y ató un hilo a cada una. Para la última parte de su plan, fue a un camino que salía de la ciudad y encontró un árbol de mesquite que serviría para su plan. Pedro subió al árbol y cuidadosamente colgó las monedas de oro, recién lavadas y relucientes, de las ramas del árbol. Luego bajó del árbol y comenzó a actuar como si estuviese cultivando el suelo alrededor del árbol. Se ocupó de rastrillar el suelo y de regar las raíces de la misma manera que cualquier granjero lo haría con una valiosa planta. Todo lo que faltaba, para que su plan fuese exitoso, era la llegada de algunas víctimas codiciosas.

Poco después dos viajeros, saliendo de la ciudad, pasaron junto al árbol. Los viajeros habían estado por varios días, y sus maneras bruscas y ruidosas habían ofendido a muchos en la ciudad. De hecho, la mayoría de las personas en la ciudad se alegraron al ver que finalmente se iban los viajeros.

Cuando los viajeros pasaron junto a Pedro, que estaba trabajando bajo el árbol, no pudieron sino notar las monedas de oro colgando de las ramas. Atraídos hacia las monedas, por sus actitudes codiciosas, los viajeros se acercaron a Pedro. Uno de los viajeros dijo: "Buenos días, señor. No podemos sino notar que su árbol parece tener monedas de oro creciendo en sus ramas". Entonces preguntó: "¿Por casualidad este árbol no está a la venta?"

Pedro se tomó un tiempo antes de contestar, pero eventualmente dijo: "No. No se vende a ningún precio. Es un árbol especial donde crece dinero, de hecho el único del mundo. Un mago en un carnaval viajero me lo dio. Le hice un favor en un momento de necesidad, y me dio este árbol. Lo lamento, pero no se vende".

Los viajeros se interesaron aún más en el árbol, tras escuchar la historia de Pedro. Uno de los viajeros volvió a preguntar: "Por favor, somos viajeros ricos y nunca hemos visto un árbol como el suyo. Nos gusta coleccionar lo inusual y lo único de los lugares por los que viajamos, y su árbol sería una magnífica adición a nuestra colección. Pagaremos el precio que pida".

Pedro comenzó a trabajar aún más cuidadosamente bajo el árbol, arreglando la tierra y las rocas de una manera más deliberada y regando las raíces del árbol con mucha ternura. Hizo una pausa en el trabajo y miró sospechosamente a los viajantes, antes de contestar: "No. Lo lamento. El árbol no se vende. Como pueden ver, es un árbol muy temperamental. Hay que atenderlo con mucho cuidado, o no dará ninguna de sus preciosas monedas de oro. Si les vendo el árbol a ustedes dos, ¿cómo podré saber que no lo matarán por descuidarlo? Y entonces el único árbol de su clase desaparecerá. No, no lo creo. El árbol me da suficiente dinero para mi familia y nuestras simples necesidades. No se vende".

Ahora, por supuesto, Pedro estaba asegurándose que el anzuelo estaba en sus víctimas, y que no se iba a desenganchar. Con toda seguridad, uno de los viajeros quedó clavado en el anzuelo y dijo: "Prometemos cuidar del árbol exactamente cómo usted nos enseñe. Le daremos suficiente dinero para que su familia nunca más carezca de nada. Y hasta le dejaremos que se lleve para usted las monedas que ahora están creciendo".

Los viajeros sacaron sus bolsas de dinero y comenzaron a poner una gran cantidad de dinero en el suelo para que Pedro viese que sus intenciones era reales. Pedro tomó su tiempo, pero se aproximó al dinero y comenzó a contarlo lentamente. "No sé", dijo Pedro. "Es mucho trabajo cuidar del árbol, y ya estoy entrando en años, y no necesito trabajar tanto. Quizá sea el momento de vender el árbol. O quizá no lo sea…"

Los viajeros ya no pudieron soportar la vacilación de Pedro. Colocaron aún más dinero en la pila y rogaron: "Por favor, véndanos el árbol. Prometemos que lo cuidaremos. Aquí está todo el dinero que tenemos".

Pedro finalmente cedió, y con un suspiro dijo: "Está bien. El árbol es de ustedes. Cuidadosamente les daré las instrucciones de cómo cuidar el árbol, pero primero necesito recoger mi cosecha".

Luego de haber recogido todas las monedas de oro, Pedro les enseñó a los dos viajeros la manera especial en que él rastrillaba la tierra y regaba las raíces. Al irse con su dinero les dijo a los viajeros: "Ahora tengan paciencia. El árbol se toma su tiempo para producir monedas de oro. Al principio parecerá que no pasa nada. Pero entonces deben cuidar la tierra y mojar las raíces aún más tiernamente". Pedro dejó entonces a los viajersos con el árbol recién comprado.

Durante meses, los viajeros acamparon junto al árbol y lo cuidaron en detalle. Removieron la tierra, arreglaron las rocas, y regaron las raíces. Después de muchos meses, finalmente comprendieron que Pedro los había engañado, y que el árbol nunca daría dinero. Por supuesto, estaban furiosos de que Pedro los había engañado y despojado de su dinero al venderles un árbol sin valor. Pero se sentían aún más humillados que un truhán como Pedro los hubiese engañado tan bien. Humillados y avergonzados, se fueron en medio de la noche sin decir una sola palabra a nadie.

Por supuesto, Pedro disfrutó del dinero que los viajeros le habían dado. Retornó a su vida de placeres fáciles, esperando el día en que, una vez más, su fortuna se terminase y tuviese que volver a sus artimañas. Esta una vez, hasta la gente de la ciudad disfrutó del truco de Pedro. No les hizo daño a ninguno de ellos, y les sacó lo mejor a los dos viajeros codiciosos.

Pedro and the Pig Tails

This Pedro de Ordimalas story tells of the time that Pedro tricked a farmer out of his own pigs. As in all of his stories, Pedro found himself out of money and down on his luck. He had recently made a lot of money through one of his legendary tricks, but as usual, he had spent it all.

This time, things looked so bleak that Pedro was forced to look for work. He finally found a job working for the owner of a pig farm. Pedro's job was cleaning the pig stalls and making sure the pigs were fed. It was very dirty work. Every night, Pedro returned home even dirtier than the pigs he tended. (And whew! Did he stink!)

The worst part of the job was working with the owner of the pig farm, who was a mean and greedy man. He would find ways to make Pedro work even harder, and then he would cheat Pedro out of his hard-earned pay. Nevertheless, Pedro needed the job and did his work the best that he could.

One morning, Pedro was cleaning the slop out of the pigs' food bins and getting ready for another hard day's work. As he was working, a man stopped to admire the pigs. He spent a long time looking at the pigs and finally said to Pedro, "You know, I've been thinking of starting a pig farm myself. Your pigs look very healthy." He then asked, "Would you please sell me some of your pigs?"

At first, Pedro began to tell the man that he had made a mistake and that he was not the owner of the pigs. He immediately realized, however, that this was an opportunity to get back at the pig owner for his cheating ways and to make a little money for himself at the same time. So Pedro answered the man, "Maybe it would be possible to sell you a few of my pigs. Pigs are easy to breed. Soon I will be able to replace the pigs I sell to you, while you have a good start on a farm. I will ask of you one thing, however. I will sell the pigs to you for a good price, but you must let me have the pigs' tails."

The man thought this was the strangest request he had ever heard. Curious, he questioned Pedro, "The pigs' tails? Why on Earth would you want the pigs' tails?"

Knowing that this was the crucial part of his plan, Pedro answered, "I've taken care of these pigs from the time that they were little piglets. I know I shouldn't, but I grow quite fond of my little pigs, and having their tails would help give me something to remember them by."

Now, the man knew that this was the oddest story he had ever heard, but he could think of no reason not to give Pedro the pigs' tails. The man gave Pedro the money for the pigs, and Pedro gave the man the pigs (minus their tails, of course).

Pedro then went out by the river where the banks were most muddy and stuck all of the pigs' tails into the mud. The tails poked out so that it looked as if the rest of the pigs' bodies were buried under the mud.

When the pig owner returned to the farm, Pedro ran out to meet him and told him an amazing story. Acting as if he were out of breath, Pedro frantically told the pig owner, "You won't believe what happened! Some of the pigs escaped from the pen when I went to get more food for them. They ran down to the river, and I chased after them to try to get them back in the pen. When I finally caught up with them, it was too late. They had fallen into the mud by the banks of the river. The mud was so deep and so much like quicksand that the pigs fell into the mud and got buried up to their tails."

The pig owner immediately rushed out to the river. He was shocked to find his pigs buried up to their tails in mud. He blew up at Pedro and fired him on the spot. He yelled at Pedro, "You're fired! This is the dumbest mistake I've ever seen. It'll take forever to pull my pigs out of this mud. Get out and don't ever let me see your face around here again!"

Pedro scurried away as fast as he could. He took the money the man had given him for the pigs, and as he left the pig farm, he had one last laugh at the trick he had pulled on the mean pig farmer. And, of course, the pig farmer got his wish. He never did see Pedro's face around his farm again.

Pedro and the Magic Pot

Once, that rascal Pedro de Ordimalas was camping by himself far out in the desert. He had been forced to return to a life of living outdoors because, as usual, he had spent all of his money and could not afford to live in a house. But Pedro was used to living by his wits, and because of his lighthearted spirit, he was able to enjoy his time in the beautiful outdoors. He especially enjoyed the quiet evenings in the desert, when he could look up at the clear starlit night and ponder all of the mysteries of life.

One day, some mule drivers were passing through the area in which Pedro was staying. They were tough men used to the rough life of the trail. They spent the evening with Pedro, forcing him to gamble at card games with them. Of course, the games were rigged, and by evening's end Pedro had lost a good deal of his meager remaining money to the men.

As the mule drivers were bunking down for the evening, Pedro overheard them laughing about how they had cheated Pedro out of his money. Pedro decided right then and there that the men deserved one of his special tricks. He would get all of his money back from them, with a little extra thrown in to make them pay for their cheating ways.

In the morning, Pedro got up before the men and dug a small hole in the dirt. He built a tiny fire inside the hole, making sure that the noise and smoke did not wake the mule drivers. After the fire had produced some strong coals, Pedro put his *frijole* pot on the embers. He then covered up the coals so that it appeared as if the pot was cooking the *frijoles* on bare ground.

Soon the aroma of cooking *frijoles* awoke the mule drivers. They all got up and prepared to eat the delicious-smelling *frijoles*. Of course, their expectation was that Pedro would cook for them and that they would eat Pedro's food instead of their own.

When they went over to where Pedro was cooking, they were amazed to find the pot of *frijoles* cooking on the bare ground, without any fire underneath it. The leader of the mule drivers asked Pedro, "How is that pot cooking the *frijoles*?"

Taking his time as he stirred the *frijoles* so they wouldn't burn in the pot, Pedro answered, "It's a magic pot. It doesn't need fire to cook the *frijoles*. All I have to do is put in the *frijoles*, the water, and the seasonings, and the pot starts cooking the *frijoles*. Couldn't be any easier."

Another mule driver asked, "Where could we get a pot like that?" He continued: "We are on the trail for weeks at a time, and such a magic pot would make cooking our meals a lot easier."

Pedro told the man, "This is the only one in the world. A potter who knew the ways of spells and magic potions made it for me after I saved his life. Unfortunately, another one of his spells blew up on him, and he was killed. There will never be another pot like this one."

The leader talked with the other mule drivers and then made a proposal to Pedro. He said, "Now you know we could easily steal the pot from you...."

Pedro quickly interrupted, "But the pot's magic wouldn't work for you. The potter made sure that it would only work for me."

The leader continued, "Good friend, we would never think of stealing the pot from you, but we are sure you could be persuaded to sell the pot to us." As he said this, he stood up to his full height and placed his hands on his hips in the most threatening manner possible. The other mule drivers did the same thing. They all circled around Pedro to make sure that he understood them.

Pedro stammered, "I see your point, and it's a good one. Of course I could be persuaded to sell the pot to such fine men as you. And I'll make sure that it is working just fine for you before I leave."

The leader asked, "Well, how much do you want for it?"

Pedro thought and thought and finally answered, "Well, it *is* a magic pot—the only one in the world. But I wouldn't need much for it." He then suggested a price that would repay him the money cheated out of him the night before plus a little extra.

The mule drivers thought the price was fair and gave the money to Pedro. They then asked Pedro to show them how to make the pot work. Pedro gave them an elaborate explanation of how it needed to be placed in a certain kind of spot and watched ever so carefully. He then added, "The most important thing is to trick the pot into thinking I am still here, or it won't work. Once it starts cooking, I can sneak away. The first person to spoon some *frijoles* out of the pot after I am gone...well then, the pot will think that person is its new master. But if I'm still around, it will still think I'm its master. We must do this very carefully." As they listened to Pedro, all of the mule drivers nodded their heads in quiet agreement.

So Pedro showed them how to get the pot to start cooking. He then gathered up his things, including the money the mule drivers gave him, and began to creep away. He motioned to the mule drivers to keep quiet and wait until he was completely gone before they did anything at all.

The mule drivers sat quietly by the pot until Pedro was completely out of sight. Then the leader put his spoon into the pot of *frijoles* and announced, "Now you are mine, little pot. Cook these *frijoles*."

Of course, the pot didn't cook anything because, by now, the coals Pedro had hidden under it had gone out. When the mule drivers discovered that Pedro had tricked them by selling them a plain, old *frijole* pot, they were furious and swore to make Pedro pay if they ever ran into him again.

By then, Pedro was miles away, enjoying a good laugh about another of his successful tricks.

Pedro y la olla mágica

Una vez, el malcriado de Pedro de Ordilamas estaba acampando solo en medio del desierto. Había sido forzado a vivir al aire libre porque, como de costumbre, se había gastado todo el dinero y no podía pagar para vivir en una casa. Pero Pedro estaba acostumbrado a vivir con sus artimañas y, por su espíritu aventurero, podía disfrutar de la hermosa vida al aire libre. Especialmente le gustaban las tranquilas tardes en el desierto, cuando podía mirar la noche iluminada de estrellas y reflexionar sobre los misterios de la vida.

Un día, unos arreadores de mulas pasaron por el área en la que Pedro estaba. Eran hombres duros, acostumbrados a la difícil vida del arreo. Pasaron la noche con Pedro y lo obligaron a apostar en juegos de cartas. Por supuesto, los juegos estaban arreglados, y al final de la noche Pedro había perdido con estos hombres el poco dinero que le quedaba.

Mientras los arrieros de mulas se preparaban para la noche, Pedro los escuchó reírse de cómo habían despojado a Pedro de su dinero. Pedro decidió ahí mismo que estos hombres merecía uno de sus trucos especiales. El recuperaría su dinero, y un poco más, para hacerles pagar por haberlo engañado.

Por la mañana, Pedro se levantó antes que los hombres y excavó un pequeño hoyo en la tierra. Encendió un fueguito dentro del hoyo, asegurándose que ni el ruido ni el humo despertasen a los arrieros de mulas. Cuando el fuego produjo buenos carbones encendidos, Pedro puso su olla de frijoles en las brasas. Luego tapó los carbones para que pareciese que la hoya estaba cocinando los frijoles sobre el suelo.

En poco tiempo, el aroma de los frijoles cocinándose despertó a los arrieros de mulas. Todos se levantaron y se dispusieron a comer los aromáticos frijoles. Por supuesto, que Pedro cocinase para ellos, y que comerían la comida de Pedro, y no la propia.

Cuando fueron a ver lo que Pedro estaba cocinando, se sorprendieron al encontrar una olla de frijoles cocinándose sobre el mero suelo, sin fuego debajo. El jefe del grupo de arrieros le preguntó a Pedro: "¿Cómo puede cocinar los frijoles esta olla?".

Tomándose el tiempo, mientras revolvía los frijoles para que no se quemasen en la olla, Pedro contestó: "Es una olla mágica. No necesita fuego para cocinar frijoles. Todo lo que hay que hacer es poner los frijoles, el agua, y los condimentos, y la olla empieza a cocinar los frijoles. No puede ser más sencillo".

"¿Dónde podemos conseguir una olla como ésta", preguntó otro arriero. "Generalmente arriamos durante semanas, y una olla mágica haría nuestras comidas mucho más fáciles", agregó.

Pedro le dijo al hombre: "Esta es la única del mundo. Un alfarero que conocía de hechizo y pociones mágicas me la hizo cuando le salvé la vida. Lamentablemente, otro de sus hechizos recayó en él, y lo mató. Nunca habrá otra olla como ésta".

El jefe habló con los otros arrieros de mulas y le hizo una propuesta Pedro. Le dijo: "Tú sabes que fácilmente podríamos robarte la olla…"

Pedro los interrumpió inmediatamente. "Pero la olla no les funcionará. El alfarero se aseguró de que solamente funcionara para mí".

El jefe agregó: "Buen amigo, nunca pensaríamos en robarte la olla, pero estamos seguros que podemos persuadirte que nos la vendas." Al decir esto, se incorporó y colocó sus manos en la cintura, de la manera más amenazadora posible. Los otros arrieros hicieron lo mismo. Se pusieron en círculo alrededor de Pedro, para asegurarse que Pedro los había entendido.

"Veo lo que quieren decir, y es un buen punto. Por supuesto que podría ser persuadido a venderles la olla a hombres tan finos como ustedes. Y antes de irme me aseguraré que trabajará para ustedes de la misma manera que lo hace para mí", tartamudeó Pedro.

El jefe preguntó: "Bueno, ¿cuánto quieres por la olla?

Pedro pensó y pensó y finalmente respondió. "Bueno, es una olla mágica, la única del mundo. Pero no necesito que me paguen mucho por ella", dijo Pedro, quien sugirió un precio que le devolvería el dinero que le habían despojado la noche anterior, y un poco más.

Los arrieros de mulas decidieron que era un precio justo y le dieron el dinero a Pedro. Le pidieron a Pedro que les mostrase cómo hacía funcionar la olla. Pedro les dio una elaborada explicación de cómo había que ponerla en cierto lugar específico y mirarla muy cuidadosamente. Luego añadió: "Lo más importante es hacerle creer a la olla que yo todavía estoy aquí, o no va a funcionar. Cuando comience a cocinar, podre irme. La primera persona que saque una cucharada de frijoles de la olla después de que me voya… bueno, la olla lo tomará como su nuevo dueño. Pero si yo todavía ando por aquí, pensará que yo sigo siendo el dueño. Debemos hacer esto muy cuidadosamente". Tras escuchar a Pedro, todos los arrieros de mulas, silenciosamente, dijeron que sí con sus cabezas.

Pedro les mostró cómo hacer que la olla empezase a cocinar. Luego reunió sus pertenencias, incluyendo el dinero que le habían dado los arrieros, y comenzó a alejarse. Les hizo gestos a los arrieros para que permaneciesen callados y esperasen hasta que él se hubiese alejado completamente antes de usar la olla.

Los arrieros de mulas se sentaron quietamente junto a la olla hasta que Pedro se perdió de vista. Entonces, el jefe puso su cuchara en los frijoles y anunció: "Ahora eres mía, ollita. Cocina estos frijoles".

Por supuesto, la olla no podía cocinar porque para ese entonces los carbones que Pedro había escondido ya se habían extinguido. Cuando los arrieros descubrieron que Pedro los había engañado al venderles una olla de frijoles vieja y simple, se enfurecieron y juraron que Pedro la pagaría si lo volvían a encontrar.

En ese momento, Pedro ya estaba a millas de distancia, disfrutando de una buena risa por otra de sus exitosas artimañas.

Pedro and the Mule Drivers

Pedro had once tricked some mule drivers into buying a "magic" pot that he convinced the men could cook *frijoles* without a flame under it. The men bought the pot from Pedro, but when the men discovered that the pot was not magic and that Pedro had tricked them, they swore to make him pay the next time they ran into him. Of course, this marked the beginning of another one of Pedro's amazing adventures.

The story begins as most Pedro de Ordimalas stories do—Pedro was struggling to find a way to make some money. He had been unlucky in his own town, so he decided to travel to another town to look for work. While he was walking along a mountain road on the way to the other town, he found a nice spot by a river to camp for the night. As soon as he had set out his bedroll, he remembered a good trick he had played on some mule drivers another time he had been camping. He laughed out loud to himself and wondered what had ever become of the magic pot he had sold to the mule drivers.

No sooner had he set out his bedroll and started a small fire to cook his supper when he heard a pack of mules coming toward his camp. For a moment, he wondered if it was those mule drivers whom he had tricked. He dismissed the thought, because if it were those mule drivers, then he would certainly be having a streak of bad luck. Those mule drivers would probably want Pedro to pay for his trick.

As soon as the mules came within sight of his camp, Pedro knew that his luck had totally run out. They were the same mule drivers! When the mule drivers saw that they had run into Pedro, they knew that their luck had finally taken a turn for the better. Now they would make Pedro pay for his trick.

When the lead mule driver saw Pedro, he yelled out, "Hey, Pedro! I still have your magic *frijole* pot, but it's broken—won't cook at all. What good luck running into you again. Maybe you can fix it."

Pedro tried to answer with some weak excuse. "Oh, the pot. Yeah. Sometimes it doesn't work. You have to be patient—real patient."

By now, the mule drivers were surrounding Pedro. As they made the ring tighter and tighter around him, Pedro knew that his game was over and began to fear for his life. In a shaky voice he asked, "*Señores,* what are you planning to do here? I know the pot might not have worked perfectly for you, but I'm willing to give you your money back." Pedro knew he had no money, but he needed a few moments to think of a plan to escape.

But it was too late. The mule drivers had already had enough of Pedro's fast talk and pounced on him. They roughed him up a little—not too much, but enough to scare Pedro. Then they tied him up in one of their empty water barrels. As they closed the top over him, Pedro asked, "What are you going to do to me?"

Laughing out loud with the other mule drivers, the leader answered, "First we're going to eat supper—your food, of course. Then we're going to get a good night's sleep. In the morning, before we leave, we're going to throw you into the river in this barrel and let you float toward the waterfall. And because you won't be needing your camp supplies anymore, we'll just take them in exchange for the money we gave you."

Pedro protested, "But what if I'm killed in the waterfall?"

The leader laughed even louder and threw the *frijole* pot into the barrel with Pedro. "Well, then you had better hope that your magic pot can save you." Laughing with all of the other mule drivers, the leader told one of his men to secure the barrel top. As soon as he was locked in, Pedro heard the men cooking their supper with his food.

Later that night, when the mule drivers were asleep and the fire had died out, Pedro struggled to escape from the barrel. To his tremendous good fortune, he discovered that the top to the barrel had only been partially secured and that, with a little effort, he could free himself. He chuckled to himself when he realized that his good luck had returned just when he needed it.

Pedro quietly crawled out of the barrel and made sure that the mule drivers were sound asleep. Then he crept around and collected all of the mule drivers' gear and supplies and put them into the barrel. As soon as he had finished, he let the mule drivers' horses loose.

When morning broke and the Sun came over the mountaintop illuminating another day, the mule drivers awoke to the greatest clamor they had every heard. Pedro was banging on the barrel and yelling at the top of his lungs. He pushed the barrel off the wagon toward the direction of the river. The mule drivers watched in astonishment as the barrel crashed into the river and broke into pieces, spilling all of their gear and supplies into the river.

Pedro yelled to the mule drivers, "Say good-bye to all of your supplies! And be careful going after them. There's a waterfall downstream!"

The last thing the mule drivers heard out of Pedro was his laugh as he raced away over the mountaintop. To this day, the mule drivers have sworn revenge on Pedro.

Pedro's luck had returned to him, but only because the mule drivers never again ran into Pedro.

Pedro and the Giant

On one of his many adventures, Pedro had the misfortune to run into a giant. Now, this was no gentle giant, rather it was a mean, bullying giant who enjoyed scaring and beating up little people. The giant, however, was not too smart, and this fact helped to give Pedro one of his greatest adventures ever.

One day, Pedro was walking through the forest when he discovered some very large footprints. In fact, the footprints were so large that no regular man could have made them. As Pedro put his foot into one of the footprints, he realized that a giant must have made them.

Pedro quickly looked around to see if the giant was still there but was relieved to find no sign of him. Now, Pedro had heard stories about giants, but never very good stories, because in all of them, the smaller person either got stepped on, thrown around, or even worse. Pedro had always lived by his wits and escaped from some very bad spots, but he had never had to face a giant. He continued to walk through the forest, being very cautious with every step.

Just when he thought that he had avoided the danger, Pedro heard the unmistakable sounds of a giant walking toward him. The trees shook, the birds flew away, and the skies darkened. Pedro knew that the giant was very close and would be upon him at any minute. Just as he saw the giant come around a bend in the road, Pedro quickly took off his sandals and threw them into the sky as high as he could. Right at that moment, the giant saw Pedro and rushed toward him.

As the giant approached Pedro, he saw that Pedro was intently looking up at the sky. He too looked up and saw two sandals falling out of the sky. The giant jumped aside to avoid being hit by the falling sandals. As he jumped, he tripped, and the forest shook with the force of his fall.

Meanwhile, Pedro yelled out, "And let that be a lesson to you! Don't ever bother me again!" Then he looked at the giant and said, "And the same goes for you."

Now, the giant had never had a little person talk to him in that manner. Usually, they ran away screaming or fell to their knees begging for mercy. The giant didn't know how to react to this new kind of little person. So he asked, "What was that all about?"

Pedro, in his deepest, strongest voice, answered, "Those were the sandals of a man I was fighting. I threw him up in the air three days ago, and this is the last of him to fall to the ground."

The giant immediately respected this little person. First, for speaking up so directly to him. And secondly, for being so strong that he could throw a man into the air with such force that it would take three days for him to return to the ground. The giant, however, had his job to do of scaring little people, so he challenged Pedro. But he did it in a careful manner because he had seen how brave and strong this little person was.

The giant said to Pedro, "If you are so strong, I challenge you to a contest to see who can punch a bigger hole in a tree."

Pedro answered the challenge. With his spirit of adventure getting the best of him, for he thought it might be fun to match wits with a giant, Pedro said, "I accept your challenge. However, I have just fought a man three days ago, and it will take me another day to get my strength back. Meet me here tomorrow, and we shall see who is the strongest."

The giant agreed to the plan then walked away from Pedro, the forest shaking with his every step. Pedro immediately began to put his plan into action. He first found a tree with a thick bark covering. He cut off a large chunk of the bark and carved a huge hole completely through the tree. He then carefully placed the bark back on the tree, covering up the large hole he had made through the tree.

The next day, the giant returned ready to defeat the little person in a contest of strength. In order to intimidate Pedro, the giant went right up to a large tree and punched his fist into it. The giant's arm had almost completely gone through the tree.

Next, it was Pedro's turn. Pedro approached the tree he had secretly prepared for the contest. He took a mighty punch at the tree, carefully aiming his fist at the spot where the hole was covered with bark. Pedro's fist crashed through the tree and came out on the other side.

The giant was surprised that he had lost the contest of strength to the little person, but he was not yet ready to give up. He challenged Pedro to another contest. He told him, "That was the warm-up contest. Tomorrow, we will see who can throw a stone the farthest. That will be a real test of strength." Then the giant angrily stomped off, shaking the forest with his every step.

Pedro thought and thought about a way to win the next contest with the giant. When he saw a bird fly overhead, he knew he had a plan that would win the contest.

The next day, the giant returned and, again, immediately tried to get the best of Pedro. The giant picked up a stone and threw it so far that it landed hundreds of feet away from where they were standing. The giant beamed at his tremendous throw, confident that he had won the contest.

Then it was Pedro's turn. As Pedro reached down to grab a stone, he secretly took out of his pocket a bird that he had captured the night before and held it like a stone. Then he made his own mighty throw into the sky, releasing the bird with it.

The instant Pedro released the bird, it flew up to the sky, disappearing out of sight into the clouds.

For a second time, the giant was amazed at the strength of such a little person. Now he was getting angry that a little person had so easily defeated him. He demanded a final contest. "These first two contests were not real tests of strength. Only one is a true contest—hand-to-hand battle. Meet me here tomorrow for your final day on Earth." Once again, the giant angrily stomped off.

Pedro knew that he could never win a battle of hand-to-hand fighting with a giant. The first two contests had been fun because he had outwitted the giant. (It was easy to outwit such a dim-witted giant.) Now, all he needed to do was to figure out a plan to outsmart the giant one more time. As he thought, he looked down at his feet, and seeing his sandals, he thought of a rather good plan. He spent all night preparing his plan

The third day, the giant returned to meet with Pedro, ready to tear him limb from limb, if necessary, to win the final contest. As he came up to the clearing where he was to meet Pedro, he saw that branches had been torn off the trees and were strewn all about. He then saw that all of the grass had been smashed down and destroyed. Blood was all over the ground. Then he saw Pedro. His clothes were all torn and he had a wild look in his eyes.

The giant asked Pedro, "What happened here? It looks as if there was a terrible battle here. And what happened to you? You look as if you got the worst of a bad fight."

Pedro walked right up to the giant and said, "I look better than the other guy. While I was waiting, a person even bigger than you came by and challenged me to a fight. I decided to fight him as a warm-up to our fight. Do you remember seeing the sandal falling from the sky when we first met?"

The giant nodded and said, "I do remember."

Then Pedro said, "Well, I've also thrown this person up into the sky, and it might take days for him to fall back to Earth, so I might as well fight you while I'm waiting for him to return."

The giant remembered that the little person had thrown a man so high into the sky that it took three days for him to come down. Then he remembered the little person's arm smashing through the tree. Finally, he remembered the stone the little person threw that flew off into the heavens. The giant began to have second thoughts about the fight. He looked around and saw the broken branches, the crushed grass, and the blood and said, "You know, I think it might be better if we don't have a hand-to-hand fight." He then turned around and ran off, shaking all of the trees with his thundering power for one last time.

Pedro laughed and laughed thinking about the dim-witted giant. But, at the same time, he hoped that he would never run into a smart giant.

Pedro and the Hanging Tree

This Pedro de Ordimalas story tells of the time that Pedro went to work for the king. Usually, whenever Pedro ran out of money, he would look for work (but secretly hoping, of course, that he wouldn't find any). He then would devise a trick to play on someone—usually a greedy person who was easily outsmarted—and he would come into enough money that he would end up not having to work at all. But this time, Pedro actually did have to find work—and soon.

Pedro went throughout the kingdom looking for work but was having no luck. He wasn't even able to find a greedy person to trick into giving him some money. Pedro was so desperate that he went to the king's castle to ask for work.

Now, the king was known as quite a clever trickster himself, and he had heard of this Pedro de Ordimalas and his tricks. The king decided that it might be fun to have Pedro work in the castle, so he offered him a job working in the king's kitchen. Pedro's job was to wash the king's banquets' dishes.

Pedro was surprised that he actually got a job, especially working for the king. Washing dishes was not Pedro's idea of a great job, but his good spirits made the job a lot of fun. The other workers enjoyed having Pedro in the castle because he was always playing lighthearted tricks on people and having fun. The king himself enjoyed Pedro's tricks and was glad he decided to give Pedro a job. He was even thinking of making Pedro the court jester, for often after the king's banquets, the people would call for Pedro to come out of the kitchen and play a few tricks on the banquet guests.

Soon the people in the castle began to say that Pedro's tricks were even better than the king's tricks. The king was a very proud man and did not like one of his dishwashers being better than him. Finally, he couldn't stand all of the talk about Pedro and decided to do something about it the next day.

At the king's banquet that night the people called for Pedro to come out and entertain them. They did not stop clamoring for Pedro until he came out of the kitchen, his dishrag on his arm. That night, Pedro was in an especially playful mood. He got carried away with the moment and ended up playing a trick on the king. The trick made the king look foolish, and the banquet room became quiet with fear. The guests knew of the king's unpredictable temper and that the king did not like being made a fool of in public.

Well, the king did lose his temper. In a fit of anger, he yelled, "Hang him at dawn!"

The people of the royal court had grown quite fond of Pedro and were heart-broken that he was to be hanged at dawn. Some of the king's most loyal and longest-serving court members approached him and asked him to reconsider. The king refused to change his mind, because if he did, it might send a message to his subjects that it is all right to make the king look like a fool.

In the morning, as dawn approached, the guards brought Pedro before the royal court. The royal judge asked Pedro if he had any last words. Pedro cleared his throat and said, "I only ask that I be given the right to choose my own hanging tree. I have served the court faithfully and well, and this is all that I ask."

All of the king's court looked to the king for his decision. In truth, the king had wished he hadn't lost his temper so quickly, for he rather liked Pedro and would miss the gaiety he had brought to the castle. But being king, he felt he had an obligation to uphold the royal image. He thought that by giving Pedro this one last request, he might soften the terrible penalty. So the king answered, "Yes, you may choose your own hanging tree."

The guards took Pedro out to the royal forest and let him choose his own hanging tree. Pedro walked and walked through the royal forest looking for the perfect tree. Finally, he spied the tree of his choice. A large sunflower plant that had grown so large that it resembled a tree.

But the sunflower plant's soft and weak trunk bent over from the weight of Pedro's body. In fact, it bent over so far that Pedro's feet returned to the ground, and the guards had to cut him loose.

The royal judge decided that the king's order had been fulfilled. They had hanged Pedro at dawn. The king accepted the decision of the royal judge, who secretly enjoyed the clever trick Pedro had pulled. However, the judge also decided that Pedro could no longer work at the royal castle. He paid Pedro for his work and released him from his job.

Pedro was overjoyed. He was finished washing dishes, had money in his pocket, and had saved his life with his clever thinking. All in all, it was a typical Pedro de Ordimalas adventure!

Pedro Goes to Heaven

The best of all of the Pedro de Ordimalas stories is his last story—the story of his death and his final journey to heaven and how he tricks both St. Peter and the devil.

After many long and happy years on Earth, Pedro finally made the journey into heaven. As he walked up the red carpet leading to the pearly gates of *la gloria*, he reminisced about the good life he had had on Earth. He remembered his many tricks and knew that he had been fortunate to have led a long and good life.

When he arrived at the gates to *la gloria*, his namesake, St. Peter, was waiting for him. St. Peter greeted Pedro by saying, "Pedro, finally you have come to the other side. Even up here in heaven I have to say that we have enjoyed many of your tricks. But I have bad news for you. The Lord says that because of these tricks, you shall not be allowed to live in *la gloria*."

Pedro was saddened to hear such terrible news and he pleaded, "St. Peter, you are my namesake, perhaps you can make a special exception in my case. None of my tricks were really meant to hurt anyone. Most of the time, the people I tricked had it coming to them anyway."

St. Peter listened to Pedro and was moved by his sincerity. He thought about it and finally told Pedro, "I'm going to make an exception in your case, because I know that inside you really do have a good heart. I'm sending you to purgatory, the place where sinners go to do final penance. If you do well there, then maybe we can consider your entry to *la gloria*."

Pedro went to purgatory and tried his best to be good. Pretty soon, however, he was causing trouble. He started to beat the other sinners. St. Peter came down to see what was causing the commotion in purgatory and was not surprised to find Pedro at the center of it all. He asked Pedro, "Pedro, what are you doing? I hear screaming and hollering coming from purgatory."

Pedro answered, "I was just trying to help these sinners pay for their sins faster, so they could get into *la gloria* sooner."

St. Peter said with exasperation, "Pedro, they have to do their own suffering. I'm sorry, but this isn't working out. You have to go to another place." He checked his heavenly manual and came up with another plan. He then told Pedro, "Pedro, you have to go to limbo. It's the place for unbaptized babies who can't get into *la gloria*. I know it's not quite the right place for you, but it'll have to do until I can think of something better."

So Pedro went to limbo. Pretty soon, another big commotion broke out in limbo. St. Peter came down to limbo and, again, was not surprised to see Pedro in the middle of it all. Pedro was dunking all of the babies in a river, making them cry and scream.

St. Peter got angry with Pedro and asked him, "Pedro, what are you doing this time? Can't you ever stay out of trouble?"

Pedro answered, "St. Peter, I was baptizing these babies so they could get into *la gloria*. I know how it feels not to be able to get into *la gloria*, and I was only trying to help."

St. Peter, now with a weariness in his voice, said, "Pedro, you're not a priest. You can't baptize these babies. Pedro, I'm sorry. I was hoping it wouldn't come to this, but only one place is left for you, the land of *el diablo*."

With the greatest sorrow in his heart, Pedro went down to the land of *el diablo*. As soon as the gates had closed, a little *diablo* came to Pedro and told him to move a pile of rocks. Pedro asked the *diablo*, "That's a small pile of rocks. What should I do when I'm finished?"

The *diablo* looked at Pedro and laughed and laughed. He then said, "You don't understand. You're to move that pile of rocks for all eternity!"

Several days later, in the land of *el diablo*, a great commotion erupted. This time, *el diablo* himself came to see what was happening. Of course, at the center of the commotion was Pedro. All of the devils were spinning around, pulling at their horns and biting their tails. When *el diablo* asked Pedro what was happening, Pedro said, "I was just saying my prayers before my meal and suddenly all of the *diablos* went crazy."

El diablo then hollered, "You can't pray here! It's not allowed! I know this has never happened before, but Pedro, you can't stay down here. You just cause too much trouble. Go back to St. Peter and see if he can figure something out."

So now Pedro was kicked out of the land of *el diablo* too. He took the long walk back up to St. Peter and told him what had happened. Pedro was greatly saddened because now he truly had no place to go.

St. Peter thought about Pedro's terrible predicament and went into *la gloria* for a conference to decide what to do. When he came out, he told Pedro, "Well, here's the plan. Everywhere you go you cause a commotion. So from now on, you will stay out here with me where I can keep an eye on you. We're going to make you a rock so you don't cause any trouble. But in order for you to see what is going on, you won't be just any rock, you'll be a *piedra con ojos*, a rock with eyes.

At last, Pedro's long journey had come to an end. He had finally found a peaceful place to spend eternity—outside the pearly gates to *la gloria*, at St. Peter's side. This is where Pedro watches everything that comes and goes, as a rock—and not just any rock, but a *piedra con ojos*, a rock with eyes.

The Wonderful Chirrionera

This story is based upon a legend of a snake that bites its own tail and becomes a round wheel rolling along the ground. The snake rolls along chasing people until it catches them. When it does, the snake unwraps itself and bites the victim.

Once there was a wealthy orchard owner named *Señor* Mariano. *Señor* Mariano had the largest orchards, the healthiest trees, and the richest soil in the valley. He grew the sweetest and best tasting fruit of any grower in the valley. At all of the state fairs, his peaches, apples, plums, and mangoes were always the blue ribbon winners. *Señor* Mariano took special pride in his orchards and spent many hours pruning his trees and making sure that the soil and water were just right for his bountiful trees.

Señor Mariano was also the meanest and stingiest man in the valley. Even though his trees produced more fruit than he could ever use or sell, he never gave any away and always made people pay for even the tiniest taste of his fruit. As he worked in the orchards, he kept a close eye on his gate so that he could catch any kids sneaking into his orchard trying to steal his fruit. And at the end of the day's work, he would sit on his porch slowly eating slices of fruit covered with sweet cream. He would make a big production of how delicious the fruit was and how much he was enjoying eating it. It was as if he were trying to purposely torment the people of the valley, especially the kids.

Three brothers, Juan, José, and Pablo, were especially tempted by *Señor* Mariano's fruit. Their mother had died several years before, and they were being raised by their father, Carlos. Their family was poor, and the boys often had to exist on nothing but *frijoles* and *tortillas*.

Carlos tried to raise his boys as best as he could, but he had to work in the fields all day long, leaving the boys alone for too many hours. As with many kids who spend too much time on their own and who eventually do something to get themselves into trouble, the three brothers were no different.

Juan, José, and Pablo would often walk past *Señor* Mariano's orchards and look hungrily at the ripe fruit on the branches. Their meager diet made them long for a meal of *Señor* Mariano's fruit.

Often on the way home from school, the brothers would stop in front of *Señor* Mariano's orchards. They would search the ground hoping to find a stray apple or mango that had fallen outside of the orchard wall or had tumbled off the fruit wagon as it went to market.

Sometimes, the boys would actually find some fruit on the ground, and they would sit under a tree to eat it, savoring every bite. When *Señor* Mariano would see them eating his fruit he would grab his whip and chase them away yelling, "You thieves! You scoundrels! Stealing the fruit of my hard work! You'll pay for this!" Of course he never caught them, because he was too old and slow, and they had the swiftness of youth in their feet.

One day, the brothers had decided that it was time to teach old, mean *Señor* Mariano a lesson. They went into the forest and chopped down some thin trees. They then trimmed the branches off the trees and, by lashing two long tree poles together with some steps made from the branches, they made a makeshift ladder. They carried the ladder to *Señor* Mariano's orchard and used it to climb over the high *adobe* wall he had built that surrounded his land.

Once on the other side of the wall and inside *Señor* Mariano's orchard, they climbed the fruit trees and started filling their bags with the best looking and largest fruit they had ever imagined. Their bags sagged under the weight of so much fruit. The boys continued to fill their bags until they decided the bags had almost gotten too heavy to carry back over the fence.

Just as the boys were ready to escape with the ill-gotten fruit, *Señor* Mariano came out of his house waving his whip in his hand and shouting, "You good-for-nothing thieves! Now I'll catch you for sure, and jail is the only place you'll be going!" *Señor* Mariano tried to catch the boys, but they abandoned their bags and fled over the wall, scampering down the dusty road back home.

Later that night, the boys were at home laughing about the sight of *Señor* Mariano chasing them with his whip. Soon after their father had come home from his day's work, they heard a knocking on their door. When Carlos opened the door, there stood *Señor* Mariano, whip in hand.

Before Carlos could even welcome *Señor* Mariano into his home, the orchard owner launched into an angry tirade. He scolded Carlos: "Your boys are nothing but common thieves. When your wife—may her soul rest in *la gloria*—was alive, she was able to keep an eye on your boys. But now that she is gone, they run loose all day long! Well, now I have caught them stealing from my orchards, and I have come to see what you are going to do about it."

Carlos looked at his boys, who were hanging their heads in shame, and told *Señor* Mariano, "I'm sorry for my boys' behavior, *Señor* Mariano. They are good boys who were raised in the church, and they will be punished for their actions.

But I do not appreciate you calling them common thieves. If you weren't so mean and stingy…" Carlos took a deep breath and decided that it was best not to continue what he was about to say. He finished by telling *Señor* Mariano, "I am gone all day trying to make a living and provide for my boys. Here is the deal I can make with you: If you see my boys stealing from you again, you have my permission to punish them on the spot with a whipping. And you may start now in punishment for today's stealing."

The three boys lined up to take their punishment. *Señor* Mariano grabbed his whip and let Juan have as mighty a blow as he could deliver across the boy's rear end. *Señor* Mariano had not realized how much the years had stolen from his strength. He was so old and feeble that the blow didn't even make Juan wince. In fact, instead of harming Juan, the blow had hurt *Señor* Mariano's arm!

Juan immediately realized that *Señor* Mariano could not harm him, so he winked at his brothers and let out a loud howl as if he were being torn limb from limb. When José and Pablo took their blows, they howled even louder. They cried in pain so convincingly that *Señor* Mariano left feeling better about the whole episode, even though his arm was killing him with pain from delivering the whippings.

Carlos warned his boys that every time they were caught stealing *Señor* Mariano's fruit, they were to receive a whipping from *Señor* Mariano. Needless to say, the whipping only convinced the boys that they had nothing to fear from stealing *Señor* Mariano's fruit. Almost every day, they would climb over the high *adobe* wall and take enough fruit for the evening meal. And every day, they would line up for *Señor* Mariano, who would administer their punishment. Afterward, they would run home laughing, while *Señor* Mariano's arm only ached worse and worse with each whipping.

Soon, *Señor* Mariano began to realize that the whippings were only hurting him and that the boys were having a grand time at the expense of his fruit and arm. He became depressed because he realized that he was no longer a young man and that, in truth, he could not protect his own orchards. He feared the day the other boys of the valley discovered what Juan, José, and Pablo had discovered—how easy it was to steal his fruit.

One morning, *Señor* Mariano was working in his orchard when he saw an amazing sight. Coming down his dusty road was a wagon being pulled by two immense oxen. The wagon driver was lying down in the bed of the wagon, appearing as if he were asleep. A whip, or something that looked like a whip, was cracking over the heads of the oxen and keeping them trudging along the road. As the wagon came closer to *Señor* Mariano, he could clearly see that no one was making the whip work the oxen. The "whip" was doing it by itself!

Señor Mariano called the wagon driver over and quizzed him, "How does your whip work? I have never seen anything like it in my whole life."

The wagon driver pulled over and stopped the wagon. He laughed loudly and told *Señor* Mariano, "This isn't a whip. This is the wonderful *chirrionera!*"

Señor Mariano was puzzled. He thought he knew everything about his valley, but he had never heard of the wonderful *chirrionera*. He asked the wagon driver, "What is a *chirrionera*, and what does it do?"

Again the wagon driver laughed heartily and said, "Never heard of the wonderful *chirrionera*?! Why the *chirrionera* is the most useful creature on Earth. It is a snake that stands on its head and whips its tail in the air, striking whatever it targets. It can be trained to do a job and can never tire of it. This one I've trained to drive my oxen while I rest in the back of the wagon."

Suddenly, *Señor* Mariano began to have a vision. As he thought about the wonderful *chirrionera*, he came up with an idea of how to teach Juan, José, and Pablo a lesson they would never forget. He asked the wagon driver, "Where could I get one of these *chirrioneras*?"

The wagon driver answered, "It's easy, if you know where to look. Next time you see a heavy rain in the mountains, hurry to them and search for the *chirrioneras*. They are hard to find, but you will know you are near them when you hear a sound that reminds you of guns shooting. Do not be afraid, though. It is only the sound of the *chirrioneras* snapping themselves dry after the rains. If you are quick, you can catch one before it dries off when it is still too wet to move quickly."

Señor Mariano thanked the wagon driver and waited for the day he would see a heavy rain in the mountains. Fortunately, he did not have long to wait. A few days later, he looked out to the mountains and saw that a heavy thundershower had settled over a high spot in the mountain ridge. *Señor* Mariano quickly saddled his horse and rode off to the mountaintop. As he approached the mountaintop, he heard the sounds of gunfire, just as the wagon driver had said. He got off his horse and carefully walked in the direction of the sound. As he came around a large boulder, he discovered the *chirrioneras*. Several were standing on their heads snapping their tails in the air. With each snap, the air cracked with a large pop that sounded exactly like a gunshot.

Señor Mariano spied one *chirrionera* that had not yet shaken off the heavy rainwater covering it. Moving quickly, *Señor* Mariano trapped the *chirrionera* with a snake-catching pole and put it in a bag.

When he returned home, *Señor* Mariano began to train the *chirrionera*. He washed and fed it, so the *chirrionera* would know that *Señor* Mariano was its master. The *chirrionera* ate the ripest and sweetest fruit every morning for breakfast and, most importantly, was taught to chase and hit a moving target. The *chirrionera* would bite its tail and roll along the ground like a wheel, suddenly stopping to stand on its head and lash out at its target with its snapping tail.

Señor Mariano called his *chirrionera* "Angelito," little angel. In the evening, he would sing a lullaby to Angelito and prepare the morning bowl of fruit for it.

One day, *Señor* Mariano saw Juan, José, and Pablo vault over his wall, and he knew it was finally the time for his revenge on the three brothers. As the brothers scampered up his trees to steal his fruit, *Señor* Mariano led Angelito out of its cage and unleashed it in the direction of the boys. As the *chirrionera* rolled along the ground toward the brothers, *Señor* Mariano yelled out, "Get them! Get them!"

The three brothers never knew what hit them. One minute they were pulling the ripe fruit off the tree limbs, and the next they were on the ground being stung with the most piercing blows and surrounded by what sounded like gunshots. They yelped and cried in pain, running around the orchard with the *chirrionera* chasing and pelting them with its snapping tail. When they finally escaped the orchard, they could barely crawl to their home they were so racked with pain. The last sounds they heard were the laughing and yelling of *Señor* Mariano, "How did you like that whipping, boys?! Come and steal my fruit again, and my Angelito will make you wish you were not even alive! Ha! Ha! Ha!"

The next night, the brothers carefully crept over to *Señor* Mariano's orchard to see what had whipped them so severely. As they peered over the wall, they saw *Señor* Mariano singing a sweet lullaby to the *chirrionera*. After the *chirrionera* had fallen asleep, they saw *Señor* Mariano lovingly cut up some ripe fruit into a bowl and place it by the *chirrionera* for its morning meal.

The brothers knew that something must be done about that snake, or else their days of eating *Señor* Mariano's tasty fruit would be over forever. They stayed up all night devising various plans until they settled on one that seemed foolproof.

Just before dawn, the three quietly entered *Señor* Mariano's yard and crept over to the place where the *chirrionera* was sleeping. They took the bowl of fruit and placed in each slice one of the hottest *chiles* grown in the valley, the fierce *habanero*. These *chiles* were so hot that they made grown men sweat and weep while eating them. In fact, people called them *diablitos*, little devils. After they had filled the fruit with the *diablitos*, the brothers hid behind some trees and waited to see if their plan would work.

When the Sun finally rose over the mountain ridge and filled the valley with its warming rays, the *chirrionera* awoke and began to eat the morning bowl of fresh fruit that it had come to expect from *Señor* Mariano. It was so hungry from the previous day's work of chasing Juan, José, and Pablo around the orchard that it gulped down all of the fruit as fast as it could.

At first, the brothers thought nothing was happening and that their plan was a failure. Then they saw the *chirrionera* suddenly bolt into the air, then fall and writhe on the ground as if it were on fire. It dashed one direction and then in another, snapping its tail in the air and filling the orchard with the sound of rapid gunshots. But the brothers were not yet rejoicing because this was only the first part of their plan.

When *Señor* Mariano heard the gunshots, he leapt out of bed and ran out of the house still in his pajamas. When he saw the *chirrionera*, he did not know what to think. The poor animal seemed to be in great pain and distress and was frantically trying to find some relief. The *chirrionera* finally found the horses' watering trough and jumped into it, gulping water as fast as it could.

When the *chirrionera* came out of the watering trough, it bit its tail and formed a circle like a wheel. It began to chase *Señor* Mariano around the orchard, and every time it caught him, it stood on its head and whipped him with its tail. The brothers howled in laughter at the sight of the *chirrionera* chasing *Señor* Mariano around the orchard in his pajamas and whipping him. Now they knew that their plan had worked. The *chirrionera* thought that *Señor* Mariano had put the hot chiles in the fruit slices, and it was now paying him back for that evil joke.

Eventually, the *chirrionera* tired of chasing *Señor* Mariano and decided life among humans was too troublesome. The last sight of the wonderful *chirrionera* was of it rolling like a wheel back to its mountain home.

From that day on, everyone had learned their lesson and tried to make life better in the valley. Juan, José, and Pablo sincerely apologized to *Señor* Mariano and gave up their thieving ways. They even went to work for *Señor* Mariano, helping him with his orchards.

In his own way, *Señor* Mariano also changed for the better. He would often put baskets of his extra fruit out by his *adobe* wall for the people of the valley to take home for their families. Every day, he would greet Juan, José, and Pablo with a bowl of fresh-cut fruit covered with sweet cream as they arrived for work. The brothers always enjoyed the bowl of delicious fruit. But they never stopped checking the slices for hidden chiles.

La maravillosa Chirrionera

Esta historia se basa en la leyenda de una serpiente que muerde su propia cola y se transforma en una gira que rueda sobre el suelo. La serpiente va así en busca de personas, hasta que las atrapa. Cuando lo hace, la serpiente se desenrosca y muerde a su víctima.

Había una vez un rico dueño de una plantación llamado Señor Mariano. El Señor Mariano tenía la plantación más grande, los árboles más sanos y el suelo más rico del valle. El producía la fruta más dulce y con mejor sabor que los otros plantadores del valle. En todas las ferias del estado, sus duraznos, manzanas, ciruelas y mangos siempre eran los ganadores del primer premio. El Señor Mariano se enorgullecía, especialmente, de sus jardines, y pasaba largas horas podando los árboles y asegurándose que el suelo y el agua fueran los justos para sus fructíferos árboles.

El Señor Mariano era también el hombre más malo y tacaño del valle. Aunque sus árboles producían más fruta de la que podía usar o vender, nunca la regalaba y siempre hacía que la gente pagase hasta por la fruta más pequeña. Mientras trabajaba en su plantación, vigilaba la tranquera para ver si algunos niños se metían en la plantación tratando de robarse frutas. Al final del día, se sentaba en el pórtico de su casa, comiendo lentamente tajadas de fruta cubiertas con crema dulce. Luego hacía ostentación de cuán deliciosas eran sus frutas y cuánto le gustaban comerlas. Era como si a propósito estuviese tratando de atormentar a la gente del valle, especialmente a los niños.

Tres hermanos, Juan, José y Pablo, eran especialmente tentados por la fruta del Señor Mariano. Su madre había muerto hacía algunos años, y ellos fueron criados por su padre, Carlos. La familia era muy pobre, y los muchachos a veces subsistían solamente con frijoles y tortillas.

Carlos trató de criar a los muchachos lo mejor que pudo, pero tenía que trabajar en el campo todo el día, dejando a los muchachos solos durante muchas horas. Como sucede con muchos niños que pasan mucho tiempo solos, y que eventualmente hacen algo que los mete en problemas, los tres hermanos no eran diferentes.

Juan, José, y Pablo a menudo iban a la plantación del Señor Mariano y miraban con hambre los racimos de frutas en las ramas. Su mísera dieta los hacía desear comerse la fruta del Señor Mariano.

A menudo, al regresar a la casa, después de la escuela, los hermanos se paraban frente a la plantación del Señor Mariano. Revisaban el suelo, con la esperanza de encontrar una manzana o un mango caídos fuera de las paredes de la plantación, o caídos del carro de frutas de camino al mercado.

A veces los hermanos encontraban algo de fruta en el suelo, y se sentaban bajo un árbol a comerla, saboreando cada bocado. Cuando el Señor Mariano los veía comer su fruta, tomada su látigo y los corría, gritando: "¡Ustedes, ladrones! ¡Ustedes, sinvergüenzas! ¡Robándose la fruta que me costó duro trabajo! ¡Pagarán por esto!" Por supuesto, nunca los atrapó, porque él era demasiado viejo y demasiado lento, y ellos tenían la velocidad de la juventud en sus pies.

Un día, los hermanos decidieron que era el momento de enseñarle al viejo y malo Señor Mariano una lección. Fueron al bosque y cortaron algunos árboles delgados. Luego cortaron las ramas de los árboles y se hicieron una improvisada escalera. Se llevaron la escalera hasta la plantación del Señor Mariano y la usaron para escalar la alta pared de adobe que él había construído, rodeando su propiedad.

Una vez del otro lado de la pared, y dentro de la propiedad del Señor Mariano, subieron a los árboles frutales y comenzaron a llenar sus bolsas con las mejores y más grandes frutas que jamás había imaginado. Los muchachos continuaron llenando sus bolsas hasta que decidieron que ya estaban casi muy pesadas como para pasarlas sobre la cerca.

Justo cuando los muchachos estaban listos para escaparse con su fruta mal habida, el Señor Mariano salió de su casa, amenazando con el látigo en sus manos, y gritando: "¡Ustedes, ladrones buenos para nada! ¡Ahora sí los voy a atrapar, y el único lugar donde van a ir es a la cárcel!" El Señor Mariano trató de atrapar a los muchachos, pero ellos abandonaron sus bolsas y huyeron saltando la pared, desapareciendo en el polvoriento camino de regreso a la casa.

Más tarde, esa misma noche, los muchachos estaban en su casa riéndose del recuerdo del Señor Mariano persiguiéndolos con un látigo. Poco después de que el padre había vuelto de su día de trabajo, alguien golpeó a la puerta. Cuando Carlos abrió la puerta, allí estaba el Señor Mariano, con el látigo en la mano.

Antes que Carlos pudiese siquiera darle la bienvenida al Señor Mariano, el dueño de la plantación lanzó un enojado discurso. Regañó a Carlos: "Sus muchachos no son nada más que ladronzuelos. Cuando su esposa, que su alma descanse en la gloria, estaba viva, ella podía vigilar a los muchachos. Pero ahora que ella se ha ido, ¡hacen lo que quieren todo el día! Bueno, ahora los atrapé robando en mi propiedad, y he venido a ver qué va a hacer usted".

Carlos miró a sus hijos, que estaban cabizbajos de vergüenza, y le dijo al Señor Mariano: "Lamento la conducta de mis hijos, Señor Mariano. Son buenos muchachos que se criaron en la iglesia, y serán castigados por sus acciones. No me gusta que los llame ladronzuelos. Si usted no fuese tan malo y tacaño…" Carlos aspiró profundamente y decidió que era mejor no continuar con lo que estaba apunto de decir. Concluyó diciéndole al Señor Mariano: "Yo voy a trabajer todo el día tratando de ganarme la vida y de proveer para mis muchachos. Este es el trato que le ofrezco. Si usted ve a mis hijos robando otra vez, tiene mi permiso de darles latigazos en ese mismo momento. Y puede empezar ahora mismo como castigo por el robo de hoy".

Los tres muchachos se alinearon para recibir el castigo. El Señor Mariano tomó su látigo y le dio a Juan un latigazo tan fuerte como pudo, en el trasero del muchacho. El Señor Mariano no se había dado cuenta cuánta fuerza le habían robado los años. Era tan viejo y tan débil que el latigazo ni siquiera estremeció a Juan. De hecho, en vez de hacer que le doliese a Juan, ¡el golpe hizo que le doliese el brazo al Señor Mariano!

Juan, inmediatamente comprendió que el Señor Mariano no podía lastimarlo, así que guiñó a sus hermanos y dejó escapar un fuerte aullido, como si le estuviesen cortando un brazo o una pierna. Cuando José y Pablo recibieron sus latigazos, gritaron aún más fuerte. Lloraron de dolor, con tanta convicción, que el Señor Mariano se fue sintiéndose mejor con lo ocurrido, aunque sus brazos lo estaban matando de dolor por haber dado los latigazos.

Carlos les dijo a los muchachos que cada vez que se los pillase robando la fruta del Señor Mariano, tendrían que recibir los latigazos del Señor Mariano. Por supuesto, los latigazos solamente convencieron a los muchachos de que nada tenían que temer al robar la fruta del Señor Mariano. Casi cada día trepaban la alta pared de adobe y tomaban fruta para la cena. Y cada día, se alineaban frente al Señor Mariano, quien administraba el castigo. Luego corrían hasta la casa riéndose, mientras el brazo del Señor Mariano le dolía cada vez más con cada latigazo.

En poco tiempo el Señor Mariano comenzó a darse cuenta de que los latigazos solamente lo perjudicaban a él y que los muchachos la estaban pasando de maravillas gracias a la fruta y al brazo del Señor Mariano. El Señor Mariano se deprimió porque comprendió que ya no era un hombre joven y que, en verdad, ya no podía proteger su plantación. Le dio miedo que un día los otros jóvenes del valle descubrieran lo que Juan, José y Pablo ya habían descibierto, cuán fácil era robar la fruta.

Una mañana, el Señor Mariano estaba trabajando en su plantación cuando vio algo asombroso. Por el camino polvoriento venia un carro tirado por dos bueyes inmensos. El conductor del carro estaba acostado en la cama del carro, como si estuviese dormido. Un látigo, o algo parecido a un látigo, resonaba sobre las cabezas de los bueyes, manteniéndolos a paso lento por el camino. Cuando el carro llegó más cerca del Señor Mariano, él pudo ver que nadie hacía resonar el látigo sobre los bueyes. ¡El "látigo" lo hacía por sí mismo!

El Señor Mariano llamó al conductor del carro y le preguntó: "¿Cómo funciona este látigo? Nunca he visto nada semejante en toda mi vida".

El conductor se incorporó y detuvo el carro. Se rió con ganas y le dijo al Señor Mariano: "Este no es un látigo. ¡Es una maravillosa chirrionera!"

El Señor Mariano estaba confundido. Pensó que conocía todo lo del valle, pero nunca había escuchado de la maravillosa chirrionera. Le preguntó al conductor: "¿Qué es una chirrionera, y para qué sirve?"

Una vez más el conductor se rió con ganas y dijo: "¿Nunca oyó de la maravillosa chirrionera? Caramba, la chirrionera es la criatura más útil de la tierra. Es una serpiente que se para de cabeza y usa su cola como látigo, golpeando todo lo que quiera golpear. Se le puede entrenar para que haga algún trabajo, y nunca se cansa. A ésta la entrené para que conduzca a mis bueyes, mientras yo descanso en la parte de atrás del carro".

De pronto, el Señor Mariano comenzó a tener una visión. Al pensar en la maravillosa chirrionera, pensó también cómo enseñarles a Juan, José y Pablo una lección que nunca olvidarían. Le preguntó al conductor del carro: "¿Dónde puedo conseguir una de estas chirrioneras?"

El conductor respondió: "Es fácil, si sabe dónde buscarlas. La próxima vez que vea una fuerte lluvia en las montañas, váyase hasta allá rápidamente y busque las chirrioneras. Son difíciles de encontrar, pero usted va a saber que está cerca de una cuando escuche sonidos que le recuerden a los disparos de armas de fuego. Pero no se asuste. Se trata solamente de las chirrioneras que se están secando después de la lluvia. Si usted se apura, puede atrapar alguna antes que se seque del todo y mientras está demasiado mojada como para moverse con rapidez".

El Señor Mariano agradeció al conductor del carro y esperó por el día en que viese una fuerte lluvia en las montañas. Afortunadamente, no tuvo que esperar mucho. Unos pocos días después, miró hacia las montañas y vio que una fuerte tormenta azotaba un cierto lugar, en las alturas de la montañas. Rápidamente el Señor Mariano puso la montura en su caballo y se fue galopando hasta la cima de la montaña. Al acercarse a la cima, comenzó a escuchar los sonidos, como de disparos, como le había dicho el conductor del carro. Se bajó del caballo y cuidadosamente fue caminando en la dirección del sonido. Detrás de una gran roca descubrió las chirrioneras. Algunas estaban de cabeza, haciendo resonar sus colas en el aire. Con cada coletazo, el aire resonaba con un "trás", sonando exactamente como un balazo.

El Señor Mariano detectó una chirrionera que todavía no se había sacudido el agua de lluvia que la cubría. Moviéndose rápidamente, el Señor Mariano atrapó a la chirrrionera con un palo para atrapar serpientes y la puso en una bolsa.

De regreso en el hogar, el Señor Mariano comenzó a entrenar a la chirrionera. La lavó y la alimentó, de modo que la chirrionera reconoció al Señor Mariano como su amo. La chirrionera comía cada mañana, en el desayuno, las mejores y más dulces frutas y, aún más importante, le enseñó a perseguir y golpear un objeto en movimiento. La chirrionera se mordía la cola, y rodaba sobre el suelo como una rueda, deteniéndose súbitamente para pararse de cabeza y golpear con su cola su objetivo.

El Señor Mariano le dio el nombre de "Angelito" a su chirrionera. Por las tardes, le cantaba una canción de cuna a Angelito y le preparaba un tazón de frutas para la mañana.

Un día, el Señor Mariano vio a Juan, José y Pablo saltar sobre la pared, y supo que era, finalmente, el momento de vengarse de los tres hermanos. Cuando los hermanos se subieron a los árboles para robarse la fruta, el Señor Mariano sacó a Angelito de su jaula y la dejó libre, en dirección de los muchachos. Mientras la chirrionera rodaba en el suelo hacia los muchachos, el Señor Mariano gritaba: "¡Atrápalos, atrápalos!"

Los tres hermanos no supieron qué los atacó. Un momento estaban sacando la fruta madura de las ramas de los árboles, y un momento después estaban en el suelo, siendo pinchados con golpes penetrantes, y rodeados por ruidos que sonaban como balazos. Gritaban y lloraban de dolor, corriendo alrededor de la plantación con la chirrionera en persecusión, golpeándolos con su cola. Cuando finalmente se escaparon de la plantación, casi no podían ni arrastrarse hasta la casa, pues tanto era su dolor. Lo último que escucharon fue la risa y los gritos del Señor Mariano: "¿Les gustó mi látigo muchachos? Vengan a robar mi fruta otra vez, y mi Angelito les hará desear no estar vivos! ¡Ja, ja ja!"

A la noche siguiente, los muchachos cuidadosamente treparon la cerca de la plantación del Señor Mariano para ver qué los había golpeado tan severamente. Cuando espiaron desde lo alto de la pared, vieron al Señor Mariano cantarle una dulce canción de cuna a la chirrionera. Cuando la chirrionera se durmió, vieron al Señor Mariano cortar cariñosamente fruta madura y colocarla en un tazón cerca de la chirrionera, para el desayuno de ésta.

Los hermanos sabían que algo deberían hacer con respecto a la serpiente, o, de lo contrario, se les habrían terminado por siempre los días de comer la deliciosa fruta del Señor Mariano. Se quedaron despiertos toda la noche, pensando en distintos planes, hasta que se pusieron de acuerdo en uno que parecía imposible de fallar.

Justo antes del amanecer, los tres entraron silenciosamente en el patio del Señor Mariano y se fueron arrastrando hasta llegar al lugar donde dormía la chirrionera. Tomaron el tazón de la fruta y colocaron pedazos de uno de los chiles más picantes del valle, el feroz habanero. Estos chiles eran tan picantes que hacía sudar y llorar a los hombres adultos que los comían. De hecho, la gente los llamaba diablitos. Tras llenar el tazón de fruta con diablitos, los hermanos se escondieron detrás de unos árboles para ver si el plan funcionaba.

Cuando finalmente salió el sol sobre las montañas y llenó el valle con sus cálidos rayos, la chirrionera se despertó y comenzó a comer del tazón de fruta fresca, que ahora siempre esperaba del Señor Mariano. Tenía tanta hambre, por el esfuerzo del día anterior de perseguir a Juan, José y Pablo en la plantación, que devoró la fruta tan rápido como pudo.

Al principio, los hermanos pensaron que no estaba pasando nada y que su plan había fracasado. Pero entonces vieron a la chirrionera saltar repentinamente por el aire, luego caer y retorcerse en el piso como si estuviese ardiendo. Corría en una dirección y luego en otra, chasqueando su cola en el aire y llenando la plantación con los sonidos de disparos rápidos. Pero los hermanos todavía no se alegraban, porque ésta era solamente la primera parte del plan.

Cuando el Señor Mariano escuchó los balazos, saltó de la cama y corrió fuera de la casa, todavía en pijamas. Cuando vio a la chirrionera, no supo qué pensar. El pobre animal parecía tener un gran dolor y molestia, y estaba, desesperadamente, buscando alguna forma de alivio. La chirrionera encontró finalmente el bebedero de los caballos y allí saltó, tomando agua tan rápido como podia.

Cuando la chirrionera salió del bebedero, se mordió la cola y formó un círculo como una rueda. Comenzó a perseguir al Señor Mariano alrededor de la plantación. Cada vez que lo alcanzaba, se paraba de cabeza y lo golpeaba con la cola. Los hermanos aullaban de risa al ver a la chirrionera perseguir al Señor Mariano correr en sus pijamas, por toda la plantación, golpeándolo. Ahora sabían que el plan había funcionado. La chirrionera pensó que el Señor Mariano había puesto los chiles picantes entre las tajadas de frutas, y ahora le había hecho pagar por su chiste diabólico.

Eventualmente la chirrionera se cansó de perseguir al Señor Mariano y decidió que la vida entre los humanos era mucho problema. Lo último que se vio de la maravillosa chirrionera fue cuando se hizo una rueda y se fue rodando a su hogar en las montañas.

Desde ese día, todos aprendieron la lección y trataron de mejorar la vida en el valle. Juan, José y Pablo se disculparon sinceramente con el Señor Mariano y dejaron de robar. Incluso fueron a trabajar con el Señor Mariano, ayudándolo en la plantación.

En su propia manera, el Señor Mariano también cambió positivamente. A menudo ponía canastas con frutas fuera de su pared de adobe, para que la gente del valle las llevase a sus familias. Cada día esperaba a Juan, José y Pablo con un tazón de fruta fresca cubierta con crema dulce, cuando llegaban para trabajar. A los hermanos les gustaban los tazones de deliciosa fruta. Pero nunca dejaron de buscar por chiles escondidos.

The Waterfall of Wisdom

High atop a towering and majestic mountain were two waterfalls. Both waterfalls flowed with deep red liquids, which gushed down to form swirling pools of ruby waters. The colors of the waterfalls were so similar that both waterfalls appeared to flow with the same liquid. But, in fact, one of the waterfalls flowed with red wine, while the other flowed with blood.

One could easily mistake one waterfall for the other, and such a mistake could have the most tragic and eternal consequences. This is because the two waterfalls were enchanted. One of the waterfalls, the waterfall of wine, gave the gift of wisdom to whoever bathed in its waters. People of the land made pilgrimages to bathe in the waters of wisdom, hoping to bring the blessed peace of wisdom to their lives. The other, the waterfall of blood, turned whoever bathed in its waters to stone. The bottom of this waterfall was encircled by caves made from the stone statues of all those who had mistaken the waters of stone for the waters of wisdom.

In this land lived a king who had a daughter whom he loved very much. She was his only daughter, and because of this, he spoiled her and gave in to all of her whims and desires. Their life was one of courtly pleasures, and the king was proud of the beautiful woman who his daughter had become.

The king desired to be a wise and just ruler. He had heard of the enchanted waterfalls and wanted to bathe in the waters of wisdom. He had also heard of the dangers of the waters of stone and knew that he would have to be careful, or else suffer the eternal cruel fate of all those who mistakenly bathed in these waters.

The king consulted with his advisors and told them, "We must travel to the outer reaches of my kingdom. There we will find two enchanted waterfalls. I desire to bathe in the waterfall of wisdom. I will use the wisdom I receive from the enchanted waters to bring peace and prosperity to my subjects."

The king's wizard cautioned him: "You must be careful that you do not bathe in the waterfall of stone. No one is immune—not even a king—to its tragic curse. The waterfall is ringed by the stone statues of both the rich and the poor who have made that fatal mistake in their search for wisdom."

The king assured his wizard, "Let us begin this journey. We will use the knowledge we have of the waterfall of stone's dangers to make the correct choice. Perhaps with the wisdom we gain we can end the curse of the waterfall of stone for all time."

After the king departed on his quest for wisdom, the princess was alone in her garden when she overheard the servants' conversations about the king's journey. She was intrigued about the idea of a waterfall that gave the gift of wisdom. She asked her servants, "Where is this waterfall of wine? I also desire to bathe in its waters and have a wisdom equal to my father's wisdom."

The servants answered, "This is not a journey for you, dear princess. A second waterfall, a waterfall of blood, also exists. Bathe in one drop of its waters, and you will become a stone statue. Many older, wiser, and more experienced persons than you have made the terrible mistake of bathing in the waters of blood and now forever remain a stone statue."

The princess was confident that she would escape the fate of those cursed people and she commanded her servants, "Prepare my horse. I too shall go in search of the waters of wisdom."

The princess raced to the waterfalls with such speed that she arrived at them before her father. When she saw the waterfalls, she was entranced by their beauty and power. In her excitement, she jumped off her horse and, without thinking, dove into the nearest pool of ruby waters.

As soon as the waters touched her skin, she felt a cold hardness begin to envelop her. She struggled to escape the waters, but it was too late. She became a stone statue and joined all of the others who had chosen unwisely in their quest for wisdom.

When the king arrived at the waterfalls, he immediately recognized his daughter of stone. The servants explained that the princess, in her headstrong manner, had rushed to the waterfalls and, in her youthful but mistaken exuberance, chosen the waterfall of stone.

The king fell to his knees and wept for his lost daughter. He cursed his fate and returned to his castle with a sad wisdom that he had never expected to gain at the enchanted waterfalls.

For years, the waters of stone washed over the princess. Eventually, she was transformed into the most exquisite and precious ruby with a royal red luster that reflected the beauty of the princess trapped within its hard case.

One day, a prince was traveling in that part of the king's land and came upon the enchanted waterfalls. He had heard the legend of the waters of wisdom and stone, but he had dismissed it as a mere tale told to entertain children. When he saw the statues of those unfortunate people who had chosen either rashly or unwisely, he knew that the legend of his childhood was true.

As he gazed into the waters of stone, he saw the most beautiful ruby resting in its waters. He carefully took the ruby from the waters and put it in his bag with the intention of having the ruby placed at the center of a protective amulet. Before leaving the enchanted waterfalls, he paused to say a small prayer for the lost souls he had seen by the waters of stone.

When he returned to his castle, he gave the ruby to the royal jewelers and asked them to make an amulet for him with the ruby at its center. As the jewelers examined the ruby stone, they felt a powerful presence emanating from it. They called on the royal wizard to examine it and explain its power.

After examining the stone, the wizard told the prince, "The red ruby has a power beyond all other stones. Trapped inside its beautiful walls is a princess. The princess called to you as you gazed into the waters of stone, and that is why you saw only this ruby and no other."

The prince looked deep into the heart of the red ruby and felt it call to his own heart. He asked his wizard, "What must I do to free her body and soul from this beautiful but cold coffin?"

The wizard told him, "You must return to the enchanted waterfalls. A second waterfall, a waterfall of wisdom, flows nearby the waterfall of stone. You must bathe this precious ruby in the waterfall of wisdom. Only then will this enchantment be broken."

The prince immediately rushed to the enchanted waterfalls. He avoided the deadly waters of the waterfall of stone and carefully lowered the ruby into the waters of wisdom. As the waters of wisdom washed over the ruby, they removed layers and layers of hardness from the stone. Eventually, nothing was left of the ruby, except the princess. She was standing alone in the waters of wisdom, as alive and beautiful as the day she first approached the enchanted waterfalls.

The prince waded into the waters of wisdom and together they bathed in its waters and drank of its truths. Before they left the enchanted waterfalls, the prince and princess washed all of the stone statues in the waters of wisdom, removing the enchantment of stone from all of the people who had suffered so long. As their final act, the prince and princess dammed up the headwaters of the waterfall of stone and forever ended its terrible and harsh enchantment.

The prince and princess returned to her castle. The king was so overjoyed to be reunited with his daughter that he gave half of his kingdom to the prince.

Eventually, the prince and princess fell in love, married, and began a royal family of their own. Peace, beauty, and wisdom ruled supreme in their kingdom. Over time, their kingdom entered the realm of legend, and they became beloved among their subjects. All of this goodness came to their world because they ruled with all of the wisdom they had gained from their immersion in the waters of wisdom so many years ago.

The Miracle of Mirajel

There once lived a man who had a daughter named Mirajel. She was the most precious daughter a father could want. Her childhood was filled with the imaginative games that only a child could create. As the father watched Mirajel immersed in her private play world, he knew that his daughter was special and that one day a special fate awaited her. As an adult, he knew of the unpredictable twists that life could take. He prayed that Mirajel's life would follow a good and strong path and that the protection of *la Santísima Virgen*, the Blessed Virgin Mary, would be with her on her long journey through life.

As Mirajel grew into womanhood, she never lost her searching imagination and yearning for more magic in her world. For Mirajel, the world of magic was not the world of evil wizards or dangerous enchantments. Rather, magic was a world of life expanded—a world where the fantastic came into the everyday life of people on this Earth. Although she was the most practical of young women in her everyday affairs, she always looked for opportunities to create the unique and unexpected in her life.

As a child, Mirajel had often delighted in the traditional stories her *abuelita* told her. She had spent many evenings listening to the *cuentos* from the old days. Her *abuelita* was a *cuentista*, a storyteller, who knew all the stories of her people and delighted in passing them on to her grandchildren. Mirajel often wished that she could live her life inside one of the stories, a place where princesses and princes outwitted dangerous opponents and where good defeated evil every time. She especially enjoyed *cuentos* in which princesses used magical objects to escape the grasp of the *el diablo* himself.

One day, Mirajel and her father were walking in their garden and she asked him, "Father, does magic really exist in the world?"

The father was startled by the question, but he tried to answer it as best as he could. He took his time, carefully choosing his words before answering. "Of course, magic exists in this world," he said. "We just don't get to see it very much. It usually remains hidden away and comes out only in very special situations."

Mirajel continued her questioning: "Does good always defeat evil?

Now her father really paused. He knew the true answer to that question, but he did not want to shatter the innocence of a young child who had only known the goodness of her family life and who believed that the world was a safe and good place. He finally decided to give her the answer he himself wished was true: "Of course, good always defeats evil."

Mirajel was quiet for a long time, and her father wondered what she was thinking. After a while she asked, "Do you think real magic will ever happen in my life? Will I meet a prince and fall in love? Will my life be spent 'happily ever after?' "

As he listened to the questions, Mirajel's father felt a sharp pain of anguish. For the first time, he truly realized that his little girl was growing up and would someday leave him to make her own life. He looked at her and softly told her, "Yes, my dearest daughter, magic will happen in your life, and you will meet a prince, fall in love, and live happily ever after—and so will your children."

Mirajel's mood changed from one of quiet thoughtfulness to one of animated excitement. With an air of impatient beseeching, almost as if she were a little girl again, she told her father, "You know what I would like? I would like to have one of those mirrors that when you look into it, you can see into the future. *Abuelita* told me a story about a girl who had one of those mirrors, and she could look into the future and see how her life would turn out. If I had one of those mirrors, I could look into it and see how my life is going to turn out. Father, do you think you could get me one of those mirrors? You just said that magic can be in my life."

Her father chuckled and, not wanting to burst her bubble, told her, "You know they are not easy to find. Magic isn't just sitting on the shelf in the store where you can easily buy it. But I'll ask around, and maybe I can find one."

Mirajel gave her father a big hug and said, "Oh father, I know you'll be able to find one."

The next day, the father was in town buying supplies and was telling the other men in the store the story about the magic mirror. They all had a good laugh at the innocence of children and jokingly wished the father good luck in his search for the mirror.

When the father left the store, a man suddenly appeared out of the darkness from between two buildings. The man came up to the father and said, "I overheard your conversation in the store and thought that I could be of some assistance in your search for a mirror that can see into the future."

The father felt a strange uneasiness about the man. He noticed that behind the man stood a large black stallion. He also smelled the faint odor of sulfur.

The man continued, "I could get the mirror for you, and you would not have to pay me anything now. My payment will come in the future."

The father was suspicious and cautiously answered, "I didn't notice you in the store. And besides, I don't really believe such a mirror exists."

The man answered, "I was there. You just didn't see me. Most people don't. And the mirror does exist. Do you really want it?"

The father was unprepared for the sudden appearance of the man and the of-. fer of the mirror. He stumbled in his reply and said, "If such a mirror really exists, it might be useful."

The man reached into his saddlebag, pulled out a hand mirror, and gave it to the father. "Here it is," said the man. "In five years, I will return for my payment."

As the man mounted his horse and rode off, the father finally realized who the man was. It was *el diablo*! The father yelled, "What is the payment?! I haven't agreed to anything! I don't want the mirror!"

He heard *el diablo* laugh and yell back, "Your daughter!" Then he left as suddenly and mysteriously as he had arrived. All that was left was the faint smell of sulfur in the air.

The father was heart-stricken. He had been tricked by *el diablo*, and now his daughter's very soul was in danger. When he returned home, he took the mirror and destroyed it, burying its evil fragments deep in a mountain cave. He never even mentioned it to his daughter. As his daughter grew up, she lived less and less in the fantasy world of the child and, eventually, forgot her request for a mirror that could see into the future. The father prayed that by destroying the mirror he had escaped his debt to *el diablo*.

Five years quickly passed, as it always does in the life of a family, and Mirajel grew into a fine young woman. Her father was very protective of her, but she dismissed his cautious ways as those of a traditional father. She knew that he was her protector and that he would always look out for her.

As Mirajel grew up, the father made special efforts to ensure that she had the blessing and protection of *la Santísima Virgen*. He would pray nightly to *la Santísima Virgen* that she would protect Mirajel in times of danger. He never mentioned to anyone his deep fear that one day *el diablo* would come for his daughter.

One day, Mirajel was walking in the family garden when a mysterious man suddenly appeared and confronted her. He tried to grab Mirajel off the ground and lift her onto his horse. Mirajel sensed that she was in great danger and grasped the medal to *la Santísima Virgen* that she kept around her neck and prayed for her help. Without explanation, the mysterious man released her and disappeared.

Mirajel told her father of the frightening encounter and mentioned that she remembered the faint smell of sulfur. She was surprised to see her father break down and cry. He then told her the complete story of the mirror and the man who was *el diablo*. He told her *el diablo* had returned to claim her soul.

Mirajel sat as still as she could during the amazing story and barely even breathed. She thought of how she had often wished as a child that her life could have the adventurous qualities of the stories her *abuelita* told her. Now she knew that sometimes even the best stories could suddenly turn into frightening and dangerous nightmares.

That night, Mirajel and her father prayed to *la Santísima Virgen*. They prayed for her eternal protection and that Mirajel's soul would know everlasting peace.

The next day, Mirajel's father smelled sulfur everywhere he went on his farm. He knew that *el diablo* had come for his daughter and that she was no longer safe. He told his Mirajel that she must flee for her safety. That night, Mirajel and her father gave each other a tearful embrace and said good-bye. Then, in the darkness of the night, Mirajel fled the only home she had ever known to begin an unpredictable journey.

Mirajel traveled to another land and eventually found work as a servant in a king's castle. Because she feared that *el diablo* would find her again, she disguised herself as a man. Her disguise was so successful that no one in the castle guessed her secret.

Mirajel diligently worked tending to the affairs of the castle. She longed to see her father and wondered if her curse would ever leave her. To comfort herself in her sad loneliness, she would spend time with the children of the castle. She soon became their favorite because of the *cuentos* she would tell them. Mirajel entertained the children by telling them all of the stories her own *abuelita* had told her so many years ago.

As she went about her work in the castle, Mirajel noticed that the prince of the castle would always find an excuse to be close to her. She was attracted to him, because he was the prince of her fairy tale *cuentos*. He was strong and handsome and would one day make a wise king. Under different circumstances, Mirajel could imagine that she was his princess and that they would live happily ever after.

One day, the prince approached her and asked: "You do not have the eyes of a man. You have the eyes of a woman. Please reveal your secret to me. Why have you come to my castle in disguise as a man?"

Mirajel had longed to tell someone her story, to meet another person in whom she could confide. She told the prince the complete story about her flight from her father and home and how she was being pursued by *el diablo*.

When she was finished with her story, the prince held her closely and revealed his heart to her. He told her, "I have known for many months that you were not a man. When I realized that you were a woman, I made every effort to be around you as much as I could. I have seen your good and gentle heart with the children of the castle. I also know that I am in love with you. Be my future queen and know that you will always have my protection."

Mirajel thought that she was inside one of her own *cuentos*, especially one in which the princess marries the prince. For a fleeting moment, she even thought that her own life might end up happily ever after.

Mirajel and the prince married in a grand festival. Mirajel had her father brought to the castle, and they had the happiest of reunions. Mirajel told her father, "The curse of *el diablo* is broken. My prince has promised to protect me for all of my life. With his protection and the protection of *la Santísima Virgen*, I will forever be safe."

The father wanted to believe Mirajel's words, but he knew that *el diablo* was the most persistent of pursuers. He knew that one day *el diablo* would find Mirajel and that a final battle would be fought for Mirajel's soul.

One day, the prince announced to Mirajel, "I must travel to another part of my father's kingdom. I will return in several days and, in my absence, am leaving my best guards to protect you."

Mirajel begged the prince, "Please don't go. I feel as if something terrible will happen if you leave me."

The prince tried to reassure Mirajel, "Do not worry, my beloved wife. You are safe in my castle. No harm will come to you inside these walls." As soon as the prince left, Mirajel prayed to *la Santísima Virgen* to protect the prince and to bring him home quickly and safely.

While the prince was gone, *el diablo* came to the castle. He had relentlessly tracked down Mirajel and had finally discovered her. This time, he vowed that she would not escape his grasp.

As part of his evil plan to capture Mirajel's soul, *el diablo* forged a letter, signing it with the prince's name. In the letter, he commanded that Mirajel be brought to the prince immediately.

When the royal servants read the letter, they commanded Mirajel to prepare to join the prince. Mirajel protested, saying that the prince had told her she would be safe only within the walls of the castle. So the servants showed her the letter and its forged signature, convincing Mirajel that the prince wanted her to join him.

Mirajel left the castle to join her prince, and as soon as she had passed the castle walls, *el diablo* descended upon her and battled the guards for her possession. The guards fought valiantly, but they were no match for the fierce strength of *el diablo*. They watched in futile horror as *el diablo* rode off with the precious Mirajel. An even worse terror came to their eyes as they watched *el diablo*'s brutal horses race off with such recklessness that they tore Mirajel to pieces and left her scattered on the open plain.

When the prince returned to the castle, his guards told him of their fierce battle with *el diablo* and the terrible death of Mirajel. They showed him the forged letter, and the prince knew that he had also been defeated by *el diablo*. The prince wept in anguish at the loss of his beloved Mirajel and asked his guards to take him to her burial place.

The guards led the prince to a mountain cave in which they had buried the remains of Mirajel. As the prince entered the cave, he was surprised by the amount of light that illuminated it. When he came to the place where Mirajel was buried, he could not find any sign of her body. In even deeper anguish, he cursed *el diablo* for taking Mirajel's body and soul to his infernal land.

As he cried, the prince looked up on the walls of the cave and noticed that the light of the cave was coming from a bright image on its walls. As his eyes adjusted to the light, he realized that the image on the walls of the cave was of Mirajel as a saint.

The prince ran to his castle and brought the *padre* to the cave to explain the image to him. When the *padre* saw the image, he knelt in worshipful prayer. He then explained to the prince, "Mirajel always had the protection of *la Santísima Virgen*. *La Santísima Virgen* protected Mirajel's soul and interceded before *el diablo* could escape with it. *La Santísima Virgen* has returned Mirajel's soul to us in this saintly image. Here is *un milagro*, a miracle, of faith. *La Santísima Virgen* has given us the image of Mirajel so we can know that she lives in eternal peace in *la gloria*, heaven itself.

The prince took the image of Mirajel back to the castle and placed it in an altar of veneration. Even in his sadness, he was comforted by the thought that Mirajel was living in eternal peace.

From that time on, the people of the kingdom would make pilgrimages to the castle to witness for themselves the image of Mirajel and to be reminded of her great life story that really did end happily ever after.

The Green Bird

There once was a woodcutter who lived on the side of a mountain with his wife and his young daughter, María. The wife was not María's real mother, but her stepmother. María's real mother had died years ago in a tragic accident in the woods.

The woodcutter had lived alone for several years trying to raise his daughter by himself. But after a while, he noticed how much María missed her mother and thought it would be good for his little girl to have a mother again.

At first, the stepmother was all kindness and sweetness toward María, but soon, her true feelings revealed themselves, and she turned into the mean person she had always been. She had only pretended that she liked children in order to trick the woodcutter into marrying her. She did not really like children very much, in particular, María. The woodcutter hoped that his wife would have a change of heart and start to like María, because to him, María was the most beautiful child in the world.

Because he knew that his wife did not like María and feared that she would harm María if the two were left alone, the woodcutter would always take María with him into the mountains as he gathered wood to sell in the village. During their long walks in the mountain woods, María and her father passed many happy hours together. Often, María thought that she and her father had been happier without the stepmother. In truth, so did the father.

One day, the woodcutter climbed a dangerously steep mountain cliff looking for dead trees to cut into firewood. He left María at the bottom of the cliff to wait for him. While her father was looking for wood, María wandered along the riverbank following a school of fish as it meandered downstream.

As nighttime fell on the mountain, María realized that she had wandered too far away from the spot where she had last seen her father. Now it was too dark for her to find her way back home by herself.

She yelled and yelled for her father, but no answer came—only the echoing of María's voice off the mountain cliffs. María gave up looking for her father and huddled under a tree, where she fell asleep.

In the morning, she resumed looking for her father. She walked and walked through the mountain forests, but only succeeded in getting herself more and more lost. She realized that she was lost for good and that she might never find her way home again. She sat down beside a mountain stream and tried to think of a way to find her father.

As she was sitting by the stream, a green bird flew by and landed beside her. María immediately spotted the bird because its feathers were the most brilliant green she had ever seen. The green bird splashed in the river water, and the drops of water on its body made the bird's feathers look as if they were covered with precious green emeralds. María was attracted to the beautiful green bird and was pleased that it stayed by her side the rest of the day. As nighttime fell, the green bird remained with María, perching in a nearby tree as María found a soft place under the tree to sleep.

María did not know it, but the bird was really an enchanted prince. An evil witch had put a spell on him that had turned him into a green bird. The prince's destiny was to hopelessly fly through the mountain forests looking for someone who would help him break his evil enchantment.

That night, María dreamed that the green bird flew to her and talked like a person. The prince flew right up to her ear and whispered, "Please help me. I am a prince with an evil enchantment on me. Please help me find my way back to my home and break this evil spell."

In her dream, María could also talk to the green bird. She asked the bird, "Where is your home? I am also lost and will help you if I can."

The green bird told her, "You must find a house on top of a tree. The tree is on top of a mountain that also has an evil enchantment on it. My beautiful city of lights has become a sad-looking mountain covered with heavy, foreboding clouds. Find that mountain, find that tree, and find that house. Then the answer to my enchantment will also be found."

In the morning, María awoke and found the green bird still hovering around her. As she looked at the bird and admired its shimmering and lustrous green feathers, she felt in her heart that her dream had been true. She slowly approached the bird so as not to frighten it away and was surprised when it peacefully flew to her and landed on her shoulder. She looked into the bird's eyes and said, "Don't be so sad, dear prince. I am a lost soul also looking for my home. I will help you find your home."

María then began a trek of hundreds of miles. For days and weeks, she wandered through the mountains looking for the prince's home. Finally, after almost giving up hope of ever finding it, she arrived at a river that encircled a sad-looking mountain covered with heavy, foreboding clouds.

When the green bird saw the mountain, it flew high into the air and swooped down around María's head in a flurry of excitement. María knew that she had found the prince's home.

María climbed the mountain and discovered a lone tree atop its peak. At the top of the tree was a small bird's house. At the base of the tree was a guard, placed there by the evil witch to keep the prince from returning to his house and breaking the enchantment.

When the guard saw the green bird, he tried to shoot it with his arrows. The bird, however, avoided the arrows and flew away to safety.

That night, María dreamed that the green bird was bathing itself in a bowl of water. She saw the guard put knives in the bowl to harm the green bird. Before María could warn the green bird, it dove into the water and crashed into the hidden knives. María then saw the bird, gashed and deeply wounded, struggle to fly out of the bowl.

When María awoke, she rushed to find the green bird. She found it lying on the ground, mortally wounded, with deep cuts all throughout its beautiful but bloodied feathers. As she tried to help the wounded bird, María knew that another of her dreams had been real.

As she leaned over the bird, she cried fearful tears of sorrow. Looking into the green bird's sad eyes she heard the prince's voice. He told her, "I must fly away from here. In order to break the enchantment, you must find me in the field and mountains of Quiquiriquí, where neither sun nor air exists. Take these shoes of iron. When they wear out, then you will have found the fields and mountains of Quiquiriquí."

María was deeply saddened to see the green bird fly away. She had fallen in love with the enchanted prince and thought she would never see him again. She believed that the prince would suffer his enchantment forever.

She then began her search for the fields and mountains of Quiquiriquí, where neither sun nor air exists. After walking for days without end, her feet ached terribly from the iron shoes. As she looked at the heavy metal shoes, she could not imagine that they would ever wear out.

At the moment of her greatest doubt that she would ever find the prince again, María came to a house on a mountaintop. In the house she found an old woman surrounded by a glowing light. The woman seemed as if she were waiting for María. When María approached the old woman, the old woman asked, "Why are you walking through here, my beautiful child?"

María told her, "I am searching for the fields and mountains of Quiquiriquí, where neither sun nor air exists. Can you help me?"

The old woman answered, "No. I cannot help you. But maybe my son, the Sun, can help you."

At that moment, the Sun rose in the east and filled the old woman's house with the bright, yellow rays of morning. As the Sun entered the house, it asked its mother, "Is a human in the house?"

The old woman told the Sun, "Yes. A beautiful young woman is in the house. She is searching for the fields and mountains of Quiquiriquí, where neither sun nor air exists. Do you know where it is?"

The Sun answered, "No. I do not. But I will take her to the Moon. Maybe the Moon has seen this place Quiquiriquí."

The Sun then took one of its rays of light and used it to carry María to the top of a faraway mountain. When they reached the mountain, the Sun told María, "You must walk for many more miles by yourself. You will come to a small house and in that house will be a woman with pale, white skin. She is the Moon. Ask her your question."

When María reached the house of the Moon, she did find a woman with the palest and whitest skin. Just as María could not look into the bright face of the Sun, she could not gaze into the clear white light reflecting off the face of the Moon. Without looking directly at her, María asked the Moon, "I am searching for the fields and mountains of Quiquiriquí, where neither sun nor air exists. Could you help me find them?"

The moon answered María, "No. I cannot help you. But if you remain here, soon the wind will blow across this mountaintop. The wind travels across the seas and the continents and knows all of the hills and valleys of the Earth. Perhaps the wind will be able to help you."

María then waited for what seemed like time without end. During the day, the Sun warmed her, and at night, the Moon illuminated her dreams of the suffering prince. Finally, the peaceful calm broke, and the gusts of the wind arrived blowing across the mountaintop.

María called to the wind, "Wind, please help me! I am searching for the fields and mountains of Quiquiriquí, where neither sun nor air exists. Can you help me find them?"

The wind howled back its answer: "No, I cannot help you. But my brother the storm can help you. He has often blown over the field and mountains of Quiquiriquí."

The wind then rose up and transformed itself into a raging storm that blew across the mountaintop. The storm raged and howled, blowing thundering storm clouds across the skies. At the height of the storm, the clouds broke, and María glimpsed the sight of Quiquiriquí in the distance. Quiquiriquí was the very sad mountain that was covered with heavy, foreboding clouds where she had begun her search so long ago. After she had seen the fields and mountains of Quiquiriquí, where neither sun nor air exists, the storm vanished and María began her final walk to Quiquiriquí.

Again, María walked for days and days. When she finally arrived at the edge of Quiquiriquí, she collapsed in pain. She looked at her feet and saw that she had walked for so long and for so far, the soles of her iron shoes were totally worn away. She had reached Quiquiriquí! As she tried to struggle to her feet to continue her journey, she slipped into a deep sleep of exhaustion.

As she slept, María dreamed that she walked to a tree, and in the tree were two doves. She could hear one of the doves saying, "There sleeps the beautiful young woman, come to save the prince. She does not know that only the ashes of our bodies can break the evil enchantment that holds him so tightly."

The other dove then said, "Be quiet! The rocks have ears, and the bushes talk."

When María awoke, she continued her search of Quiquiriquí. At last, she found her prince, almost dead under a tree. He was gasping for breath in an attempt to find another moment of life.

She heard the cooing of doves in the tree above the prince and she reached up and captured them. With a swift and lethal blow, she killed the doves. She then burned them and collected their ashes. Finally, at the end of her long and perilous journey, she stood over the green bird and sprinkled his body with the doves' ashes.

As the fine dust of the ashes covered the green bird's body, a magical transformation began to take place. The ashes swirled over the green bird until they created a tornado of ashes reaching from the Earth to the top of the sky. When the ashes finally settled down, there stood the prince, transformed to human shape again. María had broken the evil enchantment.

When the enchantment broke, the sad mountain covered with heavy, foreboding clouds transformed into the prince's beautiful city of lights. At that moment, the guard under the tree disappeared, and the house on the tree became the prince's glimmering castle at the top of the mountain.

The prince sent his servants to find María's father. They found her father, and when he came to the castle, María learned that her father no longer lived with her mean stepmother.

As at the end of all good stories, the father and daughter were joyfully reunited, the prince married María, and, of course, they all lived happily ever after.

The Enchanted Forest

Once, in a faraway land where magic was still possible, three sisters were sitting on a porch at the side of their castle. Because the three sisters were princesses, they spent most of their days in the idle activities suited to their life of privilege. As daughters of the royal court, their life was one of genteel activities and simple conversation. Servants waited on them hand and foot and delivered their every need. On the day this story begins, the princesses have no inkling of the life-changing adventures they are about to experience.

As the princesses sat on the porch sewing, they would often pass the time by playing girlish games of imagination. On this particular day, they were talking about what they would do for the kings they would marry.

The oldest princess dreamily looked into the sky and said, "If I married a king, in order to entertain him, I would make him a suit of clothes that would be so small that it could fit into a nutshell."

The second princess answered with her own dream. She told her two sisters, "That sounds all good and well. When I marry a king, however, I will make an even smaller suit of clothes. I will make a suit of clothes so small that it will fit into the shell of the pine nut."

Both of the sisters seemed very pleased with themselves. They looked at the youngest sister and asked, "Well, what will you do?"

The youngest sister did not hesitate to reply, "When I marry a king, I will give him three children. Not just any children, however. They will have signs of royalty on their heads. One son will have hair of gold. A second son will have hair of silver. The third child will be most special of all. She will be a daughter, and she will have a star on her forehead."

As the three sisters sat imagining their marriages to kings, three kings came riding up to the castle. The kings were seeking shelter from an approaching rainstorm. They found shelter under some trees that were near the porch where the princesses were sitting. The princesses were so engaged in their conversation that they did not notice the kings so close to their porch.

The kings overheard the princesses talking about the gifts that they would give the kings they married. As they listened to the princesses' stories, the kings decided it would be interesting to marry the princesses and see which one would keep her promises.

The kings revealed themselves to the princesses and asked for their hands in marriage. The princesses were so surprised and overjoyed that they, of course, agreed to marry the kings.

Almost immediately, the oldest princess did make her king a suit so small it could fit into a nutshell. Soon afterward, the second princess made her king a suit so small it could fit into a pine nut shell. Their kings were so pleased by these clever gifts that they lavished expensive gifts on both of the older sisters.

The two older sisters greatly enjoyed the special attention that they were receiving from their kings, especially the fancy gifts. They then waited to see if the youngest sister would keep her promise and give her king three children with signs of royalty on their heads. After almost a year had passed, the king who was married to the youngest sister came to the older sisters and asked them to bring a doctor to the castle because the youngest sister was ready to deliver a child.

The older sisters sensed that their kings would not be as pleased with their gifts of small suits if they saw the other king receive a son with hair of gold. They became jealous of the younger sister also because they knew that a son with hair of gold would make her the most desired and admired of the three sisters. So the sisters conspired to ensure that the youngest sister would never surpass them.

When the king asked them to get a doctor, the oldest answered, "We don't need a doctor. We will be able to attend to our sister ourselves. A doctor will be unnecessary."

When the youngest sister gave birth, it was to a son with the most beautiful hair of gold. The older sisters immediately put their plan into action. While the youngest sister was recovering from giving birth, the older sisters substituted a little dog for the golden-haired baby. They took the baby and placed it in a basket. They then threw the basket into the river and let it float away downstream.

The king soon asked, "Let me see my child. Do I have a son or a daughter?"

The sisters showed the king the dog and told him, "Here is your child."

The king was dumbfounded that his child was a dog. He cursed his fate and asked, "What kind of woman gives birth to a dog?" In order to punish his wife, he made her live in a cage with the dog.

Meanwhile, the basket with the golden-haired baby floated down the river until a *viejito* who lived alone in the forest discovered it. The *viejito* had often prayed to God to give him a child. The *viejito* had asked God, "Why am I so unfortunate? I have never had a son or daughter, and now that I am at the end of my life, I have no child to receive my inheritance."

When the *viejito* discovered the floating basket, he exclaimed, "My prayers have been answered. The Lord has sent me a child." He carefully removed the baby from the basket and cuddled it closely, tearfully looking at the baby and crying, "What a precious child. How beautiful is he with his hair of gold. Thank you Lord for this blessing. "

The *viejito* then clothed the child and raised him as the precious longed-for child for whom he had prayed so desperately. He named the beautiful boy Juan.

The youngest sister did not know what had happened to her child. She had felt a deep mother's love for her newborn child and was shocked and saddened that she had given birth to a dog. She fell into a deep misery and a profound sense of loss from which she could not escape. Her sadness was so sincere that the king relented and released her from the cage.

After another year had passed, the king again came to the sisters and said, "My wife is ready to deliver a child again. Please bring a doctor to the castle to assist my wife in childbirth."

Again the sisters conspired to steal their sister's baby. They told the king, "A doctor is unnecessary. We are capable of helping our sister give birth to her child." When the baby was born, it was indeed the promised son with hair of silver. As before, the sisters immediately took the baby, placed it in a basket, and set the basket afloat in the river.

Soon afterward, the *viejito* was walking by the river that flowed by his home and spied another basket floating in the water. He rescued the basket from the swirling river and discovered the boy with the hair of silver. When he saw the child, he exclaimed, "Thank you Lord. I am now doubly blessed. To think that I have suffered in loneliness for all of these years, and now I am blessed with two beautiful children." He took the silver-haired child home and christened him José. His prayers had been answered, and he spent many happy days and nights caring for his two sons, Juan and José.

Meanwhile, when the king asked to see his child, the sisters showed him a cat. When the king saw the cat, he raged, "What kind of woman gives birth to a dog and a cat?" He then again placed his wife in a cage with the dog and the cat, which provided her only companionship.

The youngest sister was crushed that she had given birth to a cat. All of her senses rejected such a possibility, and yet, there were the dog and the cat and no children. She mourned her cursed fate and lost children. She cried so piteously and sincerely that the king was moved by her sadness and, for a second time, released her from the cage.

The king and the youngest sister reconciled and, for a third time, attempted to have a child. Once more, the king requested that the older sisters get a doctor, only to be told for a third time that a doctor was unnecessary. This time, when the youngest sister gave birth, the sisters substituted a pig for the loveliest daughter, who had been born, as promised, with a star on her forehead.

The sisters placed the daughter in a basket and sent the basket downstream from the same place where they had released the first two baskets. The basket floated in the river until it came to rest on the riverbank at the exact spot where the *viejito* had discovered the other two baskets. The baby girl was crying with such force that the *viejito* could hear the wails in his home. He hurried to the river to investigate the crying and was amazed to once again find a beautiful baby in a basket. He held the baby girl in his arms and cooed a lullaby to put her to sleep.

When he saw the star on the baby's forehead, he knew that she was a gift from the heavens. He named the baby girl María and placed her in the same bed as Juan and José. As he gently laid María in the bed, he said, "Juan and José, the Lord has sent you the most beautiful baby sister. Now we will be an even bigger and happier family." As the *viejito* gazed at his three sleeping children, he reflected on his good fortune and counted himself among the most blessed men on the face of the Earth.

The king, however, counted himself among the most cursed on the face of the Earth when the sisters showed him the pig as his child. He shook his fists at the heavens and yelled, "How can a woman give birth to a dog, a cat, and a pig?! Where are my promised children—sons with hair of gold and silver and a daughter with a star on her forehead?"

He then threw his wife into a cage with the three animals and walked away to suffer his great sorrow. As he walked away, he looked back at his wife and told her, "Stay there with your children, the dog, the cat, and the pig. You shall live with them until the end of your days."

The youngest daughter also could not believe that she had given birth to three animals. She cried and cried over her misfortune until the tears flowed no more. As she looked at the three animals, she tried to understand why she was so cursed. But she could not bring any understanding at all to her cruel situation.

Many years passed, and one day, out of idle curiosity, the two older sisters decided to try to find out what had happened to the three children they had sent down the river in baskets. They obtained a magic mirror from a witch who lived in the forest and asked the mirror to show them the three children. They looked intently into the mirror and said, "Magic Mirror, use your powers to show us the children of our sister."

The mirror showed the sisters the three children happily playing at their home deep in the forest by the river that had delivered them to the kind and caring *viejito*. The *viejito* had died a peaceful death of old age several years earlier, and now the three children lived alone and quite happily in the only childhood home they had ever known.

When the sisters saw how beautiful their younger sister's daughter was, they were overcome with jealousy. They plotted to kill the girl and asked the mirror, "Magic mirror, please tell us how to end the life of the girl child."

The mirror answered, "An enchanted forest exists where three marvelous creations—a talking bird, a magic fruit tree, and a river of one thousand colors—can be found. The girl must go to that forest, and there she will fall under a magic spell that will turn her to stone. Send the witch to convince the girl to travel to the enchanted forest. Then the girl's life will end as she knows it."

The sisters sent the witch to the forest to find the three children. When the witch had found them, she entranced María with visions of the enchanted forest, where she would find the talking bird, the magic fruit tree, and the river of one thousand colors. When she felt that her spell was complete, the witch left to tell the evil sisters that their wish would soon come true.

As María reflected on the witch's stories of the enchanted forest, she longed to see its magical beauties. Juan and José saw that their sister was enchanted and decided to make the journey themselves in order to bring the magical creations back to the sister they loved so much. As they prepared to leave, Juan told María, "Do not worry for our safety. We will return with the magical riches of the enchanted forest."

He then took his knife and threw it into the ground until its blade was buried to the hilt. To reassure María, he said, "Check this knife every day. As long as you can pull it out of the earth, you shall know that we are safe. On the day that you cannot pull it from the ground, then you shall know that we are no longer alive."

María tested the knife and saw that it easily came out of the ground. Reassured, she kissed her brothers and wished them a safe return.

Juan and José quickly began the journey to the enchanted forest. They had been traveling for several days when they met an old hermit who lived in the forest. Juan asked the hermit, "*Ermitaño*, we are searching for an enchanted forest where we can find a talking bird, a magic fruit tree, and a river of one thousand colors. Can you help us find such a place?"

The hermit carefully eyed Juan and José and finally answered, "Such a place exists, an enchanted forest. But I must warn you that all others who have ventured into its dark beauty have never returned. You must beware of the voices that will enchant you and turn you into stone. Mind my warning and do not answer the calling voices of the forest."

José told the hermit, "*Ermitaño*, thank you for your wise word of warning. We will travel to the enchanted forest to obtain the three magical creations for our beloved sister, all the while keeping your warning in our minds. Good day, *señor*."

Juan and José traveled to the enchanted forest and soon they were deep in its lush darkness. They could sense that it was a place of enchantment and beauty. Everywhere they looked they saw looming rocks and boulders that resembled people who had been frozen in their tracks. As they wandered through the forest, they soon heard voices calling to them. The voices sounded like men in desperate trouble, calling for help. Juan and José both heeded the hermit's warning and did not answer the voices.

After searching the forest, Juan and José entered a clearing and saw the objects of their search. In the clearing was a talking bird atop a magic fruit tree beside a river of a thousand colors. As they approached this marvelous sight, they heard the voice of María call out, "Juan and José, my beloved brothers, I am saddened by your long absence. Please find the magical creations and hurry back home to me."

Overcome with joy, Juan and José forgot the hermit's warning and answered the voice, "María, we hear you. We will be home soon." As soon as they had answered the voice, they transformed into stone statues. The voices of the forest had claimed two more victims.

During the time of their absence, María had daily tested the knife in the ground. Each time she tested the knife, it had easily come out of the ground and she would return to her house assured that her brothers were alive and safe.

One day, however, the knife remained stuck in the ground. No matter how hard María tugged and pulled at the knife, it remained firmly stuck. Falling to her knees, María cried, "My brothers! They are dead. Why, oh, why has this happened? They are all I have in this world."

María gathered her strength and determined that she would find her brothers no matter how perilous the journey. After she had calmed her emotions, she began the same journey her brothers had followed to their enchantment.

When she encountered the hermit, she asked, "*Ermitaño*, have you seen my two brothers come this way? If you have, please tell me which way they went. I love them with all my heart, and I know that some great danger has fallen upon them."

The hermit told María, "Your brothers did pass this way in search of an enchanted forest. Now you must follow in their footsteps. But be warned, as I warned them, do not answer the voices of the forest. All who answer the voices of the forest are enchanted and forever turned into statues of stone."

María thanked the hermit and took the path he pointed out to her. As she went deeper and deeper into the enchanted forest, she passed many rocks and boulders that resembled people who had been transformed into statues of stone. As she approached the clearing where her brothers were standing as stone statues themselves, she heard their voices calling to her, "María, please help us. We are stone statues, and only your voice can break the evil spell that holds us. Please call to us and free us, María."

María steeled herself and disregarded the voices from the forest. She marveled at the great beauty of the talking bird, the magic fruit tree, and the river of one thousand colors but never wavered in her resolution to free her brothers. She plucked a feather from the talking bird and passed it over the heads of her two brothers. The bird's feather dropped a fine dust on the statues of the brothers, and as the dust lit upon the statues of stone, the evil spell broke, and the brothers returned to the world of the living.

The talking bird then told María to sprinkle the water from the river of one thousand colors on all of the other statues. As she sprinkled the statues, the river water disenchanted them. As the statues came to life, kings and queens returned to the world of the living after their long entrapment. They rejoiced at their freedom and announced that María and her brothers would be esteemed guests at a banquet in their honor. When the kings and queens saw that the brothers had hair of gold and silver and that María had a star on her forehead, they told them that they were royal children, because the hair colors and the star were acknowledged signs of royalty.

Before they left the forest, María, Juan, and José gathered the talking bird, the magic tree, and water from the river of one thousand colors. They carried the three magical creations home with them and decided to share their discoveries with all of those at the royal banquet.

At the banquet was María, Juan, and José's father, the king. During the festivities, their father, the king, noticed the magic fruit tree. The king reached to pluck a piece of fruit from the tree and discovered that it was a cucumber. When he opened the cucumber, he found a pearl inside of it. He marveled at the pearl and said, "How can this be? A tree gives fruit to a cucumber, and the cucumber has a pearl inside of it? This cannot be. It is impossible for a cucumber to have a pearl in it."

From the branches of the magic fruit tree the talking bird flew to the king and said, "Just as it is impossible for a woman to give birth to a dog, a cat, and a pig."

At first, the king was shocked to be addressed by a bird that talks, but he regained his composure and asked the bird to explain the meaning of its words.

The bird brought forward María, Juan, and José and told the king, "Here are your true children, swapped at birth by evil sisters for a dog, a cat, and a pig. Now you must recognize them and release their mother, your beloved wife, from her unjust imprisonment."

The king immediately recognized the three signs of royalty his children bore and rejoiced that his cruel fate had come to an end. He released his wife, and the royal family reunited in joyful bliss.

The king punished the evil sisters by throwing them into the cage where the younger sister had lived for so many years. Their punishment was to witness daily the happiness of their younger sister, the beauty of her three children, and the love the king had for her.

The dog, the cat, and the pig became royal pets, because the younger sister had come to love them, and they made perfect pets for the three children.

And, of course, they all lived happily ever after.

The Jewels of Shining Light

There once was a king who had a daughter who was soon going to be past marriageable age. The king was worried. It was almost past the time for his daughter to begin a life and family of her own.

The king believed that after a certain age, young ladies are no longer attractive to young men. He worried that his daughter might become an old maid and that he would have no heirs to his throne. He thought that his daughter was beautiful and possessed a certain charm, so he could not understand why she was not deluged with suitors.

When he spoke to his daughter, she did not seem the least bit perturbed by her lack of suitors. When the king threatened to marry her to the first suitable man who passed the king's fancy, she laughed and said, "Oh dear father, don't be so demanding. I will marry in my own time to a man of my own choosing. In fact, I will marry for love and for no other reason."

The king was furious with his daughter's headstrong attitude, but she had always been strong willed. He knew he could not force a marriage on her. Besides, his daughter was his favorite child and he knew that his own indulgences on her were one of the reasons she was still not married. He finally decided that he must take decisive action before it was too late.

The king called an emergency meeting of his ministers, and they met in special consultation in the king's star chambers. The king asked his most trusted advisors, "Tell me, why do you think my daughter has no suitors? I am in my advanced years, and my children have not yet produced an heir to the throne. It is an insult and a disgrace to my throne that I cannot marry my daughter to a suitable prince."

The king's advisors gathered together and deliberated the king's question for several hours. Finally, one of the king's ministers approached the throne and said, "Our most royal king, we have considered all of the possibilities and consulted the most sage advisors, and we have an answer to your question. Your daughter has no suitors because throughout the kingdom the young men are afraid to seek her hand in marriage. They know of her headstrong manner and believe that not one of them is rich enough to be worthy of her. In addition, the fault lies with you, our royal king. It is the tradition for the king to offer his daughter's hand in marriage in a royal contest. The young men of the kingdom do not know that you consider your daughter of marriageable age, thus they are afraid to approach the royal court."

The king reflected on the words of his ministers and he asked them further, "Then what is it that I must do? In truth, not just any young man in the kingdom is worthy to marry a king's daughter. He must be a man of status and wealth himself. He must come from a family with which a marriage would make a profitable alliance. Don't forget. He will one day inherit through marriage a good portion of the royal estate, so he must be worthy in the eyes of the royal family. But, where am I to find such a husband for my daughter?"

The royal advisors had anticipated the king's question and had their reply ready. They told the king, "You must announce a royal contest. All throughout the land you must announce that you are seeking the wealthiest man to marry your daughter. First, such a contest sends word to the young men of the land that your daughter's hand is available in marriage. Secondly, it sets the condition such that only men from the most suitable families are eligible for the contest. Finally, royal king, the young men who will enter this contest will be the finest young men in your kingdom, and surely the princess will find one of them to her liking."

The king immediately liked the idea that his ministers proposed. It had all the attributes of success. It announced that his daughter was available, and it guaranteed that only worthy men would enter the contest. Besides, he reasoned, it was time he became more forceful and acted like the king he was. His daughter would marry the winner of the contest, and that is all there was to it!

Throughout the land, the couriers of the court carried the royal proclamation. In village squares and towns of the kingdom, they posted the announcement of the contest. Young men gathered and argued who was most worthy of the princess's hand in marriage. They compared wealth and status to determine their worthiness.

At first, the princess was resistant to the idea that her father planned to marry her to the wealthiest man but, in time, she became intrigued by the idea. Her natural sense of curiosity made her wonder who would really enter the contest and what type of man might be deemed the winner. In truth, she longed to fall in love and be married. Her life as a princess was one of isolation and privilege, and her contacts with young men were severely limited. She came to see the contest as a way for her to meet a man who might win her heart. Of course, she secretly wished that the young man determined the wealthiest was also noble, handsome, brave, and wise. Like in the stories of old, she longed for her own knight in shining armor to carry her away from her life in the castle.

In one particular village far from the castle—in fact, at the outer edges of the kingdom—a poor farmer's son saw the proclamation. The farmer's son was named Juanito, and he spent his days working in the field and tending to his family's sheep. His life was one of simple pleasures: the taste of clear mountain water, the freshness of the forest air, and the aroma of home-cooked *tortillas*.

When he read the royal proclamation, he knew that he would never be the equal to the wealthiest young men in the kingdom but, for some reason, he was determined to enter the contest anyway. His father had always told him that he was the equal of any man and that with the blessing of his parents and the guidance of the holy saints, he would always find success in life.

Juanito told his parents of his intentions to enter the royal contest and they told him, "Juanito, this contest is only for the wealthiest men in the land. Do not deceive yourself. You cannot win this contest. We are a proud, hard-working people of the land and do not measure ourselves by wealth and status."

Juanito respected his parents' words, but he had made up his mind. He told his parents, "You have always taught me that I was the equal of any man. I am determined to enter this contest and ask your blessing in my journey to the royal castle."

His parents relented and agreed to give Juanito their blessing. As he knelt down before them, they placed their hands on his head and said, "You have our blessing. May the holy saints assist you in your journey, and may you return home safely."

As he packed for his journey, Juanito assessed his wealth and came up with only the sheep that were his alone. He gathered this small flock together and herded them down the road in front of him. He was taking the sheep with him as presents for the princess and hoped that the royal family would, in some way, find his humble offering worthy.

As Juanito traveled, he realized that the royal court was farther away than he had imagined. He soon knew that it would take several days for him to reach the royal castle and that he must find places to sleep along the way. He had spent many evenings in the open pasture with his sheep, so he knew how to make his bed under the open sky and how to find his food by the river's edge.

The first evening, as he settled his sheep down by a gentle mountain stream, he prayed to the holy saints and thanked them for their guidance and protection. As he fell asleep under the sparkling starry skies, he reminded himself that no matter how his journey ended he was still blessed among men because of the love of his family.

Juanito had been asleep for several hours when he was awakened by the brightest light he had ever seen. He awoke and looked to the night sky and saw a shower of stars falling. It was as if heaven itself had opened up and was sprinkling the Earth with its starry jewels.

Several of the falling fiery stars appeared to fall close to where Juanito was camped for the night. As they hit the ground, they illuminated the dark night so brightly that Juanito was easily able to find where they had fallen. First, he calmed his frightened sheep, and then he ran to the spot where he saw the fallen stars lighting the dark night. When he came upon the fallen stars, he discovered that they were stones of the brightest light he had ever seen. As he reached out and touched them, they transformed themselves into jewels of bright light of sapphire blue, emerald green, and ruby red. They cooled to his touch but retained their intense light. Juanito collected them and thanked the holy saints, for he knew that these jewels were gifts from *la gloria,* heaven itself.

Juanito continued his journey to the royal castle and soon found himself outside its gates. He knocked at the massive wooden doors to the castle and announced himself as a contestant for the hand of the king's daughter. The castle guards took one look at Juanito with his dust-covered clothes and flock of dirty sheep and laughed at him, saying, "The contest is for the wealthiest men in the kingdom, not the poorest!" They then slammed the doors shut, and Juanito was locked out of the castle.

He stayed outside the castle during the rest of the day and looked upon an unending flow of young men dressed in the finest clothes and riding the noblest horses who were entering its gates. He looked at his humble flock of sheep and his own farmer's clothes and realized the foolishness of his journey. He vowed to try one more time to enter the king's castle, and then to return to his home and family.

The next morning, Juanito awoke early and found his way into the castle by joining a group of merchants delivering goods for the king's court. Once inside the castle, he boldly found his way to the royal throne room and was soon standing in line with the other contestants for that day. When his turn came to approach the royal throne, he led his sheep before the king and his court and meekly addressed them: "Please accept my humble gift for the princess and know that my heart is pure and my desire is to be worthy of her hand in marriage."

The king looked at the sheep and at Juanito and motioned to his guards. He commanded, "Take this dirty intruder to the royal prison. He has insulted the court by bringing animals of the fields into the royal throne room and is clearly not worthy to be a contestant for my daughter's hand in marriage. Remove him and lock him up until the royal judge can determine his punishment. Now bring on the next contestant!"

The guards grabbed Juanito and dragged him out of the room. As they did, Juanito glanced at the princess sitting beside the king and, for a moment, a look passed between them. The princess was intrigued that such an obviously unfit young man had penetrated the king's throne room. She sensed a pure intention in the young man. All of the wealthy men who entered the contest had been boringly similar, and Juanito at least offered a moment's diversion.

Juanito landed in a cold dungeon below the king's castle. As he stretched out on the stone floor, he wondered how his good fortune had abandoned him. When nighttime fell, he thought of his family and home on the farm and longed to be in the open pasture with his sheep, sleeping under the open sky. As he thought of the starry night sky, he remembered his jewels of light. He took them out of the pouch where he had safely put them. As he held them in his hand, they began to shine once again with the most intense light, which illuminated his dungeon cell.

The princess was sitting by her bedroom window looking at the night sky and wondering if the king's contest would ever produce a man who would win her heart when she noticed an amazing light piercing the night. She immediately called her servants and commanded that they discover the source of the light and bring it to her.

The servants followed the light until it led them to Juanito's cell. They escorted Juanito to the princess's chamber and presented him to the princess. When the princess saw Juanito, she recognized him from the fiasco in the king's throne room earlier in the day. She knew that he had been thrown into the castle's dungeon and that it was highly improper for her to have Juanito in her chamber room, but she was still intrigued by Juanito and knew that she had the protection of her servants nearby.

She asked Juanito, "Where is the source of the amazing light I saw?"

Juanito showed her the jewels of shining light. The princess held them, and they released their light of sapphire blue, emerald green, and ruby red. Juanito told her the story of the night he saw them falling from the heavens and of his belief that they were gifts from the holy saints. The princess gazed into the jewels' light and held them as if they were the most precious objects on Earth.

Juanito told the princess of his foolish dream that he might be found worthy of her hand in marriage. The princess listened to Juanito's story and wondered what type of man would be worthy of receiving gifts from the holy saints. She remembered his honest intensity before the royal court and thought that perhaps underneath the clothes of the farmer was the heart of a true and worthy man.

She returned the jewels to Juanito and told him, "I will send my servants for you nightly, until you are removed from the dungeon. Please keep our meetings a secret. If the royal guards discover us, you will face the severest punishment."

For several nights afterward, Juanito met with the princess, and they spent the nights surrounded by the light of the shining jewels. Finally, Juanito gave the jewels to the princess. He told her, "Take these jewels. Their light is matched only by the light of your own beauty. I know that they were sent to me by the holy saints in order to win your hand in marriage, but now I see that they were meant for you to have for yourself." Juanito then left the princess, knowing that his journey was at its end.

As he left the princess's chambers, her servants called him back. They gave him a bag and told him: "The princess gives you this bag as a remembrance of her fond affection for you. She asks that you do not open it until tomorrow. Then its contents and her heart will be revealed to you." Juanito was puzzled by the gift and the strange request, but he respected the princess's wishes.

The next morning, the king gathered the royal court and announced that the contest was over. He had determined the wealthiest suitor and was ready to hand over his daughter in marriage. The king then called his daughter to join him on the royal throne.

When the princess stood beside her father, she announced, "Before I accept the hand of this man in marriage, I ask that the king consider one more contestant. My servants have discovered that the richest prince of all is in disguise among us."

A murmur of excitement sparked through the royal court. The idea of a prince in disguise was the subject of folktales. They never imagined that one might actually be among them.

The king did not like that his royal plan was being derailed by this prince-in-disguise idea, and he demanded, "If a prince is among us, then let him reveal himself now, or else I will declare this man the winner of the contest."

The princess motioned to her servants, and they led Juanito into the royal throne room. When Juanito realized that he was once again before the royal court and he saw the angry face of the king, he thought he had been brought before the king to receive his final punishment.

When the king saw Juanito, he furiously asked, "Why is this sheepherder before me again? Remove him at once and have him executed in the morning."

The princess quickly interceded and said, "This is the prince in disguise. Open the bag at his side, and his riches will be revealed for all to see."

Juanito looked down at his side and the only bag he had with him was the bag that the princess's servant had given him the night before. He had not yet looked in it and was uncertain what it held.

The servants took the bag and opened it before the king and the royal court. Out of the bag tumbled the most precious jewels and coins of gold and silver. They were the princess's own jewels and valuable coins that she had secretly placed in the bag as the first part of her plan to help Juanito win the contest. The last objects to fall from the bag were the jewels of shining light that Juanito had given to the princess. The jewels illuminated every corner of the royal throne room with their bright light of sapphire blue, emerald green, and ruby red.

When the king saw the jewels of shining light, he thought that Juanito really was a prince in disguise and was convinced by the contents of his bag that he was the wealthiest of the princess's suitors. He then proudly announced to the royal court, "The contest is concluded. We have found a husband for the princess!" At the king's announcement, the royal court exploded in cheers and celebration.

Juanito was still confused by what had happened, but when he stood next to the princess, she told him that she had fallen in love with his pure and good heart during their nightly meetings and that she knew his true wealth was in his heart. She had given him the bag containing her own wealth and the jewels of shining light so that he would win the contest.

Juanito then realized that the blessing of his parents and the gifts from the holy saints had truly brought him the hand of the princess in marriage.

BACKGROUND ABOUT JUAN OSO

Juan Oso, John the Bear, is a story about a man with the strength of a bear. The common elements shared by the traditional versions of this story include John's father being a bear, the betrayal by trusted companions, the rescue of princesses, and the happily-ever-after ending. The names of the companions vary in different versions, but they all refer to some type of mastery over natural forces.

Juan Oso

Once, in a time long ago when people still believed in the power of magic and kings ruled the land, a boy was born who had the strength of a bear. When he was little, people recognized that his strength was greater than that of any other child. As he grew, his strength was greater than that of any man. In time, he gained the reputation for having the strength of a bear and soon gained the name of *Juan Oso,* John the Bear.

As a child, Juan was constantly getting into trouble because of his great strength. Of course, he did not deliberately try to break or hurt things, for he was a very kind and gentle child. The truth of the matter is he did not know how to control his strength. He would just be playing like any other child and, suddenly, he would find himself in trouble.

One day, his mother came into the house and was angry about something. She called out, "Juan! *Juan Oso*! You come here this minute!"

Juan answered, "I'm right over here. What's wrong?"

Furious, his mother told him, "What's wrong? Everything is wrong. I just got back from the church and the *padre* had a little talk with me."

Juan couldn't imagine what the priest would say to his mother that would make her so angry. He innocently asked, "What about?"

Sitting down, she told him with an exasperated voice, "What else? You."

Juan defended himself, "Mama, you know not to believe everything the *padre* says. Especially about me."

She looked at Juan with a mother's frustrated love and answered, "Juan, this is the third time we have had to have this talk. And you know what it is about. The same thing as the last two times—your strength."

Juan knew what was coming. Even he was starting to hate that he was so strong. Also in a frustrated voice, he answered his mother, "Mama I'm not to blame. It's not my fault. I was born this way. The other kids even joke that my father was a bear, and that's why I have my strength."

Juan's mother admonished him, "Juan you have to stop using your strength to show off. You're starting to hurt other kids, and their parents are complaining."

Juan tried to explain: "We're just playing. And the other kids are always asking me to use my strength. They like to see it. And besides, my strength is the best thing I could have for the work on the farm. You yourself have told me that many times."

His mother would have nothing to do with his excuses. She wearily told him, "From the time you were born we all could see your great strength. When you were young it was cute. But now that you are almost a man, people are afraid of your strength. Juan, something has to be done. One day you really are going to hurt someone and, play or not, you will be in a lot of trouble."

Juan, starting to feel hopeless, cried out, "What am I supposed to do mama? I just play and my strength is so great that something always happens."

Looking at him for a long time before she spoke, Juan's mother finally said in a sad voice, "Juan, I never thought I would be the one to say this. Usually, it is the child who brings it up first. But now you are almost grown, and I think it is time you go into the world to seek adventure and fortune."

Juan stood still and didn't answer at first. He loved his home and his mother. He couldn't stand the idea of having to leave home. He pleaded with his mother: "I don't want to go into the world. Please don't send me away."

His mother tried to explain, "I'm not sending you away. Even if you had never had your strength, this time would have come. Sooner or later every child must go into the world to seek his fortune. Now it is your turn."

Juan sadly accepted the inevitable, and with resignation in his voice he answered, "Perhaps it is for the best. My strength has made me different all of my life. Perhaps in my adventures, my strength will bring me good fortune."

Hugging her son with a confused and torn heart, Juan's mother said the words that she knew would come one day, but words she really was not ready to say, "Juan, you have my blessing on your journeys. I know that your great strength will protect you and bring you good fortune."

Juan and his mother hugged each other, and both wiped away the tears of their sadness. Juan packed a few special things in a bag and, as all children everywhere must eventually do, left home to seek his fortune in the world.

As expected, wherever he went, Juan was able to find work. His great strength made him the most respected of all the workers in the land. In his travels, however, he soon began to hear the legends of two men whose strength was as great as his. He had never imagined that someone else could be as strong as he was. But soon he was to find out that his was not the only great strength in the world.

One day, Juan was walking through the forest and he heard a voice singing a grand, boastful song. In a powerful and clear voice, the stranger sang:

From early in the morn
Since the very day I was born
Till the end of night
I have had to work with all my might.
There has never been a man as mighty as me
I have searched the Earth from sea to sea
And everywhere I look still I have not found
A man such as me who could move a river from its ground.

Juan thought this would be a good time to have some fun, so he answered back with an impromptu song of his own:

Your boasts are like water filled with sand
Shallow and easily disturbed by another hand
Until now you say you have always ruled the day
But before my strength you should move and clear the way.

As Juan finished his song, he came upon a clearing in the forest and saw a large, powerfully built man. Juan and the man circled each other, cautiously and suspiciously eyeing one another. Finally, the man asked Juan in a thundering voice, "Who are you to challenge me in this way?" As he spoke, he threateningly shook his fist at Juan.

The man did not frighten Juan, because Juan had never been afraid of anybody in his life. Juan stood up to the man's threatening manner and, in his own thundering voice, said, "*Juan Oso*, John the Bear. My strength is as great as the bear. And who are you?"

The man took his measure of Juan and boasted, "I am *Mudarríos*, River Mover. My strength allows me to move rivers from where they run. I challenge you to a contest of strength."

Juan did not back down from this challenge. Besides, he thought it might be interesting to see *Mudarríos* move a river. Juan accepted the challenge and said, "I accept your challenge. We shall see who is to be called the strongest of men at the end of this day."

Juan and *Mudarríos* circled each other, staring intently into each other's eyes. Neither wanted to make the first move. Finally, they lunged at each other and locked arms in a wrestling grip. They grappled in a fight similar to wrestling, except they fought standing up. They were both immensely strong and evenly matched. Juan had never met anyone as strong as he was, and it surprised him.

For many minutes, they ferociously grappled. With each mighty move, they knocked down trees and shoved aside boulders. Neither seemed to have an edge over the other. The tide of the fight switched back and forth between the two mighty men. First it seemed as if Juan might win. Then it seemed as if *Mudarríos* might win. Finally, exhausted, both gave up because the struggle was so evenly matched.

Juan congratulated *Mudarríos*: "An even match!"

Mudarríos laughed and shook Juan's hand saying, "Even and well fought!"

Both Juan and *Mudarríos* then sat down and rested from their epic battle. Juan told *Mudarríos*, "I am on my journey in the world seeking adventure and fortune."

Mudarríos answered, "I am wandering the Earth finding what work I can. I am called *Mudarríos*, River Mover, because that is the work I do best. I have moved almost all of the rivers of the Earth. I always find the best path for the river to seek its way back home to the great ocean."

Juan continued the friendly conversation by telling Mudarríos, "My work has been very much the same. I have cleared forests in one day. I have moved houses to the top of the mountain. I have carried horses across raging rivers to safety."

Mudarríos stood and picked up Juan with a giant bear hug and said, "River Mover and John the Bear. Finally, I have found a *compadre* to share my work."

After *Mudarríos* put him back on the ground, Juan then said, "And I have found a friend whose strength is as great as mine."

Juan and *Mudarríos* made a camp for themselves and began cooking a supper of grilled game they had each captured. Because they were both giant eaters, they each finished off a couple of deer and washed them down with river water.

After the meal, *Mudarríos* told Juan, "I must tell you there is one other whose strength is equal to ours. His name is *Mudacerros*, Mountain Mover. Often, when I am doing the job of moving the rivers, I have seen *Mudacerros* across the valley doing his work of moving the mountains."

Juan could not believe a second person as strong as he was existed. Incredulously, he asked *Mudarríos*, "How could one man's strength be so great that he can move mountains?"

Mudarríos answered, "You will soon find out. If you listen, you will hear the footsteps of *Mudacerros*. He was working close to me this morning, and the shaking of the ground tells me that he will soon be here."

Juan put his ear to the ground and carefully listened. He could feel the earth shaking and hear the approaching footsteps of *Mudacerros*. They sounded like the loud booming of a giant. *Mudacerros* stomped into the forest clearing and immediately went over to *Mudarríos* and gave him a hearty slap on the back.

In a voice as loud as thunder, *Mudacerros* bellowed, "*Mudarríos*! My old friend. I saw you working in the other valley this morning. How many rivers have you moved today?"

Mudarríos gave *Mudacerros* a return slap on the back and told him, "Too many for one day's work. I put one right on top of the land where you had just moved a mountain."

Mudacerros then looked at Juan and asked, "And who is our good friend here?"

Juan stood tall, made his voice as deep and strong as he could, and answered, "I am *Juan Oso*, John the Bear.

Mudarríos told his friend *Mudacerros*, "His strength is as great as ours. He matched me pull for pull in an arm fight. And I must admit that he almost beat me."

Mudacerros, giving Juan a hearty slap on the back, then said, "*Juan Oso*, join us in our work. No man will be able to match the work we three will be able to do. River Mover, Mountain Mover, and John the Bear!"

Mudarríos was excited about *Mudacerros*'s idea. He quickly agreed, "With you working beside us, all of the work of the world will be ours."

Juan could not believe that he had found not only two others as strong as he was but also such good friends. He told them both, "Then I truly have found my fortune. When I left home, I knew that my strength would help me find my good fortune."

Mudarríos cheered and yelled, "*Compadres*! Let's begin our journeys! The work of the world waits for us!"

Indeed, Juan had found his good fortune. He was never without work and enjoyed the company of his two friends *Mudarríos* and *Mudacerros*.

One night, at their campsite, there appeared a strange visitor, a *duende*, a forest elf who causes mischief in the human world. Juan and *Mudarríos* were still working, while *Mudacerros* was alone in the camp tending to the fire and cooking supper.

Mudacerros was singing to himself as he stirred the coals. His great voice cleared the skies of flying birds and replenished them with sound. He sang:

> *Mudacerros, Mudacerros*
> *All the work you did today*
> *Never was there such a man*
> *They should give you twice the pay!*

As he was singing, the *duende* crept up behind him and taunted him with a song of his own:

> *Mudacerros, Mudacerros*
> *Are you sure you're not crazy?*
> *With the little work you did today*
> *I know you're very lazy!*

Mudacerros was startled and turned around to confront the *duende*. He asked the *duende*, "Who are you to talk to me in that way? Do you know who you're talking to?"

In a light, high-pitched voice, the *duende* chuckled, "*Mudacerros*—mole hill mover?"

Mudacerros reached out to grab the *duende* and yelled, "I'll teach you respect!" As he reached for the *duende*, the *duende* was too fast and dodged the blow. *Mudacerros* then said in his most threatening voice, "So you think you are fast, eh? Well, soon you will be begging for my mercy."

He attempted another blow and, as he chased the *duende*, the *duende* tripped *Mudacerros*. Now *Mudacerros* was really mad. He shook his fist at the *duende* and said, "That is the end of my kindness. Now you will pay with your life."

Again he lunged at the *duende*, and the *duende* again tripped him. With devilish laughter, the *duende* began to beat *Mudacerros* on the head. He then stole the pan of food and ran off into the forest.

Juan and *Mudarríos* had heard all of the commotion and came running back to camp. Juan arrived first and asked *Mudacerros*, "What happened? We heard you yelling."

Mudacerros dusted himself off and told his two surprised friends, "A horrible little man attacked me. He beat me up and stole our supper."

Mudarríos laughed and said, "A little man beat up the mighty Mountain Mover! I wish I could have seen that."

Mudacerros replied, "He was no ordinary little man. I'm sure he was a forest *duende*. They have magical powers that allow them to cause mischief in the world."

Juan looked around the forest and searched for the *duende*. He had never seen one and was curious about the *duendes* because he had heard so many stories about their mischief. He asked, "Why would they be here?"

Mudarríos knew of the lore of the *duendes* and explained to Juan, "Their underground caverns are nearby. It is impossible to find them. Also, I have heard that they keep princesses captive in those caverns."

Mudacerros had also heard many stories about the *duendes*, but this was the first time he had ever seen one. He agreed with *Mudarríos*'s explanation and added, "And they are guarded by giants!"

Mudarríos then said, "Well, tomorrow I will cook the supper. I know the ways of the *duendes*, and it will not get our food a second time."

The next day, it was Juan and *Mudacerros* who went to work in the mountains. *Mudarríos* stayed in the camp and waited for the *duende* to return. As he waited, he busied himself by cooking the evening meal. While he cooked, he suspiciously looked around and nervously sang to himself:

> *The night is very cold*
> *The duende had better not be so bold*
> *Mudarríos, powerful man*
> *Will catch that duende if he can.*

The *duende*, just as he had made fun of *Mudacerros*, sang back:

> *Mudarríos, Mudarríos*
> *The duende is too smart*
> *Scared and powerless man*
> *There is no way you can.*

Now it was *Mudarríos*'s turn to fight the *duende*. As he chased the *duende*, he yelled, "*Duende*! Now you will pay!"

Mudarríos chased the *duende*, but the *duende* was too fast and escaped all of *Mudarríos*'s efforts to catch him. *Mudarríos* lunged at the *duende*, but the *duende* tripped *Mudarríos* and began to beat him on the head. Then he once again stole the pan of food and ran off.

Juan and *Mudacerros* heard the fighting and ran back to camp hoping to help catch the *duende*. When they arrived, they found the camp destroyed from the fight and saw *Mudarríos* sitting in a pile of broken logs. All *Mudarríos* could say in his defense was, "He was too fast, the tricky little devil!"

Juan couldn't believe that a little fellow like a forest *duende* could trick his two strong friends. He began to pick up the camp and said, "Now we have to go another night without food. Tomorrow, I will wait, and I will catch that *duende*!"

The next night, Juan was ready. He placed a pan of food down as a trap, and then he walked around singing loudly:

Little man, little man
I dare you to show your face
If there is any way I can
You will never leave this place.

The *duende* fell for the trap and answered with his own song:

Two much better than you
Have tried and tried they said
And you have no clue
Before I beat you 'round the head.

The *duende* ran by Juan and tried to hit him on the head, but Juan was too fast and caught the *duende* by the corner of his shirt. But the *duende* broke free and ran off screaming, and Juan was left holding his shirt.

Mudarríos and *Mudacerros* had been hiding in the forest watching the incident. They quickly came running to help Juan, who was standing in the middle of the camp, holding a piece of the *duende's* shirt. He told his two amazed friends, "I caught him. Here is his shirt. He escaped, but I saw him go into a hole in the ground. It must be the opening to their underground caverns."

Mudacerros remembered all of the stories he had heard about the caverns and excitedly said, "Stolen treasures can be found under there. We could be rich. Show us the place."

Juan took them to the spot in the forest where he had seen the *duende* go down a hole and said, "It's this hole right here. I looked down this hole, but it was too deep to climb down. One of us will have to be lowered down with a rope."

Mudarríos and *Mudacerros* grabbed a rope and lowered Juan down into the cave. At the bottom of the cave, Juan did find the treasures *Mudacerros* had talked about. He also discovered a room that held captive three princesses.

The first princess was guarded by a giant, the second by a tiger, and the third by a serpent. Each tried to stop Juan, but his strength was too much for all of them. Juan was able to defeat all three guards and release the princesses from their captivity.

After freeing them, Juan found himself speechless, for he had never seen such beautiful princesses. When he was finally able to talk, he told the three princesses, "You are safe now. We must return to the mouth of the cavern, and my two friends will be able to lift you out with a rope."

One of the princesses spoke first and told Juan, "Thank you for rescuing us. Our father is the king and will reward you handsomely."

The second princess said, "No one has ever found the *duende*'s caverns. We have waited and waited to be rescued. The *duende* took care of us, but he would not let us leave."

The third princess took off her crown and gave Juan two jewels from it. As she handed Juan the two beautiful jewels, she said, "Here are two gems from my crown. I give them to you to thank you for rescuing us."

Juan could not believe the adventure he was having. He put the gems safely in his pocket, and then he told the princesses, "We had better leave. The *duende* will return any minute. My friends will pull you up with the rope. Then we can take you safely back to your castle."

He then called up to *Mudarríos* and *Mudacerros*, "Throw the rope down! The princesses are ready to come up."

Mudacerros heard Juan calling and told *Mudarríos*, "He must have rescued the princesses. The king will generously reward whoever brings them back."

Mudarríos agreed, "Yes. A handsome reward is possible."

Mudacerros went on further with an evil plan, "A reward split in two produces larger shares than a reward split in three. This is our one chance to make our fortune."

Sensing his idea, *Mudarríos* answered, "Perhaps you are right. We have been together long before he joined us. Yes. Two parts are greater than three parts."

Mudarríos and *Mudacerros* then threw down the rope. Juan helped the three princesses climb up the rope to their freedom. When the last princess had climbed the rope, *Mudarríos* and *Mudacerros* pulled up the rope, leaving Juan stranded at the bottom.

Juan yelled to his friends, "Hey! Throw down the rope! Get me out of here!"

One of the princesses asked *Mudarríos*, "Aren't you going to help him?"

Mudacerros answered, "No. We made an agreement that he would stay down and further explore the caverns, and we would come back for him later."

Then *Mudarríos* and *Mudacerros* left to take the princesses back to their castle. They threw the rope away, making sure that Juan remained abandoned in the cavern.

Meanwhile, Juan didn't know why it was taking so long for his friends to throw down the rope to him. He again yelled up to them, "Help! *Mudarríos*, throw down the rope! *Mudacerros*, pull me up! Help!"

Just then, the *duende* entered the cavern where Juan was yelling. He asked Juan, "What are you doing in my caverns? And where are the princesses? Did you see where the treasures are hidden?"

The *duende* jumped on Juan and began to hit him on the head, but this time Juan was too strong for the *duende*. He simply picked up the *duende* and dangled him in the air by his feet.

Juan threatened the *duende* by telling him, "Duende, you'd better show me the way out of this cavern, or you will never leave it again yourself! This is your last chance! Show me the way out of this cavern!"

The *duende* begged for mercy and pleaded, "Put me down! Ouch! You're hurting my neck." He then pointed to the way out: "The path out begins right over there. Ouch! Not so hard. Ouch!"

Meanwhile, *Mudarríos* and *Mudacerros* took the princesses back to their father's castle. When the king saw his three daughters returned safely, he told *Mudarríos* and *Mudacerros*, "I wish to reward you two for rescuing my daughters."

The queen also said, "The whole kingdom owes you its gratitude. The princesses are most beloved throughout the kingdom. You have brought back joy to our land."

The king then said, "The princesses have told me that a third man was the one who actually rescued them from the caverns."

Quickly, *Mudarríos* answered, "No. They are mistaken. They were so scared, and it was so dark in the caves that they imagined a third man. It was just my friend and me."

As *Mudarríos* was speaking, Juan entered the king's throne room and pointed to Mudarríos and said, "Your majesty, those words are a lie!"

The king motioned to his guards and said, "Who are you who so rudely bursts into the king's throne room? Guards!"

The first princess ran up to Juan and told the king, "Father, this is the man who rescued us."

The second princess also ran up to Juan and said, "It is him." She then turned to Juan and said, "They said you were dead."

Mudarríos pushed Juan aside and said to the king, "Your majesty, this man is an impostor."

Mudacerros agreed with him: "It was dark in the caves, and your daughters were suffering from their captivity. They could not see clearly enough to identify the man. This man is not our partner. He is a thief trying to gain our reward."

Juan approached the king and asked, "Please, your majesty, may I speak?"

The third princess also beseeched her father, "Please, let him speak, father."

The king was curious about the turn of events and told Juan, "You may speak."

Speaking very deliberately, Juan addressed the king, "Your majesty. Examine closely the crown of your third daughter. It is missing two gemstones. Here are the stones your daughter gave me in the caverns as I was rescuing her and her sisters."

The king took the crown of the third princess and examined it along with the two gems Juan had handed him. He returned the crown to his daughter and the gems to Juan.

The king gestured to *Mudarríos* and *Mudacerros* and commanded, "Guards! Throw these two men into the dungeon." Then he addressed Juan, "And you, good sir, join us in a celebration of the rescue of the princesses. And know that those two gems you hold are but the first of many you shall receive as your reward for rescuing the princesses."

Ashes for Sale

Once, there were two close friends (*dos compadres*)—one rich and one poor, as is common in *dos compadres* stories. The rich *compadre* constantly lorded his wealth over the poor *compadre*. He would belittle the poor *compadre* by saying how lazy and dumb he was and by reminding him of his bad luck. Even though they had been *compadres* for many years, there really wasn't much friendship left between the two men.

The poor *compadre*, nevertheless, worked hard all his days, struggling to provide a meager life for his family. While he was sweating in the fields working his crops under the scorching hot sun, the poor *compadre* dreamed of the day when he would have more money and his family would not have to struggle so much. He saw himself sitting at the same fine table as the rich *compadre*, and the rich *compadre* was asking *him* for advice. As with most dreams, they helped to pass the time spent doing tedious work, but eventually, they would fade under the harsh light of reality. For the poor *compadre*, reality came every time he met up with the rich *compadre* and was reminded of his poverty and the rich *compadre*'s wealth.

One day, the rich *compadre* was carrying a sack of flour to the baker when he ran into the poor *compadre*. The rich *compadre* greeted the poor *compadre*, "*Compadre*, what has you walking on the road so early in the morning?"

The poor *compadre* responded, "I am going to town to look for work. The crops have been damaged this year because of the hot weather. My family needs to eat, so I must find a job soon."

Just then, the poor *compadre* noticed the large sack the rich *compadre* was carrying. He was curious about what it contained. He asked the rich *compadre*, "What do you carry in your sack?" He went on, "Please tell me if it has anything to do with work or money, because I am looking for a way to find both."

The rich *compadre* looked at his sack and decided it would be fun to play a little joke on the poor *compadre*. He replied to the poor *compadre*, "This old sack? It is just a sack of ashes. Every few days, I clean out my fireplace and take the ashes to town to sell. For some reason, the townspeople need extra ashes and are willing to pay a lot of money for them. Listen, *compadre*, I know that you are always in need of a little extra money. Perhaps you can make some by selling the ashes from your fireplace."

The poor *compadre* could not believe that the rich *compadre* had finally seen it in his heart to offer some kindness to him. He knew that the rich *compadre* was very good about finding ways to make money. Maybe at last he could share in one of the rich *compadre's* moneymaking plans. He looked at the sack the rich *compadre* was carrying and asked, "They are willing to pay good money for a simple bag of ashes?"

The rich *compadre* slapped him on the back and said, "Lots of it, *compadre*!"

The poor *compadre* hurried home and told his wife about his new plan. As he scooped the ashes from the fireplace into a sack, he excitedly told her, "Soon our worries will be over. I know a plan that will make us lots of money."

Now, the wife had seen her husband come home with a lot of crazy ideas for making money, but this one seemed worse than all the others. She could not believe that any person would pay money for something they could get at home for free. She warned her husband: "The rich *compadre* has never helped us before. I'm suspicious of this plan of yours. Whatever you do, don't lose any of our own money."

The poor *compadre* finished filling his sack with ashes and raced out the door calling back to his wife, "Don't worry. This is a foolproof plan." He then hurried to town to make his fortune.

When he arrived in the town, he went to the town square, put the sack down on the ground before him, and opened it up. He proudly stood over his sack and called out, "Ashes for sale! Ashes for sale!"

People walked by looking at him as if he were crazy. Some stopped to look at the ashes and then walked away laughing. Others crossed the street so they would not have to pass in front of the poor *compadre*.

By the end of the day, the poor *compadre* was tired, covered in dust, and hoarse from yelling, "Ashes for sale!" He finally asked a man who had been selling masks next to him all day, "Good *señor*, please tell me why nobody will buy my ashes. My *compadre* told me everybody in town would buy them."

The mask seller looked at him sympathetically and said, "I'm afraid you've been the victim of a cruel joke. Nobody is going to buy ashes from you. We have all the ashes we need in our own fireplaces at home."

The mask seller took pity on the sad plight of the poor *compadre* and handed him one of his paper masks. He told him, "Here, take this mask. I have had a good day and you look as if you need your luck to change. Maybe this mask will be of some use to you some day."

The poor *compadre* took the mask and looked at it. It was a mask of *el diablo* himself. It was red, with horns, and had a fierce expression on it. He didn't know how the mask would ever be of any use to him, but he accepted it and thanked the mask seller.

As the sun set and nighttime approached, the poor *compadre* realized that his plan was a failure. His foolproof plan had only proved him to be a fool. He then realized that once again the rich *compadre* had gotten the best of him. Dejectedly, he emptied his ashes onto the ground and began the long walk back home.

As he walked home, he imagined what he would tell his wife. Even more, he fantasized about all the ways he would get revenge on the rich *compadre*.

But it had gotten too late for him to make it all the way home that night. He searched the area and saw a cave that looked as if it would provide a warm and safe spot for a night's rest.

He went into the cave and discovered that it was a labyrinth of tunnels, with each tunnel leading farther back into the cave. He followed one of the tunnels until he found a secluded spot to spend the night. As he lay down to rest, he felt water from the roof of the cave dripping on his face. He moved to another spot, but the water still dripped in his face. Finally, he put the mask on his face, thinking that maybe it would be of some use after all. The water just dripped on the mask, and the poor *compadre* was finally able to fall asleep.

Later in the night, after the poor *compadre* had been sleeping for several hours, he awoke to strange noises. The cave was pitch dark, and he couldn't see anything. As the noises got closer, he realized that he was hearing voices. He became frightened because he remembered stories about thieves and murderers using caves for hiding places. He was so scared that he forgot that he still had the mask on his face.

Soon, a wild-looking group of men came to the place where the poor *compadre* sat hiding against the walls of the cave. The men were indeed bandits who had come to their hiding spot in the caves. As they came closer, the poor *compadre* could see them because of the lit torches they carried. The men had bags of money—many, many heavy bags of money. The poor *compadre* sat as still as he could in fear of what the men would do to him if he were discovered.

One of the men spoke in a fierce, mean voice that sent a shiver down the spine of the poor *compadre*. He growled to the other men, "This is where we'll stop for the rest of the night. In the morning, we will split up the money and go our separate ways."

As the poor *compadre* sat shaking with fear, he felt something crawling up his leg. Imagining that it was a scorpion or a tarantula, he let out a yell. But it had only been a spider.

With knives drawn and ready to kill whomever they found, the bandits immediately ran to the spot from where they heard the yell. One of the bandits stumbled over the poor *compadre*. He shoved a fiery torch in the *compadre*'s face. The flames of the torch lit the *diablo* mask the poor *compadre* was still wearing and made it appear ferocious and evil.

The bandit screamed, "We've gone down too far into the Earth. *El diablo* himself has come to get us for our evil ways!" The bandit was so frightened that he let out a terrible scream, causing all the bats in the cave to start flying around. Then he dropped the torch, which set the ground on fire.

Now, the poor *compadre*, still wearing the mask, started screaming and running around trying to find a way out of the cave. He did not realize that while he was doing this, he was surrounded by flames of fire and flying bats.

What the bandits saw was *el diablo* himself rising out of the flames of his land, accompanied by his evil bats, screaming and yelling, come to take them to their eternal punishment. The bandits ran crazily through the tunnels of the caves trying to escape *el diablo*. They were running in such desperate fear, they all unfortunately fell off a steep cliff and drowned in a subterranean river raging below.

Meanwhile, the poor *compadre* had run around in such a fearful frenzy that he smacked into one of the cave's walls and knocked himself out. When he awoke, the fires were out and all he heard was a deathly silence in the cave. He searched the ground and found one of the fallen torches. He relit it and began walking back through the tunnels, alert for the return of the bandits. He eventually discovered the bodies of the bandits floating away on the river to their watery graves. The poor *compadre* couldn't help thinking that maybe *el diablo* had come for the bandits in punishment for their evil ways.

The poor *compadre* then found the bags of money the bandits had dropped in their mad flight. He tried to count the money, but he gave up because there was too much of it. All he knew was that it was enough for his family to live comfortably for the rest of their lives.

When the poor *compadre* returned home, he told his wife the whole fiasco of trying to sell ashes in town. He then told her the amazing story about the bandits and the cave, including the part about the *diablo* mask. But he had saved the best part for last. When he finished his story, he took her out to the barn and showed her the bags of money. She saw all of those shining coins and fainted dead away.

The poor *compadre* tried to find out from where the bandits' money had come, but the bandits must have stolen it in a land far from the poor *compadre*'s. Eventually, he decided to keep the money and do good works with it. He gave a significant amount to the church and gave small bags filled with money to those in need. The poor *compadre* remembered his own days of poverty and vowed he would always assist those in need.

Meanwhile, the rich *compadre* noticed that the poor *compadre* had suddenly become rich. He saw that the poor *compadre* had so much money, he even gave some of it away. The rich *compadre* was jealous and had to know how the poor *compadre* came into such wealth. He walked to the poor *compadre*'s house and said, "*Compadre*, I have noticed that your luck has changed. Perhaps you would share with me the story of your wealth."

The poor *compadre* knew that this was the situation for which he had been waiting. In his most sincere voice he said, "Well, to tell the truth, I owe all this money to your good advice. As you suggested, I went to town to sell my ashes. What you said was true. The people of the town really *did* need extra ashes. They bought so much that I was able to set up a little business selling ashes to them. And from that simple idea, I became rich. In fact, so rich that I don't need to work anymore. I have retired from the ash-selling business, and if you wish to continue it, I am sure that the people of the town still need ashes."

The rich *compadre* couldn't believe that his silly idea of selling ashes worked. He knew the poor *compadre*'s story had to be true because he couldn't imagine any other way the poor *compadre* could have come into so much money. He told the poor *compadre*, "I can see that the plan worked for you, and I just might take you up on your offer of taking over the business."

From then on, the life of the poor *compadre* and his family changed. They lived a life of comfort and leisure, and throughout the valley they practiced their good works of charity for the poor. They also spent many enjoyable moments laughing about the stories they heard of the rich *compadre* standing on a corner in town calling out, "Ashes for sale! Ashes for sale!"

Se venden cenizas

Había una vez dos amigos cercanos, dos compadres, uno rico y uno pobre, como es común en las historias de dos compadres. El compadre rico hacía constantemente ostentación de su riqueza frente al compadre pobre. El rico rebajaba al compadre pobre diciéndole cuán perezoso y tonto era, y recordándole cuánta mala suerte tenía. Aunque habían sido compadres por muchos años, realmente no había mucha amistad entre los dos hombres.

El compadre pobre, sin embargo, trabajaba duro todos sus días, esforzándose para proveer una mísera vida a su familia. Mientras él estaba sudando en el campo, trabajando entre los sembradíos debajo del sol abrasador, el compadre pobre soñaba con el día en que tendría suficiente dinero y su familia ya no pasaría tanta necesidad. Se veía a él mismo sentado a la misma fina mesa que su compadre rico, y el compadre rico le pedía consejos a él. Como con la mayoría de sus sueños, éstos lo ayudaban a pasar el tiempo que se iba en ocupaciones tediosas, pero eventualmente se disipaban a la luz de la dura realidad. Para el compadre pobre, la realidad lo esperaba cada vez que se encontraba con el compadre rico y recordaba su pobreza y la riqueza del compadre rico.

Un día, el compadre rico llevaba una bolsa de harina al panadero cuando se encontró con el compadre pobre. El compadre rico saludó al compadre pobre: "Compadre, ¿qué hace caminando por la calle tan temprano en la mañana?"

"Voy a la ciudad a buscar trabajo. La cosecha se ha dañado este año debido al calor. Mi familia tiene que comer, así que debo encontrar trabajo pronto", respondió el compadre pobre.

En ese momento, el compadre pobre notó la gran bolsa que el compadre rico llevaba. Sintió curiosidad sobre qué contendría. Le preguntó al compadre rico: "¿Qué llevas en esa bolsa?" Y agregó: "Por favor, dime si tiene algo que ver con trabajo o con dinero, porque estoy buscando ambos".

El compadre rico miró su bolsa y decidió que sería divertido hacerle una pequeña broma a su compadre pobre. Le respondió al compadre pobre: "¿Esta bolsa vieja? Es solamente un saco de cenizas. Cada dos o tres días, limpio mi chiminea y vengo a la ciudad a vender las cenizas. Por alguna razón, la gente de la ciudad necesita más cenizas, y me pagan buen dinero por ellas. Escucha, compadre, yo sé que tú siempre necesitas un poco de dinero extra. Quizá podrías hacer algo de dinero vendiendo las cenizas de tu chimenea."

El compadre pobre no podía creer que el compadre rico finalmente había decidido en su corazón ofrecer un poco de amabilidad. Sabía que el compadre rico era muy bueno en cuanto a encontrar maneras de hacer dinero. Quizá por fin podría compartir uno de los planes del compadre rico para hacer dinero. Miró la bolsa que el compadre rico llevaba y preguntó: "¿Pagan buen dinero por una simple bolsa de cenizas?"

Con una palmada en la espalda, el compadre rico respondió: "¡Mucho dinero, compadre!"

El compadre pobre regresó apresuradamente a su casa y le contó a su esposa el nuevo plan. Mientras juntaba las cenizas de la chimenea y las ponía en una bolsa, le dijo a su esposa lleno de entusiamo: "En poco tiempo se terminarán nuestras preocupaciones. Tengo un plan que nos dará mucho dinero".

Ahora bien, la esposa había visto a su esposo llegar a la casa con muchas ideas locas para hacer dinero, pero ésta parecía peor que todas las otras. Ella no podía creer que ninguna persona pagase por algo que todos tenían gratis en sus propias casas. Le advirtió a su marido: "El compadre rico nunca nos ayudó antes. Tengo mis sospechas de este plan tuyo. Sea lo que fuere que hagas, no pierdas nada de tu dinero".

El compadre pobre terminó de llenar el saco de cenizas y salió corriendo por la puerta, dándose vuelta para decirle a su esposa: "No te preocupes. Este plan es infalible". Luego se dirigió a prisa a la ciudad para hacer fortuna.

Cuando llegó a la ciudad, fue a la plaza central, puso su bolsa en el suelo delante de él, y lo abrió. Con orgullo se paró junto a la bolsa y comenzó a anunciar: "¡Se venden cenizas, se venden cenizas!"

La gente pasaba y lo miraba como si estuviera loco. Algunos se paraban a ver las cenizas y luego seguían caminando, riéndose. Otros cruzaban la calle para no pasar junto al compadre pobre.

Al final del día el compadre pobre estaba cansado, cubierto de polvo y afónico de tanto gritar "¡Se venden cenizas!" Finalmente le preguntó a un hombre que estaba vendiendo máscaras junto a él todo el día: "Buen señor, por favor dígame por qué nadie me compra mis cenizas. Mi compadre me dijo que todos las compran en la ciudad".

El vendedor de máscaras lo miró con simpatía y le dijo: "Temo que usted ha sido víctima de una broma pesada. Nadie le va a comprar las cenizas. Tenemos todas las cenizas que necesitamos en las chimeneas de nuestros hogares".

El vendedor de máscaras sintió lástima de la triste condición del compadre pobre y le dio una de sus máscaras de papel. "Tome, tenga esta máscara. Tuve un buen día y parece que usted necesita cambiar su suerte. Quizá esta máscara le será útil algún día", le dijo.

El compadre pobre tomó la máscara y la miró. Era la máscara del mismo diablo. Era roja, con cuernos, y con una expresión feroz. No sabía cómo ni cuándo usaría la máscara, pero la aceptó y le agradeció al venderor de máscaras.

Al ponerse el sol y al llegar la noche, el compadre pobre se dio cuenta que su plan era un fracaso. Su plan infalible solamente había probado que él era un tonto. Comprendió que una vez mas el compadre rico lo había engañado. Con abatimiento vació las cenizas en el suelo y comenzó a recorrer el largo camino de regreso al hogar.

Al caminar hacia la casa se imaginó lo que le diría a su esposa. Pero más fantaseaba con la manera en que se vengaría de su compadre rico.

Pero ya se había hecho tarde esa noche para llegar hasta la casa. Buscó a su alrededor y vio una cueva que parecía podría proveerle un lugar seguro y cálido para pasar la noche.

Entró en la cueva y descubrió que era un laberinto de túneles, con cada tunel perdiéndose en el interior de la cueva. Siguió uno de los túneles y encontró un lugar apartado donde pasar la noche. Al recostarse para descansar, sintió que agua goteaba del techo de la cueva y le caía en la cara. Se movió a otro lugar, pero el agua seguía cayéndole en la cara. Finalmente, se puso la máscara en la cara, pensando que después de todo le era útil. El agua goteaba sobre la máscara, y el compadre pobre finalmente pudo dormir.

Más tarde esa noche, luego de que el compadre pobre había estado durmiendo por varias horas, ruidos extraños lo despertaron. La cueva estaba completamente oscura, y no pudo ver nada. Cuando los ruidos se acercaron, comprendió que estaba escuchando voces. Se asustó al acordarse de las historias de ladrones y asesinos escondiéndose en las cuevas. Tenía tanto miedo que se olvidó que todavía tenía la máscara puesta.

Poco después un grupo de hombres de apariencia salvaje llegó al lugar donde el compadre pobre estaba sentado, escondiéndose contra las paredes de la cueva. Los hombres eran en verdad bandidos, que habían venido a la cueva a esconderse. Al acercarse, el compadre pobre pudo verlos por la luz de la antorcha que llevaban. Los hombre tenían bolsas de dinero, muchas y pesadas bolsas de dinero. El compadre pobre se sentó tan quieto como pudo, por miedo de lo que los hombres le harían si lo descubrían.

Uno de los hombres habló con una voz feroz y malvada, que envió escalofríos a la espalda del compradre pobre. Les gruñó a los otros hombres: "Aquí es dónde nos detendremos a pasar la noche. Por la mañana dividiremos el dinero y nos separaremos".

Mientras tanto, el compadre pobre estaba sentado, temblando de miedo. Sintió algo que le subía por la pierna. Imaginando que era un escorpión o una tarántula, dejó escapar un grito. Pero era solamente una araña.

Blandiendo cuchillos y listos para matar a quienquiera que los hubiese encontrado, los bandidos corrieron hacia el lugar donde se había escuchado el grito.

Uno de los bandidos se trastabilló sobre el compadre pobre. Puso una antorcha ardiente en la cara del compadre. La llamas de la antorcha iluminaron la máscara del diablo que el compadre pobre todavía llevaba puesta, y que lo hizo aparecer como feroz y malévolo.

El bandido gritó: "Hemos descendido mucho en la tierra. ¡El mismísimo diablo ha venido a castigarnos por nuestras malas maneras!" El bandido tenía tanto miedo que se le escapó un terrible grito, haciendo que todos los murciélagos de la cueva comenzacen a volar. Entonces se le cayó la antorcha, lo que hizo que se prendiese fuego al suelo.

Ahora bien, el compadre pobre, todavía con la máscara puesta, comenzó a gritar y a correr alrededor de la cueva, tratando de encontrar la salida. No se dio cuenta que al hacer esto estaba rodeado de llamas de fuego y de muerciélagos voladores.

Cuando los bandidos vieron que el diablo mismo se elevaba de las llamas del suelo, acompañado de sus maléficos murciélagos, gritando y aullando, pensaron que venía a llevarlos a su castigo eterno. Los bandidos corrieron como locos a través de los túneles de las cuevas tratando de escapar del diablo. Corrían con tanto temor y desesperación que, desafortudamente, todos se cayeron por un despeñadero y se ahogaron en un río subterráneo que corría allí abajo.

Mientras tanto, el compadre pobre corrió con un miedo tan frenético que chocó contra una de las paredes de la cueva y quedó demayado. Cuando se despertó, el fuego se había apagado y todo lo que escuchó fue el mortal silencio de la cueva. Buscó en el suelo y encontró una de las antorchas. La encendió y comenzó a caminar por los túneles, alerta, por miedo al regreso de los bandidos. Eventualmente descubrió los cuerpos de los bandidos flotando en el río, de camino hacia su tumba de agua. El compadre pobre no pudo sino pensar que quizá el diablo había venido a buscar a los bandidos para castigarlos por sus malas conductas.

El compadre pobre encontró entonces las bolsas de dinero que los bandidos habían dejado caer en su loca huída. Trató de contar el dinero, pero abandonó la tarea porque era mucho. Lo único que supo fue que era suficiente para que él y su familia viviesen cómodamente el resto de sus vidas.

Cuando el compadre pobre volvió a su casa, le dijo a su esposa de todo el fiasco de vender las cenizas en la ciudad. Le contó entonces su asombrosa historia sobre los bandidos en la cueva, incluyendo la parte de la máscara del diablo. Pero dejó lo mejor para el final. Cuando terminó su historia, la llevó al granero y le mostró todas las bolsas de dinero. Ella vio todas esas relucientes monedas de oro y se desmayó como muerta.

El compadre pobre trató de averiguar de dónde había venido el dinero que los bandidos tenían, pero, seguramente, los bandidos debían haberlo robado en un lugar muy lejos de donde vivía el compadre pobre. Eventualmente, decidió quedarse con el dinero y hacer obras de caridad. Le dio una importante suma a la iglesia, y les daba bolsitas de dinero a los necesitados. El compadre pobre recordaba sus días de pobreza y prometió que siempre ayudaría a los necesitados.

Mientras tando, el compadre rico notó que el compadre pobre se había vuelto rico de repente. Vio que el compadre pobre tenía tanto dinero que incluso repartía parte de ese dinero. El compadre rico estaba celoso y quiso saber cómo era quel el compadre pobre tenía ahora tanta riqueza. Caminó hasta la casa del compadre pobre y le dijo: "Compadre, he notado que tu suerte ha cambiado. Quizá te gustaría compartir conmigo la historia de tu riqueza".

El compadre pobre reconoció que ésta era la ocasión que él estaba esperando. En su tono de voz más sincero dijo: "Bueno, te diré la verdad. Debo este dinero a tu buen consejo. Como me sugeriste, fui a la ciudad a vender mis cenizas. Lo que me dijiste era verdad. La gente de la ciudad realmente necesitaba cenizas extras. Compraron tanto que pude comenzar una pequeña empresa vendiéndoles cenizas. Y por esa simple idea me hice rico. De hecho, soy tan rico que ya no necesito trabajar. Me he retirado del negocio de vender cenizas. Si tú quieres continuarlo, estoy seguro que la gente de la ciudad todavía necesita cenizas".

El compadre rico no podía creer que su tonta idea de vender cenizas hubiese funcionado. Creyó que la historia del compadre pobre era verdad, porque no pudo imaginarse ninguna otra manera en que el compadre pobre pudiese haber hecho tanto dinero. Le dijo al compadre pobre: "Veo que el plan funcionó para ti. Y creo que hasta aceptaré tu oferta de hacerme cargo del negocio".

Desde ese día, la vida del compadre pobre y de su familia cambió. Vivieron una vida de comodidad y placer, y practicaron sus buenas obras de caridad con los pobres de todo el valle. También tenían sus buenos momentos de risa cuando escuchaban las historias del compadre rico parado en una esquina de la ciudad y gritando: "¡Se venden cenizas, se venden cenizas!"

The Magic Cap

Once there were two *compadres*—one rich, and the other poor. The rich *compadre* was a man of great wealth who had land, cattle, and a large *hacienda*. The poor *compadre* was not as fortunate. His home was a small plot of barren land outside of town, and he struggled to put food on his family's table. No matter how hard he worked, he never seemed to be doing any better.

One day, the poor *compadre* told his wife, "My *compadre* and I have been friends for many years. You and I have struggled so hard and have so little to show for it, while he is the most admired man in the valley because of his great wealth. I am going to go and ask him for help. Although I am a proud man, it isn't right that we should starve. Perhaps he would see fit to help us."

The next day, the poor *compadre* went to his friend's house. With his beaten and worn cap in his hand, he asked his *compadre* for help to make it through his difficult time.

The rich *compadre* laughed when he heard his friend's tale of woe. He said, "If you would only work harder and use your wits more, you would have wealth like I do. I cannot help you, because it would be wrong to help someone who does not help himself." He then looked at the poor *compadre*'s cap and offered a suggestion, "Why don't you take your cap to town and try to sell it as an antique? It is so old and worn, people would pay just to see such a cap."

The poor *compadre* left with his cap in hand and vowed someday to make the rich *compadre* realize how much he had humiliated him.

For a full year, the poor *compadre* worked harder than ever. During this time, his luck began to change. His crop was his largest harvest ever, and he was even able to put a little money aside. He was still not as well off as the rich *compadre*, but his family was happy and healthy, and they appreciated not having to struggle as much as before.

One day, the poor *compadre* told his wife, "Now it is time for me to play a little joke on my friend. He never realized how humiliated I was the day I asked him for help. He was so discourteous to me. It is time for him to learn a lesson."

The poor *compadre* took a little of his hard-earned money and went into town. His first stop was a hat store, where he bought a beautiful new cap—one trimmed with leather and silver. Then he set about his plan.

He went to a jewelry store and purchased a cheap watch. He told the owner of the store, "I need your help. A rich man has humiliated me, and I want to play a little joke on him. Would you take this watch I just bought and change the price tag so it appears to be an expensive watch? I will return later with the rich man and once again buy my watch. When I start to pay for it, I will point to my new cap and say, '*Cárgueselo a la gorra,* charge it to the cap.' You are to say: 'You owe me nothing. Take it. It is yours.' "

After the jewelry store owner had agreed to help him, the poor *compadre* went to another store. In this one he bought an imitation string of pearls. Again he asked the store owner to help him. He explained the situation to him and said, "Would you take this string of cheap pearls I just bought and change the price tag so it appears to be an expensive necklace? I will return later with the rich man and once again buy my necklace. When I start to pay for it, I will point to my new cap and say, '*Cárgueselo a la gorra,* charge it to the cap.' You are to say: 'You owe me nothing. Take it. It is yours.' "

His last two stops were at a clothing store and a restaurant. In the first he bought a new suit and in the second he paid for two meals. At each place, he explained his situation and asked for the help of the owner. Each agreed to say: "You owe me nothing. Take it. It is yours," when the poor *compadre* said, "*Cárgueselo a la gorra,* charge it to the cap."

With his plan now set, the poor *compadre* went to see his friend. As he approached the house, the rich *compadre* came out and invited his friend into the house. He admired the new cap and suit of clothes the poor *compadre* was wearing, and said, "Well you certainly seem to be doing much better for yourself. You must have taken my advice. *Compadre,* you look like a man of great wealth. How did your fortunes change so quickly? Why, just a few months ago, you and your whole family looked as poor as ever. Is there some secret to your new wealth? Perhaps you could share it with me. You know, if you ever came asking for help again, I would surely help you this time."

The poor *compadre* told his friend, "Yes, my luck has changed. First, let me treat you to a fine meal, and then perhaps we can talk about the secret to my change of fortunes."

The rich *compadre* was never one to turn down a free meal, and besides, he was desperate to know the secret of his friend's wealth.

As they went into town, the poor *compadre* stopped at the first jewelry store they passed. He said, "I have bought myself a new watch. Let's stop and pick it up before we go to eat."

Once inside the store he pointed to a watch with an expensive price tag on it. The rich *compadre* looked on in amazement. When it came time to pay for the watch, the poor *compadre* pointed to his cap and said, "*Cárgueselo a la gorra,* charge it to the cap."

The store owner, as prearranged, said, "You owe me nothing. Take it. It is yours."

As they left the store, the rich *compadre* said to himself, "So it must be the cap. It must have some magical powers or be very valuable."

As they passed a second store, the poor *compadre* again said to his friend, "I have an expensive new necklace here. I promised my wife I would pick it up on the way home. Please excuse me while I do this for my wife."

Inside this store the same events happened as had occurred in the first store. The poor *compadre* selected a very expensive string of pearls and said, "*Cárgueselo a la gorra,* charge it to the cap." And again the store owner said, "You owe me nothing. Take it. It is yours."

Now the rich *compadre* was sure it was the cap. He vowed to have the cap for himself before the day was over.

At the restaurant, the poor *compadre* treated his friend to the finest meal he had ever had.

At the end of the meal, the poor *compadre* simply pointed to his cap and said, "*Cárgueselo a la gorra,* charge it to the cap." The rich *compadre* could not believe it as he watched the restaurant owner say to the poor *compadre*, "You owe me nothing. Come again anytime, for you are always welcome here."

Finally, the rich *compadre* could stand it no more. He said to his friend, "I have seen enough. I know that your cap is the secret to your new wealth. It must be a magic cap to turn your fortunes around so completely. Please sell it to me. I will give you whatever you want for it."

The poor *compadre* answered, "Believe me, my cap is not magic. It has nothing to do with my change in fortunes. It is a cap much like one you could buy yourself."

But the rich *compadre* would not hear it. He was determined to have the cap. Finally, the poor *compadre* accepted his offer of $10,000 for the cap.

As he left the restaurant, the poor *compadre* felt sorry for his friend. But he felt that his trick was a turn well deserved, as he knew that his friend's greedy ways would never change. Meanwhile, the rich *compadre* rushed home to tell his wife about the cap.

As he entered his home, the rich *compadre* excitedly told his wife about the cap. He said, "Get ready. We are going into town, and I am going to buy you the most expensive necklace. Then we will dine with more luxury than ever before and will be the envy of everyone who sees us."

At the same jewelry store as before, the rich *compadre* ushered in his eager wife and selected the largest diamond necklace he could find. After his thrilled wife had put it on, the rich *compadre* winked at his wife, looked at the store owner, pointed to his cap, and loudly said, "*Cárgueselo a la gorra,* charge it to the cap."

The store owner looked at the rich *compadre* and replied, "That cap will buy you nothing. Now pay up."

The rich *compadre* curtly answered back, "I will do no such thing! I said "*Cárgueselo a la gorra,* charge it to the cap."

The store owner immediately called the police and had the rich *compadre* arrested for attempted robbery.

The rich *compadre* was eventually let out of jail. But his reputation as a madman grew every time he told the story about the magic cap that, with the phrase "*Cárgueselo a la gorra,* charge it to the cap," could buy you anything in the world.

Meanwhile, the poor *compadre* carefully used the money he had received from the rich *compadre* to improve his fortunes. He continued to work hard, and his family was always thankful for the meager but good life they had. And through the years, the poor *compadre* entertained his children with the story about a magical cap that would buy whatever you wanted if you just said "*Cárgueselo a la gorra,* charge it to the cap."

The Art of Lying

There once lived two *compadres*—one smart, and one not so smart. The smart *compadre* was something of a con man. He fancied himself the world's greatest storyteller because of the tall tales he could tell. Some people might say he was the world's greatest liar, but he would disagree.

The smart *compadre* didn't consider himself a bad man for lying. He had traveled all over the world and had always been able to make a living solely through the use of his wits. He just figured that his clever wits were to use as he saw fit, and if they sometimes provided a better life for himself, then so much the better. Besides, he had always felt that no real harm came from his tall tales and that people probably enjoyed the trickery as much as he did.

One day, he was trying to teach his friend, the slow *compadre*, the art of lying. He called his friend over and said, "I am going to give you a lesson on the art of lying. If you learn and become even half as good as I am, then we can become partners. Now, just listen to me and try to do as I do."

He felt that it was his obligation to help his friend. His friend had always been a good person, but because he was a little slow, he had not amounted to much. He felt that by giving his friend a few lessons, he could make him a partner in his fun.

He began the lesson by telling his friend, "Now, pay close attention. I have traveled the world over and have seen many miraculous things. Some of those things your eyes would not believe. Why, once I saw a pumpkin so large that a shepherd used it as a barn for his sheep."

The slow *compadre* really enjoyed the tall tales his friend would tell. He had always secretly wished that his friend would take him on as a partner. Often he had heard his friend working his magic on groups of people, and he had learned a few things along the way. He knew that one of the secrets was to tell a taller tale than the one just told.

He thought and thought as hard as he could and, finally, he replied to his friend, "Well, once in my travels, I saw an oven so big that it took 10 men to keep the fire going."

The smart *compadre* liked what he was hearing. Perhaps his friend would be all right after all. Out of genuine curiosity, he replied, "Why was the oven so large, my friend?"

The slow *compadre* laughed and said in reply, "To cook your pumpkin in, my *amigo*."

The smart *compadre* laughed and laughed and knew that his friend was ready. He told him, "That was very good. You have learned a few things by hanging around me over the years. Now we can become partners, and my work will be easier with a friend who can help out."

He continued to explain his plan to the slow *compadre*, "By working together we will earn an easy living through lying. I will tell them, and then you will swear to their truth. But we must have a signal to stop if things are getting out of hand. I have had occasion when a lie has backfired, and I wished I had stopped sooner. This will be our plan: We will each keep our shirttails out. Whenever we feel a story is getting out of hand, we will just give a tug on the other's shirttail. Then we will know it is time to stop and be satisfied with what we have up to that point. Agreed?"

The slow *compadre* agreed. He was so excited to begin his new life as his friend's partner.

They immediately went into town and approached a group of men in the plaza. The smart *compadre* was the first to speak, "*Buenas tardes, amigos.* And then he began to work a story, "My *compadre* and I just came from a country where rattlesnakes are a mile long."

As he watched the reaction of the men to what the smart *compadre* was saying, the slow *compadre* became unsure of himself. He had not actually ever told such a tall tale to a group of strangers and was afraid to say anything at all. So, he just tugged at his friend's shirttail.

The smart *compadre* knew that his friend might give them away at any moment, so he tried to soften his lie, "Well, maybe not quite a mile. Maybe it was more like a half a mile."

The dumb *compadre* looked at the men's sober faces and tugged at his friend's shirttail again.

In exasperation, the smart *compadre* nervously told the men, "OK. Not quite a half a mile, but they were a least as long as our shirttails."

When they heard this final lie, the men shouted out, "These two are trying to trick us with their feeble lies! Run them out of town!"

As they escaped from the town's angry crowd, the smart *compadre* told his friend, "See, I told you. People do not like a bad lie. A bad lie is an insult to their intelligence. But a good lie is a thing of beauty, and people will greatly reward you for it. Now, learn from this lesson! We have nothing for our efforts and will go hungry tonight. From now on, we will work on making our tall tales better stories. And forget about the shirttails. All that did was cause confusion."

In the next town, the *compadres* once again approached a group of men in the plaza. As before, the smart *compadre* spoke first, "*Amigos*, in the village we just came from a baby was born with seven heads." He anxiously looked at his friend and waited for him to back up his story.

One of the town's men scratched his beard, looked at the slow *compadre*, and said, "Is this the truth? It does not seem possible."

The dumb *compadre* quickly tucked his shirttail into his trousers and replied, "Well, I didn't exactly see the baby with my own eyes. But as we left the village, I did see hanging on a clothesline a baby's little shirt with seven little collars."

The town's men could not believe what they were hearing, but they were enjoying the story so much that one of the men said, "*Compadres*, obviously you have traveled much and seen even more than we can imagine here in our little village. Come to the *cantina* and tell us more of what you have seen. You will be our guests for supper and breakfast."

From that day on, the two *compadres* traveled the world earning an easy living through their tall tales of wonder. Some people say they were the world's greatest liars, but they thought of themselves as the world's greatest storytellers, for all they had done was perfect the art of lying.

The Fox and the Coyote

This story begins with *Señor* Farmer, who had a problem. Somebody had been stealing his chickens. This was someone smart and tricky, because no matter how many traps *Señor* Farmer set, the thief always managed to escape with some of his chickens.

Soon the chicken stealing had become critical because almost all of his best and fattest chickens were gone, stolen by the chicken thief. *Señor* Farmer had to do something he was sure would work to catch the thief.

Señor Farmer finally devised a plan that he thought was foolproof. This time he would catch the chicken thief and make him pay for his thievery. *Señor* Farmer worked all day building and securing his trap, which sat by the door to the chicken coop. He made sure that everything was in place as evening approached, because the chickens were usually stolen during the nighttime. Then he went into his house, sure that by morning he would have the thief trapped.

That evening, Fox was searching for food as usual. On most days, Fox was unsuccessful in his search for food and would go back to his cave hungry. On his best days, however, he would find a rabbit or a chicken to eat and would return home with a full belly and a content heart.

It just so happened that this was not one of Fox's best days. He had been searching for food and, as nighttime approached, had still not found anything to eat. Resigned to sleeping with a growling stomach that night, Fox was walking by *Señor* Farmer's house when he heard a sound he liked. In fact, he heard a sound he really liked, even loved: the sound of chickens in the chicken coop.

Now Fox had been stealing chickens from this chicken coop for some time, but he had decided not to steal from it anymore. *Señor* Farmer, who owned the chickens, had been trying to capture him, and the last time, the trap had been so good that Fox barely escaped with his life.

But Fox was so hungry, and the chickens were so close that Fox decided to chance it one more time. He leapt over the fence and crept up to the chicken coop. As he reached the door to the chicken coop, Fox was surprised to find a little man guarding the door. Fox growled at the little man, but the little man said nothing. Fox then snapped at the little man, and again the little man said nothing. Finally

Fox said, "Little man, move out of my way. I'm hungry, and nobody, especially a little man, is going to stop me from getting a chicken or two."

Still the little man was silent, and in frustration, Fox struck out at him. As soon as Fox's paw hit him, it stuck fast to the little man. So Fox hit the little man with his other paw, and that one also got stuck. Fox then tried to use his hind legs to pull off his paws, but instead found himself totally stuck to the little man.

Fox then realized that the little man was the trap *Señor* Farmer had set for him. The little man was really a doll covered with tar, and now Fox was totally glued to the doll and could not escape at all. The more Fox struggled, the more he got stuck.

Fox knew that he had to get loose before *Señor* Farmer came and found him, or else he was a dead fox, for sure. But Fox also knew that he would need help to escape. Just as Fox was ready to give up hope he heard Coyote walking by *Señor* Farmer's yard. Fox called out, "Coyote! My dear friend Coyote. What brings you by *Señor* Farmer's house so late at night?"

Coyote answered, "I was just out looking for food and am now on my way home. I haven't found a single thing to eat and I'm so hungry."

Sensing that this would be his one chance for escape, Fox replied, "Coyote, this is your lucky night. I'm just getting ready to catch some chickens for myself, and if you come and help me, I will get a few for you too."

Coyote knew that Fox was one of the best chicken thieves and, being very hungry, he climbed the fence to see what Fox was talking about. When he saw Fox, all tangled up with the little man, he laughed out loud and asked, "Fox, what are you doing? It looks as if you are dancing with that little man."

Fox then said, "I'm not dancing with him. I'm holding him down. This little man was trying to run and tell *Señor* Farmer I was here. But I tackled him, and now I need your help to hold him down while I steal a few chickens. Come here and help me, and I'll get a couple of especially fat ones for you."

Coyote was so hungry that he could almost taste the fat chickens. So he rushed over and grabbed onto the little man. With Coyote holding the little man, Fox was able to pull himself free. Now Fox laughed at Coyote and said, "Now it's your turn to dance with the little man." Then Fox ran into the chicken coop and grabbed a big fat chicken. He then leapt over the fence and ran off into the night's darkness, leaving Coyote stuck to the little man.

In the morning, *Señor* Farmer came out to the chicken coop to see if his trap had worked. When he saw Coyote stuck to the little man, he said, "So it was you, Coyote, stealing my chickens!"

He then picked up a large stick and began beating Coyote. Coyote howled for mercy, but *Señor* Farmer would give him none. He only beat him harder. Then *Señor* Farmer threw Coyote into a shed and said, "Now I'm going to get my rifle, and soon my chickens will be safe again. Don't try to escape, because I've set another trap even worse than the little man."

As soon as *Señor* Farmer had left to get his gun, Coyote desperately struggled to get out of the shed. He finally succeeded in squeezing himself out through a gap in the window.

He jumped down from the window and fell into a tub of boiling water *Señor* Farmer had placed underneath it. Yelling in pain at the top of his lungs, Coyote ran off swearing to get revenge on Fox.

A few nights later, Coyote ran into Fox by a pond. Fox was staring intently at the water and did not notice Coyote sneaking up on him. Coyote pounced on Fox and prepared to give him a good thrashing.

Fox yelled out, "Coyote, you're going to ruin everything!"

Coyote did not understand what Fox was talking about, so he answered, "Ruin what? The only thing I'm going to ruin is you for that trick you pulled on me with the little man."

Thinking quickly, Fox replied, "Coyote, I'm so glad you brought that up. I've been looking for you because I have your chicken. I saved the fattest for you because you helped me out the other night. Now if you'll let me up, I'll go get your chicken. I already ate one of them, and I can tell you they are the plumpest, juiciest, and most delicious I've ever tasted."

Now Coyote was still mad at Fox, but when he heard Fox talking about the chickens, his mouth started to water. He really wanted to taste one of them. So he let Fox get up and told him, "Fox, you had better not be tricking me again. This time I'm going with you."

Fox immediately said, "No, you have to stay here and try to get the cheese."

Coyote asked, "Cheese! What cheese?"

Fox took Coyote over to the pond and pointed to a large round thing floating in the pond. He then told Coyote, "Right there. That is the cheese I'm talking about. You stay here and grab it when it floats closer, and I'll go get the chickens. Then we'll have a feast of chicken and cheese." Fox moved Coyote to a place where he could see the cheese better and then he ran off.

Coyote could almost taste the chicken and cheese. He kept his gaze fixed on the cheese, and as soon as it got close enough, he reached out to grab it. When he did, Coyote came up empty-handed and fell right into the pond. Totally drenched, he thrashed around looking for the cheese. He looked up at the night sky and realized that the cheese had been the reflection of the full moon in the pond water and that Fox had again tricked him. Now he really wanted to catch Fox and make him pay for his evil ways.

Coyote had searched and searched for Fox when he finally spied him creeping into a cave. Coyote said to himself, "Ha! Now I've got him trapped." He then ran into the cave and saw Fox sleeping on the ground. Coyote yelled out, "Now I've got you. And there will be no tricks or escape this time."

When Fox heard Coyote, he immediately rolled on his back and stuck his legs into the air, with his paws touching the roof of the cave. He then cried to Coyote, "Coyote don't move, or we will both be killed!"

Coyote knew that Fox was up to some trick and said, "Not this time Fox. This time I've got you for sure."

Fox replied to Coyote, "I know that last trick wasn't very nice, but believe me this time. The roof of the cave is about to fall in, and it's all I can do to hold it up."

Just then Fox moved suddenly, and some rocks from the roof of the cave fell on Coyote's head. Coyote yelped, "Ouch! It is falling in!" He then rolled over on his back and placed his paws against the roof.

Fox looked at Coyote and said, "Thanks for helping. With both of us holding up the roof, we'll be safe."

Coyote shook with fear and said, "But we can't hold it up forever. We need help."

Fox saw his chance and said, "Coyote, you're much stronger than I am. You stay here holding up the roof, and I'll run for help. Now don't move, or it will all come crashing down on you." Then, as before, Fox ran off.

Soon Coyote's legs and arms began to tire. Shaking with fear, Coyote finally collapsed in fatigue. Only then did he realize that the roof wasn't falling and that he had been tricked again.

Coyote furiously ran out of the cave and eventually found Fox sitting under a tree. As Coyote ran up to Fox, Fox rolled over and began poking a stick into a bag hanging from a tree limb. As he got closer to Fox, Coyote heard him saying, "Come on out. Come on out." Curious, Coyote crept even closer. Fox continued to say, "Come on out. Come on out." Finally, his curiosity getting the best of him, Coyote asked, "What are you doing?"

Fox turned around and said, "Shhh. Be quiet. Little bitty children are stuck inside this bag, and their mother has died. I'm trying to get them out to help them, but I can't do it."

Feeling sorry for the trapped children, Coyote asked, "Can I help? Show me what to do."

Fox gave Coyote the stick and instructed him: "Hold the stick just like this. Poke it in the hole. When you hear the children crying a little bit, just stir the stick around quickly and they'll come out."

Coyote did as he was instructed. He put the stick in the hole and, at first, stirred the stick slowly. He listened carefully, and when he heard a slight crying coming from the bag—almost like a buzzing sound—he immediately stirred the stick as hard as he could. Coyote was stirring with such force that the bag fell from the tree. It broke open and hundreds of bees stormed out and began to sting poor Coyote. The bag was a beehive all along, and Coyote had made the bees angry with his crazy stirring and breaking of their hive.

Coyote ran to the river and jumped in, howling in pain from the bee stings. Coyote then stayed in the river until the bees had flown away. He climbed out, and while nursing his bee stings, he decided that his efforts to get even with Fox had only caused him to get burned in hot water, drenched in a pond, and now, stung by bees. He swore that the next time he ran into Fox, Fox would be the one to end up in pain.

For weeks he searched for Fox, until he finally found him hiding in some tall grass. This time, he was careful to sneak up on Fox so Fox wouldn't see him. When he got close to Fox, he reached out and tried to grab him. But Fox was too fast, and he evaded Coyote's grasp.

Fox then said to Coyote, "Now just be careful. I know that you have a good reason to be angry, but now is not the time to try to get even with me. Any minute now, the king's servants are going to be walking by carrying the food for the king's banquet. If we're careful and quiet, we can surprise them and get some of the food for ourselves. Just stick your nose up in the air and you can almost smell the food."

Coyote stuck his nose up in the air and was sure that he did smell food. Maybe this time Fox was telling the truth.

Fox then said, "I'll go over to the other side of the road and wait there. Hide here in the tall grass and, when you hear my signal, jump out and grab some of the food."

Coyote crouched down as low as he could and waited for Fox's signal. After a while, he thought he smelled fire. He carefully poked his head above the tall grass and he saw flames coming his way. Fox had set fire to the tall grass in an attempt to burn Coyote's hide.

Coyote eventually outran the fire. To this day, Coyote is still looking for Fox, determined to make Fox pay for all his tricks.

El zorro y el coyote

Esta historia comienza con el Señor Granjero, quien tenía un problema. Alguien estaba robando sus pollos. Era alguien astuto y listo, porque no importaba cuántas trampas ponía el Señor Granjero, el ladrón siempre se las ingeniaba para escaparse con alguno de los pollos.

En poco tiempo el robo de pollos se hizo crítico, porque casi todos sus mejores pollos, los más gordos, habían desaparecido, robados por el ladrón de pollos. El Señor Granjero tenía que hacer algo para asegurar la captura del ladrón.

El Señor Granjero finalmente ideó un plan que consideró infalible. Esta vez atraparía al ladrón de pollos y le haría pagar por sus robos. El Señor Granjero trabajó todo el día construyendo y probando la trampa, la que puso cerca de la puerta del gallinero. Se aseguró de que todo estuviera listo cuando llegase la noche, porque el ladrón de pollos, usualmente, robaba durante la noche. Se fue a su casa, seguro que por la mañana el ladrón estaría atrapado.

Esa noche, como siempre, el Zorro estaba buscando comida. La mayoría del tiempo el Zorro no tenía éxito al buscar comida y tenía que regresar hambriento a su cueva. En sus mejores días, sin embargo, encontraba un conejo o un pollo para comer, y volvía a su cueva con la panza llena y el corazón contento.

Sucedió que éste no era uno de los mejores días para el Zorro. Había buscado comida todo el día, y al llegar la noche no había encontrado nada para comer. Resignado a dormir con un estómago crujiente esa noche, el Zorro caminaba por la casa del Señor Granjero cuando escuchó un sonido que le gusto. De hecho, escuchó un sonido que de verdad le gustaba, que incluso amaba: el sonido de los pollos en el gallinero.

Ahora bien, el Zorro había robado algunos pollos de vez en cuando, pero había decidido no robar más. El Señor Granjero, el dueño de los pollos, había tratado de capturarlo, y la última vez la trampa había sido tan buena que el Zorro por poco pudo escapar con vida.

Pero el Zorro tenía hambre, y los pollos estaban tan cerca que el Zorro decidió aprovechar la oportunidad una vez más. Saltó sobre la cerca y se arrastró hasta el gallinero. Al llegar a la puerta del gallinero, el Zorro se sorprendió al encontrar a un hombrecito custodiando la puerta. El Zorro le gruñó al hombrecito, él no dijo nada. El Zorro le chasqueó al hombrecito, pero éste no dijo nada. Finalmente el Zorro dijo: "Hombrecito, quítate de mi camino. Tengo hambre y nadie, ni siquiera un hombrecito, va a impedir que me coma uno o dos pollos".

El hombrecito seguía en silencio. Frustrado, el Zorro lo golpeó. En el instante en que la pata del Zorro tocó al hombrecito, la pata se quedó pegada en el hombrecito. El Zorro golpeó al hombrecito con la otra pata, y ésta también se quedó pegada. El Zorro trató de usar las patas traseras para liberar las delanteras, pero, por el contrario, se encontró totalmente pegado al hombrecito.

El Zorro se dio cuenta de que el hombrecito era la trampa que el Señor Granjero le había puesto. El hombrecito era en realidad un muñeco recubierto con resiná y ahora el Zorro estaba totalmente pegado al muñeco y no podía escaparse. Cuanto más intentaba el Zorro despegarse, más pegado quedaba.

El Zorro entendía que tenía que liberarse antes que el Señor Granjero viniese y lo encontrase, o sino de seguro seriá un zorro muerto. Pero el Zorro también sabía que para escapar necesitaría ayuda. Justo cuando el Zorro estaba a punto de perder la esperanza, escuchó que el Coyote se acercaba al patio del Señor Granjero. El Zorro dijo: "¡Coyote! Mi querido amigo Coyote. ¿Qué te trae a la casa del Señor Granjero a estas horas de la noche?"

El Coyote respondió: "Estaba buscando comida y ahora ya me voy a mi casa. No encontré nada para comer y todavía tengo mucho hambre".

Sintiendo que ésta podría ser una oportunidad para escaparse, el Zorro dijo: "Coyote, ésta es tu noche de suerte. Yo mismo estaba a punto de atrapar algunos de los pollos, y si tú vienes y me ayudas, te daré algunos".

El Coyote sabía que el Zorro era uno de los mejores ladrones de pollos y, al tener tanta hambre, se subió a la cerca para ver de qué hablaba el Zorro. Cuando vio al Zorro, todo abrazado al hombrecito, se rió y le preguntó: "Zorro, ¿qué estás haciendo? Parece que estás bailando con este hombrecito".

El Zorro le dijo entonces: "No estoy bailando con él. Lo estoy deteniendo. Este hombrecito trató de correr para avisarle al Señor Granjero que yo estaba aquí. Pero lo atrapé, y ahora necesito que me ayudes a retenerlo mientras yo robo algunos pollos. Ven y ayudarme, y robaré especialmente para ti un par de pollos gordos".

El Coyote tenía tanta hambre que hasta sentía el sabor de los gordos pollos. Así que corrió y agarró al hombrecito. Con el Coyote sosteniendo al hombrecito, el Zorro pudo librarse. El Zorro se rió y le dijo al Coyote: "Ahora es tu turno de bailar con el hombrecito". El Zorro corrió hasta el gallinero y agarró un pollo gordo. Luego saltó la cerca y se perdió en la oscuridad de la noche, dejando al Coyote atrapado con el hombrecito.

Por la mañana, el Señor Granjero fue hasta el gallinero para ver si la trampa había funcionado. Cuando vio al Coyote atrapado en el hombrecito, le dijo: "¡Así que tú, Coyote, te estabas robando mis pollos!"

Tomó entonces un palo largo y comenzó a golpear al Coyote. El Coyoté aullaba pidiendo misericordia, pero el Señor Granjero no le dio ninguna. Lo golpeó incluso más fuerte. El Señor Granjero arrojó entonces al Coyote en un galpón y le dijo: "Ahora voy a buscar mi rifle, y dentro de poco mis pollos estarán otra vez seguros. No trates de escaparte, porque he puesto otra trampa todavía peor que la de este hombrecito".

Tan pronto como el Señor Granjero se fue para ir a buscar su pistola, el Coyote trató desesperadamente de escaparse del galpón. Finalmente lo consiguió, escurriéndose por una rajadura en la ventana.

El Coyote saltó por la ventana y se cayó en una tina de agua hirviendo, que el Señor Granjero había puesto precisamente allí. Gritando de dolor con todos sus pulmones, el Coyote huyó a la carrera, jurando vengarse del Zorro.

Unas pocas noches después, el Coyote se encontró con el Zorro en una laguna. El Zorro estaba mirando fijamente al agua y no se dio cuenta que el Coyote se estaba acercando. El Coyote saltó sobre el Zorro y se preparó para darle una buena paliza.

El Zorro gritó: "¡Coyote, vas a arruinarlo todo!"

El Coyote no entendió de qué estaba hablando el Zorro, y le preguntó: "¿Arruinar qué? A lo único que voy a arruinar es a ti por el truco que me hiciste con el hombrecito".

Pensando rápidamente, el Zorro respondió: "Coyote, estoy tan contento que lo mencionas. Te estaba buscando porque tengo tus pollos. Guardé el más gordo para ti porque me ayudaste la otra noche. Ahora, si me dejas ir, iré a buscarlos. Ya me comí uno de ellos, y te aseguro que son de los más tiernos, jugosos y deliciosos que jamás he probado".

El Coyote todavía estaba enojado con el Zorro, pero cuando lo escuchó hablar de los pollos, se le hizo agua la boca. Realmente quería comerse uno. Así que dejó que el Zorro se levantase y le dijo: "Zorro, más te vale que esta vez no me engañes. Esta vez voy contigo".

"No, tienes que quedarte aquí y traer el queso", dijo inmediatamente el Zorro.

"¿Queso? ¿Qué queso?", preguntó el Coyote.

El Zorro llevó al Coyote hasta la laguna y apuntó a un largo objeto flotando en la laguna. Le dijo al Coyote: "Allí. Ese es el queso del que estoy hablando. Quédate aquí y lo atrapas cuando pase cerca. Yo voy a buscar los pollos. Tendremos un banquete de pollo y queso". El Zorro movió al Coyote hasta un lugar desde donde el queso se veía mejor, y luego se fue.

El Coyote casi podía saborear el pollo y el queso. Se quedó mirando fijamente al queso, y tan pronto como se acercó lo suficiente, se acercó para agarrarlo. Cuando lo hizo, el Coyote se quedó con las manos vacías y se cayó al agua. Totalmente empapado, buscó el queso a su alrededor. Entonces miró al cielo y se dio cuenta que el queso era el reflejo de la luna llena en el agua de la laguna. El Zorro lo había engañado otra vez. Ahora sí que quería atrapar al Zorro y hacerle pagar por sus diabluras.

El Coyote buscó y buscó al Zorro hasta que finalmente lo encontró entrando en una cueva. El Coyote pensó: "¡Ja! Esta vez lo tengo atrapado". Corrió hasta la cueva y vio al Zorro durmiendo en el piso. El Coyote gritó: "¡Ahora sí te tengo. Y esta vez no hay ni trucos ni escapes!"

Cuando el Zorro escuchó al Coyote, inmediatamente se puso de espaldas con las patas hacia arriba tocando el techo de la cueva. Le dijo entonces al Coyote: "Coyote, ¡no te muevas, o los dos moriremos!"

El Coyote sabía que el Zorro estaba usando otro de sus trucos y dijo: "No esta vez, Zorro. Esta vez te tengo por seguro".

El Zorro le respondió al Coyote: "Yo sé que el último truco no fue muy lindo, pero créeme esta vez. El techo de la cueva está a punto de caerse, y todo lo que puedo hacer es sostenerlo".

El Zorro se movió de repente y algunas piedras del techo de la cueva cayeron sobre la cabeza del Coyote. "¡Ay!", gritó el Coyote. "¡Se cae el techo!" Se puso entonces de espaldas y puso sus patas contra el techo.

El Zorro miró al Coyote y dijo: "Gracias por ayudar. Si los dos sostenemos el techo, estaremos a salvo".

El Coyote temblaba de miedo. Dijo: "Pero no podemos mantenernos así por siempre. Necesitamos ayuda".

El Zorro vio su oportunidad y dijo: "Coyote, tú eres más fuerte que yo. Quédate aquí sosteniendo el techo, y correré a buscar ayuda. No te muevas, o el techo se caerá y te aplastará". Como antes, el Zorro salió corriendo.

Al poco tiempo las piernas y los brazos del Coyote comenzaron a cansarse. Temblando de miedo, el Coyote finalmente se dejó vencer por la fatiga. Solamente entonces se dio cuenta que el techo no se caía y de que una vez más lo habían engañado.

El Coyote salió furioso de la cueva y eventualmente encontró al Zorro sentado bajo un árbol. Mientras el Coyote corría hacia el Zorro, el Zorro se incorporó y comenzó a introducir un palo en unabolsa que colgaba de una de las ramas del árbol. Al acercarse al Zorro, el Coyote lo escuchó decir: "Salgan. Salgan". Curioso, el Coyote se acercó cuidadosamente aún más. El Zorro continuó diciendo: "Salgan. Salgan". Finalmente su curiosidad pudo más, y el Coyote preguntó: "¿Qué estás haciendo?"

El Zorro se volteó y le dijo: "Shhh. Silencio. Unos niñitos están atrapados dentro de esta bolsa, y su madre se murió. Estoy tratando de que salgan para ayudarlos, pero no puedo".

Sintiendo lástima por los niños atrapados, el Coyote preguntó: "¿Puedo ayudar? Muéstrame que puedo hacer".

El Zorro le dio el palo al Coyote y lo instruyó: "Sostiene este palo de esta manera. Ponlo en este agujero. Cuando escuches a los niños llorar un poquito, solamente agita el palo rápidamente y ellos saldrán".

El Coyote hizo lo que se le había dicho. Puso el palo en el agujero y primero lo movió lentamente. Escuchó cuidadosamente, y cuando oyó un pequeño llanto viniendo de la bolsa, casi como un zumbido, inmediatamente agitó el palo tan fuerte como pudo. El Coyote agitó el palo con tanta fuerza que la bolsa se cayó del árbol. Se abrió, y cientos de abejas salieron y comenzaron a picar al pobre Coyote. La bolsa era una colmena, y el Coyote había irritado a las abejas al agitar el palo y al quebrar la colmena.

El Coyote corrió hasta el río y se zambulló, aullando de dolor por las picaduras de las abejas. El Coyote se quedó en el río hasta que las abejas se fueron. Salió del río y, lamiéndose sus heridas, decidió que sus esfuerzos de vengarse del Zorro lo habían llevado a quemarse en agua hirviendo, empaparse en la laguna y, ahora, ser picado por abejas. Juró que la próxima vez que viese al Zorro, el Zorro terminaría sufriendo el dolor.

Durante semanas buscó al Zorro, hasta que finalmente lo encontró escondido entre el pasto alto. Esta vez, cuidadosamente se acercó al Zorro para que el Zorro no lo viese. Cuando se acercó al Zorro, saltó y trató de atraparlo. Pero el Zorro era muy rápido, y esquivó el intento del Coyote.

El Zorro le dijo al Coyote: "Ten mucho cuidado. Sé que tienes buenas razones para estar enojado, pero ahora no es el momento de tratar de vengarte. En cualquier momento los siervos del rey van a pasar llevando la comida para el banquete del rey. Si tenemos cuidado y estamos en silencio, podremos sorprenderlos parte de la comida será para nosotros. Olfatea y casi podrás sentir el aroma de la comida".

El Coyote levantó su nariz y pudo jurar que olía el aroma de la comida. Quizá esta vez el Zorro estaba diciendo la verdad.

El Zorro dijo: "Vé al otro lado del camino y espera allí. Escóndete en el pasto alto y cuando escuches mi señal, salta y agarra algo de comida".

El Coyote se agachó tan bajo como pudo y esperó la señal del Zorro. Después de un rato, creyó olfatear fuego. Con cuidado asomó su cabeza por encima del pasto alto y vio que las llamas se estaban acercando. El Zorro le había prendido fuego al pasto alto para intentar quemar el escondite del Coyote.

El Coyote pudo escaparse del fuego. Hasta el día de hoy el Coyote sigue buscando al Zorro, determinado a hacer que el Zorro pague por todos sus trucos.

The Lion and the Cricket

One of the best stories about the animal kingdom is the story of the lion and the cricket. At the beginning of time, all of the big animals of the forest thought that might makes right and that the bigger animal always wins the battle. The idea behind this story, however, is that, every so often, the smaller animal is smarter and fiercer than the bigger animal and comes out victorious. This is especially true if that small animal has the help of friends.

A long time ago—so long ago that the animals were still deciding who was the strongest, the fastest, and the bravest—a lion was strolling through the forest. The lion had already decided that he was king of the forest and that all of the other animals should bow down to him. In fact, the lion was so sure that he was the strongest, fastest, and bravest that he didn't even look where he was walking. He assumed that other animals would just move out of his way as he walked by them.

After he had been walking for a long time, the lion decided to lie down in the cool shade of a tree and take a little rest. Just as he was about to fall asleep, he heard a small, annoying noise. A very definite "crick, crick, crick" sound was coming from under a nearby leaf.

The lion tried to ignore the sound, but once he became aware of it, all he heard was the irritating "crick, crick, crick." He finally got fed up with the sound and reached over to smash whatever was under the leaf making the noise. The lion was thinking to himself, "How dare it—whatever is under that leaf—keep making that terrible sound to annoy the sleep of the king of the forest."

A gust of wind suddenly blew the leaf over, and there sat a tiny black cricket. The cricket was startled to see the lion and said, "Hey, watch what you're doing! I was under that leaf."

An animal had never talked to the lion in such a tone of voice. He angrily answered, "Don't you talk to me like that. I'm the king of the forest, and you're lucky I didn't smash you for making that infernal racket. Now, move along and leave me alone."

The cricket reared up and told the lion, "You can't boss me around like that. You're not the king of *me*. In fact, you're the king of nothing, as far as I'm concerned."

Now the lion was really angry. He knew he had to teach the cricket a lesson, or else word would get around the forest that a little cricket had bossed around the lion. He swatted the cricket and warned him, "You had better be careful, or else you'll be sorry you ever ran into me."

The cricket wasn't at all afraid of the lion. He looked the lion right in the eye and told him, "You're the one who had better be careful. I'm going to go get my friends, and we'll teach you a lesson!"

The lion roared back, "Go get your friends! And I'll get mine, and we'll see who will teach *whom* a lesson."

The cricket replied, "We'll meet you right here tomorrow."

So the lion and the cricket went off to gather their friends for the big fight.

The lion let out one of his deep, loud roars and called all of his clawed friends to help him in the fight. His friends included the bear, the wolf, the coyote, and the tiger. When they answered the call of the lion, they all laughed at the idea of a fight with the cricket and his friends. The bear said, "It's almost not worth having a fight. We're all the strongest and best hunters of the forest. How could a cricket ever think he and his friends could defeat us?" The tiger laughed and added, "The nerve of those little creatures."

Meanwhile, the cricket had gathered all of his biting and stinging friends to help him. His friends included the bee, the scorpion, the tarantula, the mosquito, the ant, and the wasp. When he told them they would be fighting the lion and his friends, they all cheered and yelled. The bee spoke for them all when he said, "It's about time we taught those animals a lesson. All they do is strut around as if they were the greatest animals on Earth. Well, tomorrow they'll find out different."

The cricket and his friends talked long into the night about their fighting strategies. When they were sure that they had devised the best plan possible, they went to sleep for the night to rest up for the big fight.

The next day, the lion and his friends arrived at the designated fighting spot but didn't find the cricket or his friends anywhere. The lion huffed and puffed around and roared as loud as he could to try to impress all of the animals with his great strength. He told his friends, "See, I told you that the cricket and his friends would be too afraid to fight us. They're probably far away hiding under a leaf, hoping we don't come looking for them."

Coyote raced around looking for the cricket and yelling, "Oh, I wanted a fight so badly! I was ready to fight!" The lion and his friends looked high and low, but they could not find the cricket and his friends anywhere. The coyote gave up and sat down on a pile of leaves to rest.

Suddenly, the coyote jumped up screaming and crying, "Owwww! Something bit me!" As he was carrying on, the cricket leapt out from under a leaf and yelled, "Attack!"

The cricket and his friends flew out from under the leaves and logs where they had been hiding. They attacked the lion and his friends, biting and stinging them over and over again.

The lion and his friends jumped and ran about howling for mercy. The cricket and his friends, however, showed no mercy and continued to bite and sting the clawed animals until they finally decided that the clawed animals had been taught a good enough lesson. The clawed animals limped off to their lairs and caves and nursed their wounded bodies, which were covered with bites and stings.

From that day on, all the clawed animals of the forest had more respect for the smaller animals. The cricket and his friends had proven that it's not who is bigger that matters most, rather it's who is smarter and fiercer. So from the beginning of time, the animal kingdom has learned not to judge an animal by its size.

El león y el grillo

Una de las mejores historias del reino animal es la historia del león y el grillo. En el principio del tiempo, todos los grandes animales de la selva pensaban que la fuerza les daba el derecho y que el animal más grande siempre ganaba la batalla. La idea de esta historia, sin embargo, es que algunas veces el animal más pequeño es más astuto y más feroz que el animal más grande, y resulta victorioso. Esto es verdad, especialmente si el animal pequeño cuenta con la ayuda de sus amigos.

Hace mucho tiempo, cuando los animales estaban todavía decidiendo quién era el más fuerte, el más rápido y el más valiente, un león caminaba por la selva. El león había decidido que él era el rey de la selva y que todos los otros animales deberían reverenciarlo. De hecho, el león estaba tan seguro que él era el rey de la selva y que él era el más fuerte, el más rápido y el más valiente que ni le importaba por donde caminaba. Asumía que los otros animales simplemente se harían a un lado para darle paso.

Luego de caminar durante un largo tiempo, el león decidió recostarse en la refrescante sombra de un árbol y descansar un rato. Justo cuando comenzaba a quedarse dormido, escuchó un ruidito molesto. Un muy claro "crick, crick, crick" venía de abajo de una hoja cercana.

El león trató de ignorar el ruido, pero una vez que le prestó atención, ya no pudo dejar de escuchar el irritante sonido "crick, crick, crick". Finalmente se cansó del ruido y se levantó dispuesto a aplastar a lo que fuera que estuviese debajo de la hoja haciendo el ruido. El león pensaba: "Cómo se atreve, quienquiera que esté debajo de la hoja, a hacer un sonido tan horrible para molestar al rey de la selva".

Una ráfaga de viento súbitamente dio vuelta la hoja, y allí estaba un grillito negro. El grillo se asombró al ver al león y le dijo: "¡Eh, cuidado con lo que haces, que yo estoy debajo de la hoja!".

Jamás animal alguno le había hablado al león con ese tono de voz. Enojado, el león respondió: "No me hables de esa manera. Soy el rey de la selva, y tienes suerte que no te voy a aplastar por hacer ese ruido infernal. Ahora, desaparece y déjame solo".

El grillo se incorporó y le dijo al león: "A mí no me des órdenes de esa manera. Tú no eres *mi* rey. De hecho, desde mi punto de vista, no eres ningún rey".

Ahora sí que el león estaba enojado. Decidió enseñarle una lección al grillo, pues de lo contrario se sabría en la selva que un grillito había desafiado al león. Atrapó al grillo y le advirtió: "Mira, mejor ten cuidado, o si no lamentarás haberte encontrado conmigo".

El grillo no tenía miedo del león. Lo miró fíjamente y le dijo: "Mejor tú ten cuidado. Voy a buscar a mis amigos y te enseñaremos una lección".

El león rugió y dijo: "¡Vé a buscar a tus amigos! Yo voy a buscar a los míos, y vamos a ver quién le enseña una lección a quién"

El grillo respondió: "Nos encontraremos aquí mismo mañana".

El león y el grillo se fueron a buscar a sus amigos para la gran pelea.

El león usó uno de los estruendosos y profundos rugidos para llamar a todos sus aguerridos amigos, para que lo ayudasen en el combate. Sus amigos eran el oso, el lobo, el coyote y el tigre. Cuando respondieron al llamado del león, se rieron de la idea de luchar contra el grillo y sus amigos. "Casi ni vale la pena pelear", dijo el oso. "Somos los más fuertes y los mejores cazadores de la selva. ¿Cómo puede pensar el grillo que él y sus amigos pueden derrotarnos?" El tigre se rió y añadió: "Los nervios que tienen estas criaturitas".

Mientras tanto, el grillo había reunido a todos sus amigos, los que picaban y mordían, para que lo ayudasen. Los amigos eran la abeja, el escorpión, la tarántula, el mosquito, la hormiga y la avispa. Cuando les dijo que lucharían contra el león y sus amigos, gritaron de alegría. "Ya es hora de que les demos una lección a esos animales", dijo la abeja hablando en nombre de todos. "Todo lo que hacen es pavonearse, como si fuesen los mejores animales del planeta. Bueno, mañana se encontrarán con otra realidad".

El grillo y sus amigos pasaron parte de la noche hablando de la estrategia para su combate. Cuando estuvieron de acuerdo que tenían el mejor plan posible, se fueron a dormir para descansar para la gran pelea.

Al día siguiente, el león y sus amigos llegaron al lugar designado para la pelea, pero no pudieron encontrar al grillo o sus amigos. El león resopló y rugió tan fuerte como pudo para impresionar, con su gran poder, a todos los animales. Les dijo a sus amigos: "Ven, les dije que el grillo y sus amigos tenían mucho miedo de pelear con nosotros. Probablemente ya están muy lejos, escondidos bajo una hoja, rogando que no los vayamos a buscar".

El coyote corría de un lado a otro buscando al grillo y gritando: "Oh, ¡yo tenía tantas ganas de pelear!" El león y sus amigos buscaron arriba y abajo, pero no encontraron ni al grillo ni a sus amigos en ningún lugar. El coyote se dio por vencido y se sentó a descansar en una pila de hojas.

De repente, el coyote dio un salto, gritando y llorando: "¡Aaaayyyyy! ¡Algo me picó!". Mientras el coyote gritaba, el grillo salió de debajo de una hoja y ordenó: "¡Al ataque!"

El grillo y sus amigos salieron volando de las debajo de hojas y los troncos donde se habían escondido. Atacaron al león y a sus amigos, mordiéndolos y picándolos una y otra vez.

El león y sus amigos saltaban y corrían pidiendo misericordia. El grillo y sus amigos, sin embargo, no mostraron misericordia y continuaron picando y mordiendo a los animales con garras hasta que decidieron que los animales con garras habían aprendido una muy buena lección. Los animales con garras volvieron a sus guaridas y cuevas para lamer sus lastimados cuerpos, cubiertos con mordidas y picaduras.

Desde ese día, los animales con garras en la selva tuvieron más respeto por los animales más pequeños. El grillo y sus amigos habían demostrado que no importa quién es el más grande, sino quién es más astuto y más atrevido. De esa manera, desde el principio del tiempo, el reino animal aprendió a no juzgar a los animales por su tamaño.

The Mouse and the Ant

Once, on a flat desert plain, there lived a small ant. She was always searching for food under decaying wood or piles of leaves or by the remains of abandoned houses. Often she was lonely and wished for a companion to keep her company, but she continued to work hard and kept her faith that soon her fortunes would change.

One day, as she searched by a spot where soldiers had camped for the night, she found a silver dollar. The minute she saw it, she recognized it as something valuable. Although it was very heavy for her, she was able to drag it into town and show it to the store owner.

As soon as the store owner saw the silver dollar, he told the ant, "This is a very valuable coin. You have been very fortunate to find it. Now, you may buy whatever you want in the store."

The ant could not believe her good fortune. She waltzed around the store and picked out a beautiful new dress and hat.

She dressed herself in her new finery and took a stroll through the plaza. She imagined that because her luck was obviously changing, she might as well go looking for her longed-for companion.

As soon as the dog saw the ant dressed in her beautiful clothes, he bounded up to her and began a conversation. But the dog's rough ways were not to the liking of the genteel ant, and she told the dog to go on his way.

Next, the cat approached the ant. But his wild meowing was a noisy racket to the ant, and she bid the cat to also go on his way.

Throughout the day, the animals of the town were smitten by the ladylike manner of the ant, and each approached the ant and tried to win her hand. But the ant had lived for many years by herself and was not about to give up her freedom for a less-than-suitable companion.

Near the end of the day, she was beginning to think that perhaps the silver dollar was the extent of her new good fortune and that she was destined to live a life alone. As she was preparing to return to her home, she passed by a small door and heard the most attractive voice singing. As she poked her head through the door, she saw a mouse singing to himself. Now, to most other animals, the thin, squeaky voice of the mouse was not a sound of beauty. But just as beauty is in the eye of the beholder, a beautiful singing voice is a matter of personal taste. To the ant, the mouse's voice was a lyrical beauty.

She quietly waited until the mouse had finished his song. When he sensed her presence, the startled mouse turned and said, "Oh, my! You surprised me. May I help you in some way? What is it that you want?"

The ant replied, "I was just enjoying your singing. May I stay a little while longer and keep listening?"

Now, the truth of the matter is that the mouse had led a lonely life himself. He often passed the day by singing songs to himself to make the time pass by faster. He was delighted that someone was willing to spend time with him.

Time passed and the ant and the mouse were enjoying each other's company. They both felt that at last they had found a true companion. Soon, they recognized their love for each other, got married, and began a life together.

Through the years, the mouse and the ant lived a life of shared joys and happiness. Many a night, the ant went to sleep listening to the voice of the mouse as he serenaded her to sleep.

One day, the ant went into town to do some errands. She had begun to cook a pot of soup and asked the mouse if he would watch over it while she was away. Of course, the mouse said he would watch it as carefully as he could.

Now, the pot was very large, and the mouse was very small. So, in order to stir the soup so it wouldn't burn, he stacked two chairs on top of one another. As he was stirring, he began to lose his balance and fell into the soup. He couldn't pull himself out, and he drowned.

After that tragic accident, the ant continued to live in the home she and the mouse had made together. She longed for her dearest companion and would pass the hours remembering their happy days. Often, when the people of the village passed by the house late at night, they could hear the voice of the ant as she sang the beautiful songs the mouse had sung to her during their years together.

Because two people who have spent a lifetime together eventually develop the same habits, the ant had learned from the mouse how a beautiful song can comfort the soul and help pass the days.

The Owl and the Painted Bird

A long time ago, during the time when the world was new, animals across the Earth were busy developing their natures and appearances. The birds of the world were especially active at this time.

Each bird was learning the songs that would be their own and that would identify that particular bird to the other animals. They were also trying on feathers that would mark each type of bird as distinct and beautiful.

One bird, Pi-coo, was having an especially difficult time. She could not make up her mind about which feathers she should wear. The more she tried on, the more confused she became. Soon, almost all of the feathers were spoken for, and she was left with almost nothing to cover her naked body. Because she had no feathers, she was very ashamed and refused to come out of her nest.

The other birds felt sorry for her. They gathered together and talked about a way they could help Pi-coo.

The eagle, who spoke first, said, "Why don't we each give her one feather? We all have so many. It wouldn't be missed and would really help her."

The other birds were not so sure about the idea, but not one bird could come up with another plan. The birds worried that if they each gave a feather to Pi-coo, she might become the most beautiful of all the birds.

Finally, the wise old owl spoke up. He said, "Why don't we each just loan her a feather? Then she will be covered. As soon as her own feathers grow in, then she will return our feathers. I myself will be responsible for the return of the feathers."

The other birds agreed to this plan only because of the guarantee by the wise old owl to return their feathers.

Soon all the birds had given Pi-coo a feather. She gathered all of the feathers and carefully arranged them on her naked body. As soon as she saw her reflection in the still waters of the river, she realized that she was the most beautiful of all the birds. She looked like a painted bird, with all the colors of the rainbow shining on her magnificent body. Realizing that the other birds would be jealous and would never allow her to keep their feathers, she immediately flew high into the sky, never to return.

It was not long before the birds realized that Pi-coo was not returning. Incensed, they searched for the wise old owl, but he was nowhere to be found. They could not stand the idea that Pi-coo was now the most beautiful of the birds and demanded that the wise old owl keep his word and return the donated feathers.

The wise old owl knew how angry the other birds were. So he hid in the trees during the day and came out only at night when he knew that the other birds were sleeping. During the night, he would quietly fly around and call out for Pi-coo, "Pi-coo. Pi-coo."

And that is why, to this day, the owl is a nocturnal bird, only coming out at night to fly through the air with its plaintive, searching cry of "Pi-coo. Pi-coo."

La lechuza y el pájaro pintado

Hace mucho tiempo, en aquella época cuando el mundo era nuevo, los animales de toda la tierra estaban ocupados desarrollando sus naturalezas y sus aspectos. Los pájaros del mundo estaban especialmente activos en ese momento.

Cada pájaro estaba aprendiendo las canciones que serían las suyas propias y que indentificarían a ese pájaro ante los otros animales. También se estaban probando las plumas que caracterizarían a cada pájaro como algo distinto y hermoso.

Una de las aves, Picú, tenía dificultades. No podía decidir qué plumas usar. Cuanto más lo pensaba, más se confundía. En poco tiempo casi todas las plumas ya estaban reservadas, y Picú no tenía casi nada para cubrir su cuerpo desnudo. Como no tenía plumas, se sentía avergonzada y no quería salir de su nido.

Los otros pájaros se compadecieron de ella. Se reunieron y hablaron sobre cómo ayudar a Picú.

El águila habló primero y dijo: "¿Por qué no cada uno de nosotros le regala una pluma. Todos tenemos muchas. No echaremos de menos una pluma, y realmente podría ayudarla".

Los otros pájaros no estaban tan seguros de la idea, pero ninguno tenía otro plan. Los pájaros temían que si cada uno le daba una pluma a Picú, ella se convertiría en la más bella de las aves.

Finalmente, la sabia lechuza habló. "¿Por qué no le prestamos las plumas? Ella tendrá cómo cubrirse. Luego, tan pronto como le crezcan sus propias plumas, nos devolverá las nuestras. Yo me hago responsable por la devolución de las plumas", dijo la lechuza.

Los otros animales accedieron al plan solamente porque la vieja y sabia lechuza garantizaba la devolución de las plumas.

Poco después cada pájaro le había dado una pluma a Picú. Ella reunió todas las plumas y con mucha diligencia se las acomodó en su cuerpo desnudo. Tan pronto como vio su imagen reflejada en las aguas del río, comprendió que era la más bella de las aves. Parecía un pájaro pintado, con todos los colores del brillante arco iris sobre su magnífico cuerpo. Se dio cuenta que los otros pájaros estarían celosos y que nunca le permitirían quedarse con las plumas, Picú inmediatamente salió volando hacia las alturas del cielo, y nunca regresó.

No pasó mucho tiempo para que los pájaros se diesen cuenta que Picú no iba a regresar. Enardecidos, se fueron a buscar a la vieja lechuza sabia, pero no pudieron encontrarla. No podían aceptar la idea que Picú fuese la más bella de las aves y pidieron que la vieja y sabia lechuza cumpliese su palabra y devolviese las plumas donadas.

La vieja y sabia lechuza vio cuán enojados estaban los pájaros. Por eso se esconde en los árboles durante el día y sale solamente por la noche, cuando sabe que los otros pájaros están durmiendo. Por la noche, vuela casi silenciosamente y llama a Picú: "Picú, Picú".

Por eso, hasta este día, la lechuza es una animal nocturno, que sale a volar de noche, recorriendo el aire con su grito de búsqueda y demanda: "Picú, Picú".

The Ant Who Learned to Play the Flute

Once there was a little ant, an *hormiguita*. The *hormiguita* was one of the hardest working ants in the anthill. All day and night, he helped dig out tunnels so the anthill could continue to grow and support the many new ants who were constantly being born. He was also one of the strongest ants. He was always the ant who took the job of traveling long distances away from the anthill to search for food. He almost always successfully returned, dragging behind him a large piece of bread or a chunk of dried fruit. Throughout the anthill, the other ants recognized his strength and hard-working nature.

He wasn't king of the anthill, however. He was just a regular worker ant with the responsibilities of a worker ant—which are mainly to work hard, and then work even harder some more. All of this constant hard work made the ant daydream about a life in which he did not have to work so hard. He was not lazy or afraid of hard work. He just sometimes wished there was more to his life than working like a slave. But his father and his father before him had been worker ants, so he was resigned to the same fate.

One day, when he was on one of his journeys searching for food, the *hormiguita* discovered an abandoned flute hidden underneath a pile of leaves. The flute must have belonged to a very special ant because it had been carved out of precious wood and had the decorations of a lord. The *hormiguita* carried it back to his anthill and asked around to see if it belonged to any ant he knew. Nobody claimed the flute, so the ant decided to keep it for himself.

At the end of every workday, the *hormiguita* would take out his flute and teach himself how to play it. At first, he could hardly make a single sound on it, but he persevered and soon was able to make quite a lovely sound on it. Before long, he had created different melodies and, soon after that, could play the most beautiful songs on it. All of the other ants would gather around and enjoy his music. His music brought a certain peacefulness to the hectic din of the anthill.

One day, the *hormiguita* decided to leave his anthill and go into the world to seek his fortune. He had decided that his hard work as a slave to the anthill had to end and that, with his new talent playing the flute, he could possibly find work playing at weddings.

The *hormiguita* had made a very brave decision. Few ants ever leave the anthill, because life outside their tunnels can be very dangerous. Not only is it difficult to find food but the big people seem to get a certain pleasure out of stepping on ants. Life for an ant on his own is very perilous.

The *hormiguita* took nothing with him but his flute. He had been traveling for several days when he came upon the largest anthill he had ever seen. The anthill rose like a majestic pyramid out of the ground and seemed to be bustling with the activity of a million ants. Normally, it can be very dangerous for an ant to approach an anthill other than his own, because the new ants might think that he is an intruder looking to steal food or a scout from another anthill intent on taking over their anthill.

The *hormiguita* approached the new anthill and began playing a tune on his flute. The new ants were so shocked to see and hear the *hormiguita* playing the flute that they stopped working, which is practically unheard of for ants. The *hormiguita* stepped inside the anthill and asked to see the queen. Word spread throughout the anthill that an ant who played the flute had entered the anthill.

Very quickly, word reached the queen of the anthill. She summoned the *hormiguita* and asked him to play for her. Nervously, he played a simple tune to see if she would like it. The queen seemed pleased, so he played a longer tune, and soon he was playing his best songs and even improvising a few new tunes. Ants began to follow the sound of the flute, which echoed throughout the anthill tunnels. They were surprisingly moved by the music. A few even began to dance.

The queen announced that the *hormiguita* could stay in the anthill and that he would be the queen's official musician. The *hormiguita's* dream had come true. His life as a worker ant was over, and he had forged a new beginning as the musician to the queen herself. The *hormiguita* spent many happy days in the anthill, entertaining the worker ants and being on special call whenever the queen wanted to hear music.

One day, a messenger ant raced into the anthill with terrible news. A rival queen had decided to attack the anthill and take it over. The fierce army ants were approaching the anthill as he delivered the message and no time was left to prepare a defense.

The *hormiguita* could see how saddened the queen was by this news. The queen knew that her colony could not defend the anthill from the army ants and that her anthill would be destroyed in the battle. She quietly and nobly awaited her fate as all of the worker ants scurried for their own safety.

The *hormiguita* approached his queen and tried to comfort her. She had helped him when he was in need, and now he felt it was his duty to try and help her save her anthill. He told the queen that he had a plan that just might work.

He would leave the anthill to face the army ants by himself. He would hide in the tall grass and play his flute as the army ants passed by. He knew that his flute music was irresistible and hoped that it would cast a spell on the army ants. If his plan worked, the army ants would be distracted by the flute music and would start dancing. While the army ants were distracted, the queen's soldiers could launch a surprise attack on the army ants. The queen had no other options, so she agreed to try the *hormiguita*'s plan.

The *hormiguita* bravely marched out of the anthill carrying only his flute. He hid in the tall grass and began playing as the army ants passed by. At first, the army ants ignored the flute music, but soon they began to sway in rhythm to its melody. After a while, they stopped their crisp marching and began to dance to the melodious music of the *hormiguita*'s flute.

As planned, the queen's soldiers attacked and conquered the army ants while they were distracted and their defenses were down. The *hormiguita's* plan had saved the anthill.

The *hormiguita* returned to the anthill as a hero, but he was just thankful that he could continue to entertain the ants in the anthill with his beautiful music. Eventually, the queen fell in love with the *hormiguita*, and they were married in a grand ceremony. To this day, all of the ants of the anthill tell the amazing story of the simple worker ant who used his beautiful flute music to save the anthill, marry the queen, and become king of the anthill.

The Burro and the Fox

Like many other animals in the animal kingdom, the burro is a beast of burden, spending his life toiling in the hot sun in order to make his master's life a little easier. The burro knows no other existence and is destined to a life of service and loyalty to his master.

The worst fate for a burro, however, is to have a cruel master. Some masters love and care for their burro, respecting that their own life is dependent on this creature. Others take the burro for granted and just expect the burro to always be there to carry their heavy load. Others, the worst ones, take their own mean temperament out on the poor, defenseless burro by whipping, beating, and starving their burro. They have little or no concern for the burro's well-being, and if the burro dies, no remorse or sense of loss is felt by the master.

It just so happens that in this story, our burro has one of these mean masters. This master would beat the burro if it walked too fast, walked too slowly, stopped too abruptly, or started too suddenly. He would beat the burro if it tripped on the steep, rocky mountain path or if it stopped for water by a mountain stream. Some days, he would beat the burro just for being in the way.

Finally, the burro had had enough of his master's beatings and decided to run away. Late one night, while the master was sleeping, the burro broke out of the corral and took off down the road with a quick trot. He was free—free at last!

The burro loved his new freedom. He strolled along a shady mountain path, eating the new spring grasses. He lounged by a mountain stream, sipping its cool, fresh waters. He paused and rested when he wanted, and he walked along when he wanted. Most of all, he did not pass his days in fear of a beating.

One day, as he walked along a forest path, the burro ran into a fox. The fox asked the burro, "Why are you walking alone so far in the forest? Where is your master?"

The burro replied, "I have run away from my master, because he beats me all of the time. I am a free burro, and I will walk wherever my spirit leads me."

The fox then told the burro, "I am a servant of the lion, the king of the forest. Perhaps you should come to meet the lion and see if you could join our band of free animals. The lion is a strong and wise ruler, and perhaps he could help you find a new life. Come with me, and I will announce you to the lion. You will be well received by him."

The burro followed the fox. He was thankful that he had at last met up with other free animals and was hopeful that the lion could help him find a new life. He had been enjoying his free wanderings, but he did not want to be a nomad and never have a home again.

The fox and burro arrived at the home of the lion. The fox went to the lion and announced the burro's arrival, "I have run into an old burro who has run away from his master. I have brought him here so that you may meet him and have told him that he will be well received by you."

The lion told the fox, "Bring this burro to me right away. I do want to meet him."

The fox brought the burro to the lion. He introduced the burro to the lion and then left so the lion could question the burro by himself.

While the lion addressed the burro, he paced around and around the burro. The burro began to get nervous, because lions usually only pace when they are hungry. As the lion circled the burro, he got closer and closer, making the circle around the burro tighter and tighter with each pass.

Finally, the lion suddenly jumped toward the burro and nipped at his flanks. He continued to circle and nip at the burro with such strength that he almost knocked the burro over with his attacks.

The burro finally got the idea that the lion was trying to bite him—probably even eat him. The burro turned and struck out at the lion with his hooves. The lion was old and had already spent many years as a fierce hunter, but those years were behind him. He did not have the speed or reflexes he once had.

The burro's hooves slammed into the lion and knocked him to the ground. As the lion hit the ground, the burro bolted away from the lion and raced away down the forest path.

On his way from the lion, the burro again ran into the fox. As he whizzed by the fox, the fox called out, "Why are you in such a hurry?! Did your meeting with the lion not go well? The lion is always anxious to meet new animals. I was sure you would be well received."

Without even stopping, the burro called back, "That was the trouble. I was too well received by the lion. He liked me so much that he wanted to eat me! He even tried to bite me and start his evening meal early."

The fox yelled back, "No! No! The lion was only trying to give you a good welcome!"

The burro did not believe the fox. He told the fox, "Thank you for your good welcome. But now I am running away from the lion too."

As the burro disappeared into the distance, the fox yelled, "Don't run that way! That way leads back to your master!"

The burro answered, "I am going back to my master. I'd rather be with a master who beats me than a lion who wants to eat me!"

GLOSSARY OF SPANISH WORDS

abuelita little grandmother, a term of endearment

adobe dried mud and straw brick used for construction in the American Southwest

alebrige the invented name of Oaxacan wood carving

amigo friend

ancianos the elderly, the old ones

atlatl spear-thrower detail on Toltec statues

buenas tardes good afternoon

cantina a bar or nightclub

caravelas Spanish ships or galleons

cárgueselo a la gorra charge it to the cap

charro rural horseman from Jalisco; a traditional Mexican horseman

chiles a hot pepper typical of Mexican cuisine

chirrionera a legendary Mexican snake that can bite its tail and roll like a wheel

Cinqo de Mayo May 5th, a celebration of Mexico's victory over France at the Battle of Puebla in 1862

compadre technically, the godparent of one's child; more commonly, a very close friend

con with

conquistadores conquerors; can refer specifically to Spanish conquerors

copalillo copal

criollos pure Spanish people born in the New World

cuentista storyteller

cuento story

danzante dancer, Zapotec stone carvings

diablito little devil

diablo devil

duende mischievous wandering goblin or elf. The legend of the *duendes* involves the events after the Lord and the devil had their arguments at the beginning of time. During the epic battle, some of the angels stayed with the Lord and some went with the devil. When the Lord closed the doors to heaven and the devil closed the doors to hell, many angels were caught in between the two and had no place to go. These angels came to Earth and became the *duendes*. *Duendes* spend their time on Earth causing mischief in human affairs.

El diez y seis de Septiembre September 16th, Mexican Independence Day

El grito de Delores the cry of Delores, the call for Mexican Independence Day by Father Hidalgo on September 16, 1810

ecomienda Spanish land grant system in the New World

ermitaño hermit

filipinas simple, buttoned up, white shirts

folklórico Mexican traditional dance

friole pinto bean

guyabera traditional Mexican men's shirt

habanero small, very hot chile

hacienda estate

hijo son

historia story or tale

hormiguita little ant

huipil Mayan sleeveless tunic dress

Indios native Mexican Indians

jarabe tapatío the Mexican Hat Dance

la gloria heaven

leyenda legend

la lorna the weeping woman

maize corn

Mara'akame Huichol Shaman

mariachi Mexican strolling folk musicians

mestizos persons of mixed Indian and Spanish heritage

metate stone surface used for grinding corn

milagro miracle

mito myth

mulatos persons of mixed Black and Spanish heritage

nierika Huichol stone tablets

nopal type of cactus

ojo eye

ojo de dios eye of god; a handcrafted spiritual symbol of the Huichol Indians

oso bear

padre father; priest

papel picado punched paper; colorful, intricately designed paper cutouts

Partido Revolucionario Institucinal the Industrial Revolutionary Party, Mexico's most important political party

Pastorela Mexican Christmas drama depicting the Nativity story

patron land owner of a hacienda

peninsulares the pure Spanish born in Spain

peones native laborers on haciendas

pesos the standard Mexican monetary unit

Piedra con ojos rock with eyes

piñata clay pot filled with prizes and sweets; a children's game

poncho woolen blanket with a hole in the middle, to be worn pulled over the head

posadas inns, with Las Posadas being a Christmas ceremony

ranchera a type of Mexican folk music

rebozo shawl

Santísima Virgen The Blessed Virgin Mary

señor sir; title for man

señora lady; title for married woman

señorita young lady; title for unmarried woman

telemones Toltec statues

tilma poncho

tortillas unleavened flour bread

vaquero Mexican cowboy

viejito old man

Viva Mexico long live Mexico

Zambos persons of Black and Indian heritage

Zapote an abundant tree in Oaxaca

SUGGESTED READINGS

Barbash, Shepard. *Oaxacan Woodcarving: The Magic in the Trees.* San Francisco: Chronicle Books, 1993.

Barlow, Genevieve, and William N. Stivers. *Stories from Mexico.* Lincolnwood, Ill.: Passport Books, 1995.

Bierhorst, John, ed. *The Hungry Woman: Myths and Legends of the Aztecs.* New York: William Morrow, 1984.

_____. *The Mythology of Mexico and Central America.* New York: William Morrow, 1990.

Brenner, Anita. *The Boy Who Could Do Anything, and Other Mexican Folk Tales.* Hamden, Conn.: Linnet Books, 1992.

Brusca, Maria Cristina, and Tona Wilson. *Pedro Fools the Gringo.* New York: Henry Holt, 1995.

Bunson, Margaret, and Stephen M. Bunson. *Encyclopedia of Ancient Mesoamerica.* New York: Facts on File, 1996.

Cabello-Argandoña, Roberto. *Cinco de Mayo: A Symbol of Mexican Resistance.* Encino, Calif.: Floricanto Press, 1993.

Caso, Alfonso. *The Aztecs: People of the Sun.* Norman, Okla.: University of Oklahoma Press, 1958.

Chabrán, Richard, and Rafael Chabrán, eds. *The Latino Encyclopedia.* New York: Marshall Cavendish, 1996.

Coe, Michael D. *Mexico, From the Olmecs to the Aztecs.* London: Thames and Hudson, 1997.

Cordry, Donald B. *Mexican Masks.* Austin, Tex.: University of Texas Press, 1980.

Cordy, Donald B., and Dorothy M. Cordry. *Mexican Indian Costumes.* Austin, Tex.: University of Texas Press, 1968.

Díaz del Castillo, Bernal. *The Discovery and Conquest of Mexico: 1517–1521.* London: George Routledge & Sons, 1928.

Dobie, J. Frank, ed. *Puro Mexicano*. Dallas: Southern Methodist University Press, 1935.

Dolch, Edward W., and Marguerite P. Dolche. *Stories from Mexico*. Champaign, Ill.: Garrard, 1960.

Enciso, Jorge. *Designs from Pre-Columbian Mexico*. New York: Dover, 1971.

_____. *Design Motifs of Ancient Mexico*. New York: Dover, 1947.

Giddings, Ruth Warner. *Yaqui Myths and Legends*. Edited by Harry Behn. Tucson, Ariz.: University of Arizona Press, 1959.

Janvier, Thomas A. *Legends of the City of Mexico*. New York: Harper and Brothers, 1910.

Johnson, William Weber, and the Editors of *LIFE*. *Mexico: LIFE World Library*. New York: Time, 1964.

Lyons, Grant. *Tales People Tell in Mexico*. New York: Julian Messner, 1972.

Madrigal, Antonio Hernández. *The Eagle and the Rainbow: Timeless Tales from Mexico*. Golden, Colo.: Fulcrum, 1997.

Meza, Otilia. *Leyendas Mexicas y Mayas*. Mexico D.F.: Panorama Editorial, 1991.

_____. *Leyendas Prehispánicas Mexicanas*. Mexico D.F.: Panorama Editorial, 1988.

Miller, Elaine. *Mexican Folk Narrative from the Los Angeles Area*. Austin, Tex.: University of Texas Press, 1973.

Miller, Robert R. *Mexico: A History*. Norman, Okla.: University of Oklahoma Press, 1985.

Paredes, Américo. *Folktales of Mexico*. Chicago: University of Chicago Press, 1970.

Piggott, Juliet. *Mexican Folktales*. New York: Crane Russak, 1973.

Rael, Juan B. *Cuentos Españoles de Colorado y Nuevo Méjico*, New York: Arno Press, 1977.

Robe, Stanley L. *Amapa Storytellers*. Berkeley, Calif.: University of California Press, 1972.

_____. *Mexican Tales and Legends from Vera Cruz*. Berkeley, Calif.: University of California Press, 1971.

Robe, Stanley L., et al. *Antologia del Saber Popular: A Selection from Various Genres of Mexican Folklore across Borders*. Los Angeles: University of California Chicano Studies Center Publications, 1991.

Sabloff, Jeremy A. *The Cities of Ancient Mexico: Reconstructing a Lost World*. New York: Thames and Hudson, 1997.

Sayer, Chloë. *Arts and Crafts of Mexico*. San Francisco: Chronicle Books, 1990.

_____. *Mexican Costume*. London: British Museum Publications, 1985.

Schwendener, Norma, and Averil Tibbels. *Legends and Dances of Old Mexico*. New York: A. S. Barnes, 1933.

Sedillo, Mela. *Mexican and New Mexican Folkdances*. Albuquerque, N. Mex.: The University of New Mexico Press, 1935.

Spence, Lewis. *The Myths of Mexico and Peru*. New York: Dover, 1994.

Storm, Dan. *Picture Tales from Mexico*. Philadelphia: J. B. Lippincott, 1941.

Taube, Karl. *Aztec and Mayan Myths*. Austin, Tex.: University of Texas Press, 1993.

Tedlock, Dennis. *Popol Vuh: The Definitive Edition of the Mayan Book of the Dawn of Life and the Glories of Gods and Kings*. New York: Simon & Schuster, 1996.

Thompson, Stith. *The Folktale*. New York: Holt, Rinehart, & Winston, 1946.

Toor, Frances. *A Treasury of Mexican Folkways*. New York: Crown, 1947.

Townsend, Richard. *The Aztecs*. London: Thames and Hudson, 1992.

Valadez, Susan. *Huichol Indian Sacred Ritual*. San Francisco: Amber Lotus, 1997.

Verti, Sebastián. *Tradiciones Mexicanas*. Mexico D.F.: Editorial Diana, 1991.

Vigil, Angel. *The Corn Woman: Stories and Legends of the Hispanic Southwest*. Englewood, Colo.: Libraries Unlimited, 1994.

_____. *¡Teatro! Plays from the Hispanic Culture for Young People*. Englewood, Colo.: Libraries Unlimited, 1996.

_____. *Una Linda Raza: Cultural and Artistic Traditions of the Hispanic Southwest*. Golden, Colo.: Fulcrum, 1998.

Wheeler, Howard T. *Tales from Jalisco, Mexico*. Philadelphia: The American Folk-Lore Society, 1943.

PERMISSIONS AND CREDITS

Illustrations by Carol Kimball, found throughout this book, are reprinted with her permission.

Icon designs by Alfredo Cárdenas, found throughout this book, are reprinted with his permission.

Book's cover image of the Mexican flag is adapted from Corel Gallery Clipart Catalogue.

Icon designs are adapted from *Design Motifs of Ancient Mexico* and *Designs from Pre-Columbian Mexico*.

"History of Mexico," pages xix–xxviii, is adapted from *Una Linda Raza*, Fulcrum Press, 350 Indiana, Suite 350, Golden, CO 80401. Adapted by permission.

The map of Mexican states on page xxviii is reprinted from *The Latino Encyclopedia*, edited by Richard Chabrán and Rafael Chabrán, by permission of Marshall Cavendish Corporation, 99 White Plains Road, Tarrytown, NY 10591.

The stories *The Magic Cap* and *The Art of Lying* are adapted from *Charge This to the Cap* and *Keep the Shirt-Tail In* by Riley Aiken in *Puro Mexicano*, publication of the Texas Folklore Society, no 12, © 1935 by Texas Folklore Society. Adapted by permission.

The story *The Wonderful Chirrionera* is adapted from a story by Dan Storm in *Puro Mexicano*, Publication of the Texas Folklore Society, no.12, © 1935 by Texas Folklore Society. Adapted by permission.

In "Mexican Folk Arts," Color Plates 1–13 and 18–20 are from the collection of Rod and Kim Wagner, Galeria Mexicana, Denver, Colorado. Reprinted by permission.

In "Mexican Folk Arts," Color Plates 14–17 are from the collection of Ted Thomas and Paula Crane, Manos Folk Art, Denver, Colorado. Reprinted by permission.

Photographs of Mexican dance costumes are by Judy Miranda. Reprinted by permission. The models are Indalesia Gonzales and Lorenzo Ramírez.

Traditional Mexican folk dance costumes are provided by Grupo Folklórico Sabor Latino, Denver, Colorado.

Index

Ah Kin Xooc (Mayan god), 66–67
Animal fables
   Ant Who Learned to Play the
      Flute, The, 203–5
   Burro and the Fox, The, 206–7
   Fox and the Coyote, The, 181–90
   Lion and the Cricket, The, 191–93
   Mouse and the Ant, The, 197–98
   Owl and the Painted Bird, The,
      199–200
Ant Who Learned to Play the Flute,
   The, 203–5
Ants, 197–98, 203–5
Art of Lying, The, 178–80
Ashes for Sale, 164–68
Aztec people
   as Mexica people, 4–5
   and poinsettias, 22
   and Spanish missionaries, 5–6, 7
   Sun Stone, 41–42
   Tenochtitlan, founding of, 3
Aztec stories
   Broken Bones, The, 52–53
   Creation of the World, The, 41–44
   Eagle on the Cactus, The, 4–5
   El Nopal, 64–65
   Into the Fire, 49–50
   Flowing Waters, The, 48
   Food from the Gods, 54–55
   Music from the Gods, 58–60
   Our Lady of Guadalupe, 5–11
   Rain of Five Years, The, 85–86
   Trail of Stars, The, 51
Aztlan, 3, 4

Badger Names the Sun, 74
Badgers, 74
Bird stories, 133–37, 199–200
Blessed Virgin Mary, 8–11, 127–32.
   See also *Our Lady of*
   Guadalupe
Bridge of Many Colors, The, 75–77
Broken Bones, The, 52–53
Burro and the Fox, The, 206–7
Burros, 206–7

Cactus, creation of, 64–65
Chalchiuhtlicue (Aztec god), 44
Charro, defined, 28
Chicomostoc, 4
Christianity, Spanish missionaries
   and, 5–6, 7
Christmas stories, 21–27, 23–27
Cihuacoatl (pre-Columbian goddess),
   17
Coatepec, 4
Comet and the Tiger, The, 83–84
Copil (Aztec god), 64–65
Cortés, Hernán, 17
Costume, national, 27–28
Coyotes, 81–82, 181–90, 191–93
   Creation of the World, The, 41–44
Creation stories
   Badger Names the Sun, 74
   Bridge of Many Colors, The,
      75–77
   Broken Bones, The, 52–53
   Comet and the Tiger, The, 83–84
   Creation of the World, The, 43–44

El Nopal, 64–65
Into the Fire, 49–50
Flowing Waters, The, 48
Food from the Gods, 54–55
Gift of the Toad, The, 72–73
Murmur of the River, The, 66–67
Music from the Gods, 58–60
Possum's Tail, The, 70–71
Rain of Five Years, The, 85–86
Song to Three Stars, 81–82
Trail of Stars, The, 51
Creator Pair (Aztec gods), 43
Crickets, 191–93
Cuetlaxochitl (poinsettia), 22

Dances, 28
De Chávez, Doña Margarita *(La China Poblana),* 29
De Ordimalas, Pedro
Pedro and the Giant, 105–7
Pedro and the Hanging Tree, 108–9
Pedro and the Magic Pot, 97–99
Pedro and the Money Tree, 89–91
Pedro and the Mule Drivers, 103–4
Pedro and the Pig Tails, 95–96
Pedro Goes to Heaven, 110–11
De San Juan, Catarina *(La China Poblana),* 29–30
De Sosa, Captain Miguel *(La China Poblana),* 29
Dead, land of the, 52–53
Diego, Juan *(Our Lady of Guadalupe),* 5, 7–11
Doña Marina *(Our Lady of Guadalupe),* 17–18
Dos Compadres stories
Art of Lying, The, 178–80
Ashes for Sale, 164–68
Magic Cap, The, 174–77
Duality, Lord and Lady of (Aztec gods), 43

Eagle on the Cactus, The, 4–5
Eagles, 4–5, 64–65
Earth, creation of, 43–50
El Jarabe Tapatío, 28
El Nopal, 64–65
Enchanted Forest, The, 138–45

Fables, animal
Ant Who Learned to Play the Flute, The, 203–5
Burro and the Fox, The, 206–7
Fox and the Coyote, The, 181–90
Lion and the Cricket, The, 191–93
Mouse and the Ant, The, 197–98
Owl and the Painted Bird, The, 199–200
Fire, creation of, 70–71, 72–73
Five Suns, 41–42
Flag, Mexican, origin of design, 3–5, 64–65
Flood stories, 48, 75–77, 85–86
Flowing Waters, The, 48
Food from the Gods, 54–55
Fox and the Coyote, The, 181–90
Foxes, 181–90, 206–7
Friends stories. *See* Dos Compadres stories

Giant stories, 105–7
Gift of the Toad, The, 72–73
Goddess of the Earth (Huichol goddess), 85–86
Goddess of Water (Aztec goddess), 44
Green Bird, The, 133–37

Huichol people, 85–86
Huitzilopochtli (Aztec god), 4, 17, 64–65
Humanity, creation of, 52–53

Insect stories, 191–93, 197–98,
203–5
Into the Fire, 49–50
Ixtlaccihuatl *(The Legend of the Two
Volcanoes),* 33–35

Jewels of Shining Light, The, 146–52
John the Bear, 152–63
Juan Oso, 152–63
Juanita *(The Weeping Woman),*
19–21
Juanito *(The Jewels of Shining
Light),* 146–52

La China Poblana, 27–30
La Malinche, 17
Lady of Jade Skirts (Aztec goddess),
44
Lake Texcoco, 3, 4, 64–65
Las Posadas, 22, 23–27
Legend of the Poinsettia, The, 21–27
Legend of the Two Volcanoes, The,
33–35
Legends, essential
Eagle on the Cactus, The, 3–5
La China Poblana, 27–30
Legend of the Poinsettia, The,
21–27
*Legend of the Two Volcanoes,
The,* 33–35
Our Lady of Guadalupe, 5–11
Weeping Woman, The, 17–21
Lion and the Cricket, The, 191–93
Lions, 191–93, 206–7

Magic Cap, The, 174–77
Magic stories
Enchanted Forest, The, 138–45
Green Bird, The, 133–37
Jewels of Shining Light, The,
146–52

Juan Oso, 152–63
Miracle of Mirajel, The, 127–32
Waterfall of Wisdom, The, 124–26
Wonderful Chirrionera, The,
112–17
Maize, creation of, 54–55
María *(The Green Bird),* 133–37
Mariano, Señior *(The Wonderful
Chirrionera),* 112–17
Marina, Doña *(The Weeping
Woman),* 17–18
Martínez Family *(The Legend of the
Poinsettia),* 23–27
Mayan people, 66–67
Mazatec people, 70–71
Mexi (Aztec god), 4
Mexica people, 4–5, 83–84. *See also*
Aztec people
*Mexican and New Mexican
Folkdances* (Sedillo), 28
Mexican Costume (Sayer), 28
Mexican Hat Dance, 28
Mexico City, 3, 5, 41. *See also*
Tenochtitlan
Mice, 197–98
Mictlan (Aztec land of dead), 52–53
Mictlantecuhtli (Aztec god), 52–53
Milky Way, creation of, 51
Miracle of Mirajel, The, 127–32
Mirajel *(The Miracle of Mirajel),*
127–32
Money stories, 89–91
Moon stories, 49–50, 83–84
Mouse and the Ant, The, 197–98
Mudacerros *(Juan Oso),* 155–63
Mudarríos *(Juan Oso),* 155–63
Murmur of the River, The, 66–67
Music, creation of, 58–60, 66–67
Music from the Gods, 58–60

Nahua people, 4, 33
Nahuatl language, 6, 8

Nanahuatzin (Aztec god), 49–50
National costume, 27–28

Ometeotl (Aztec gods), 43
Oppossums, 70–71
Our Lady of Guadalupe, 5–11
Owl and the Painted Bird, The,
 199–200

Pedro and the Giant, 105–7
Pedro and the Hanging Tree, 108–9
Pedro and the Magic Pot, 97–99
Pedro and the Money Tree, 89–91
Pedro and the Mule Drivers, 103–4
Pedro and the Pig Tails, 95–96
Pedro Goes to Heaven, 110–11
People, creation of, 52–53
Pi-coo *(The Owl and the Painted
 Bird),* 199–200
Pigs, 95–96
Poinsett, Joel R., 22
Poinsettias, 21–22
Popocatepetl *(The Legend of the Two
 Volcanoes),* 33–35
Possum's Tail, The, 70–71
Princess Mirrah *(La China Poblana),*
 29–30
Puebla, 27, 29–30

Quauhtlatoatzin. *See* Diego, Juan
Quetzalcoatl (Aztec god), 42–44, 48,
 51–55, 58–60
Quiquiriquí *(The Green Bird),*
 135–37

Rain of Five Years, The, 85–86
Rainbows, 75–77
Rebozo, defined, 27–28

Sayer, Chloë, 28

Sedillo, Mela, 28
Snake Skirt (pre-Columbian
 goddess), 17
Snakes, 112–17
Spanish colonists, Mexico City built
 by, 5
Spanish missionaries, conversion of
 Indians by, 5–6, 7
Stars, 51, 81–82, 83–84
Sun
 Aztec Sun Stone, 41–42
 Badger Names the Sun, 74
 creation of, 49–50
 Creation of the World, The, 43–44
 Into the Fire, 49–50
 Music from the Gods, 58–60
Sun Stone, 41–42

Tamoanchan (Aztec land of gods), 53
Tarahumara people, 81–82
Tecuciztecatl (Aztec god), 49–50
Tenoch, 5
Tenochtitlán, founding of, 3, 5,
 64–65
Tepeyac *(Our Lady of Guadalupe),* 6,
 7–11
Tezcatlipoca (Aztec god), 42–44, 48,
 51–53, 58–59
Miracle of Mirajel, The, 127–32
Tigers, 83–84
Tlaloc (Aztec god), 43–44, 55
Tlaltecuhtli (Aztec Earth monster),
 41–42, 48, 51
Toads, 72–73
Tonacatepetl, 54–55
Tonantzin (Aztec goddess), 6, 7, 8
Tonatiuh (Aztec Fifth Sun), 41–42
Toor, Francis, 28
Treasury of Mexican Folkways
 (Toor), 28

Trickster tales
    Pedro and the Giant, 105–7
    Pedro and the Hanging Tree,
       108–9
    Pedro and the Magic Pot, 97–99
    Pedro and the Money Tree, 89–91
    Pedro and the Mule Drivers, 103–4
    Pedro and the Pig Tails, 95–96
    Pedro Goes to Heaven, 110–11

Virgin of Guadalupe. *See* Our Lady
    of Guadalupe

Volcanoes, 33–35

Waterfall of Wisdom, The, 124–26
Weeping Woman, The, 17–21
Wonderful Chirrionera, The, 112–17

Yaqui people, 72–73, 74

Zapotec people, 75–77
Zocalo Plaza, 41
Zumarraga, Bishop, 9–11

AUTHOR'S BIOGRAPHY

Photo credit: Jan Pelton

ANGEL VIGIL

Angel Vigil is Chairman of the Fine and Performing Arts Department and Director of Drama at Colorado Academy in Denver, Colorado. He is an accomplished performer, stage director, and teacher. As an arts administrator, he has developed many innovative educational arts programs for schools and art centers.

Angel is an award-winning educator and storyteller. He has appeared at national storytelling festivals throughout the United States. His awards include the Governor's Award for Excellence in Education, a Heritage Artist Award, a Master Artist Award, a COVisions Recognition Fellowship from the Colorado Council on the Arts, and the Mayor's Individual Artist Fellowship.

Angel is the author of several books on Latino culture. His book *The Corn Woman: Stories and Legends of the Hispanic Southwest* won the prestigious 1995 New York Public Library Book for the Teen Award. He is also the author of *¡Teatro! Plays from the Hispanic Culture for Young People* and *Una Linda Raza, Cultural and Artistic Traditions of the Hispanic Southwest*. Additionally, he cowrote *Cuentos*, a play based on the traditional stories of the Hispanic Southwest. Angel is the featured storyteller on *Do Not Pass Me By: A Celebration of Colorado Folklife*, a folk arts collection produced by the Colorado Council on the Arts.